Leaving Home at 72

Leaving Home at 72

Don and Dana Manges

iUniverse, Inc.
New York Lincoln Shanghai

Leaving Home at 72

iUniverse books may be ordered through booksellers or by contacting:

iUniverse
2021 Pine Lake Road, Suite 100
Lincoln, NE 68512
www.iuniverse.com
1-800-Authors (1-800-288-4677)

ISBN-13: 978-0-595-37362-8 (pbk)
ISBN-13: 978-0-595-81759-7 (ebk)
ISBN-10: 0-595-37362-3 (pbk)
ISBN-10: 0-595-81759-9 (ebk)

Printed in the United States of America

About the Authors

Don and Dana Manges live in Pittsburgh. They have three sons, David, Ted and Hardy, and four grandchildren.

In this travel memoir, they tell their stories separately. You'll recognize their voices through the typography. Don writes in this serif type face. He grew up in Berwind, W.Va., graduated from Michigan State in journalism, and retired as a partner in a Pittsburgh advertising agency.

Dana writes in this plainer type face, a sans serif. She's a native of Fox Chapel near Pittsburgh. After graduating from Wells College in chemistry, she was a member of Edwin Land's team developing color film at Polaroid. She's also been a writer and bookkeeper.

Don = serif

Dana = sans serif

Special Thanks

We met Philip Rostek, our next door neighbor, when we came back from Europe in Summer 2003. A professor of drawing and painting at Seton Hill University in Greensburg, Pennsylvania, Phil asked if he could contribute some drawings to our book—an unexpected delight. He is a graduate of Penn State and Carnegie Mellon University.

David Gates first designed our covers, then indeed became totally invaluable. He art directed the entire book. We first worked together in 1976 at Van Dine Horton McNamara Manges, Inc., our advertising agency. And, as you can see, we've never stopped. David graduated from the Cleveland Institute of Art.

Karen Reber took our pock-marked manuscripts and Zip drives and turned them into this, our first book. Karen, too, worked for our agency. When her one child, Amanda, goes to college next year, Karen expects to leave Pittsburgh and live her dream in the Outer Banks.

Melinda Beard edited our book in the beginning, while encouraging us. Her son Philip Beard II informed our travels through the publishing obstacle course as he met success with his novel "Dear Zoe."

Don Manges
Fall 2005

Contents

ROME

LONDON

RETURNING

– #1 –
No Trekking the Himalayas, No Swimming With the Sharks

Our story is in many ways ordinary. Travel, our hobby for 50 years, increased in tempo as we retired in 1997. Surveying options at age 72, we decided to make it all travel all the time. We sold the house we had lived in for 35 years in Pittsburgh. We sold a piano and two cars, pushed old things onto our children and stored the rest. Then we rented apartments for 18 months in Rome, Vienna, London and Paris.

Our timing was not superb; we left home several months after September 11, 2001. We lived in France when the French hated the Iraq war.

Looking back on 18 months encouraged us to look back even further. Where does this itch to travel come from? Is it genetic? Dana's grandmother sailed to France during World War I to help the troops. Her parents, it seems, were swinging New Yorkers living on an ashram in the 1920s. I write about growing up in a coal town in southern West Virginia, with an occasional traumatic visit to New York. We write these scenes as if they're from different movies, with only an implied, family narrative to hold them together. So we don't start writing about The Trip until we leave for Rome.

With creeping years and creaking joints, despite health issues, we made a long-term plan and stayed with it. After 18 months, we knew another change awaited—a return to earth not as the suburbanites we had become over four decades—with pond, deck and garden, living among established gentry—but now as city dwellers who take the bus and return home to an apartment among neighbors a third our age. It's not as hair-raising as trekking the Himalayas or swimming with the sharks, but neither is it the comfortable humdrum of ever-repeating patterns.

Major change late in life is an adventure in itself. We pulled ourselves out of a field of knowns—sons and their wives, grandchildren, friends, house and garden, neighborhood, doctors and routines—onto a mountain of unknowns. Writing about all this has made it more real for us; it might make it more possible for you.

You'll recognize our stories this way:

Don's are in this serif type face.

◆   ◆   ◆

Dana's are in this sans serif.

Dana and Don Manges
Pittsburgh, Pennsylvania

FAMILY
STORIES

A 50-Year Trip From
Berwind, West Virginia to Istanbul

How did it happen, at the age of 72, that a couple married for 45 years would suddenly sell their house and move to Europe for 18 months? The urge may have started 62 years before.

In the summer of 1940 I walked to the post office. Our family had moved from Windber, a coal town in Pennsylvania, to Berwind, a smaller coal camp in southern West Virginia. My father was the buyer for everything in company stores in 13 towns, from car loads of potatoes to refrigerators to aspirin. Berwind was very quiet. And I was a dreamer.

At the post office, dreams were waiting. Cutting coupons from travel ads in Colliers or The Saturday Evening Post almost made my legs twitch: "Visit Colorado." "Travel Nova Scotia." "Two weeks in California." I would bring home thick packets addressed simply to Donald Manges, Berwind, West Virginia, sit in the red leather chair in our living room, and piece by piece, unfold the map, absorb the brochure, <u>walk</u> those mountains and beaches.

In the late forties, my Dad would take us to the New Jersey shore, then spend a few days in New York City, all four of us in one room in a hotel in Times Square. My dad Ted, my mother Kitty, my sister Lois, 13, and I, aged 18. I still remember looping over the Pulaski Skyway, a raised highway from New Jersey, seeing New York ahead. Lois and I would sneak out at night to Bop City to hear Jackie Cain and Roy Kral sing jazz. I was transfixed. No other travel can compare with seeing New York City as a teen-aged boy from West Virginia.

Now, move on to 1952. That summer I was in the Army in Stuttgart, Germany. As a Pfc and editor of the Seventh Army Sentinel, I had only 15 days of leave to see Europe, thanks to the Army's ironic gift of 15 days' leave back in the hometown of Windber, Pennsylvania. (On one of those weeks, flying to Rome from Stuttgart, I waited in the Nice airport with Rex Harrison and his wife, Kay Kendall, with their piles of luggage, languid as only Brits can be.)

But those two weeks of vacation in Europe, the one week to Rome and Florence, the other to Paris, Brussels and Amsterdam, opened an unforgettable window for me. I'd had a few History of Art courses in college, studied up at the army camp, but nothing prepared me for that first trip to Italy. It was the art, it was the food, it was another life. The Pantheon and Bernini in Rome...Michelangelo, da Vinci and the Renaissance paintings in

Florence...absolutely astounded me, as they still do now, 50 years later.

In Paris I was lucky enough to arrive the same day as the May 1953 issue of Holiday magazine, the cover shouting "Paris! Paris!" Irwin Shaw rhapsodized about Café Deux Magots and the left bank; I saw the Eiffel Tower and Notre Dame through his eyes and never got over it.

Some years later, Dana Fulton and I were married, had two sons, David and Ted, and bought a house in the suburbs of Pittsburgh, where our third son, Hardy, was born. In 1964 we had an invitation from my sister Lois and Jim Gillespie, now married and living in San Antonio. They wrote, "Come see us in Texas." "Nooooo," we wrote back, "how about meeting in Mexico City? They speak Spanish, have pyramids, eat dinner at 8:00 p.m."

We left the boys with my parents and flew to Mexico City for a February week of people-watching in the *zocalo*, the main square of the city, a trip through the gardens at Xochimilco, a *Folklorico* ballet at the Bellas Artes. Then we four got on the wrong bus for a hot, dusty 12-hour trip south. But we saw the old silver city of Taxco, and the parched, brown mountains of central Mexico (so different from the green Appalachians I'd grown up with) and finally, the beautiful curving bay at Acapulco.

Here, we found our hotel, from Frommer's "Mexico on $5 a Day," lounged on hammocks on the deck, just across the street from the cliff-divers at La Quebrada. On the beach, we had drinks with tiny parasols and watched the sun set into the Pacific. We took the funicular down to the seaside pool at the Mirador, we heard the mariachi bands and sipped tequila.

In 1971, it was Italy and France for Lois and Jim, Dana and me, and a first for the other three. The apricot colors of Rome are mixed in memory with the Sistine Chapel and St. Peters; in Florence...the pink and green of the Duomo with Michelangelo and Botticelli. Then a rental car...to Portofino, to the palace at Monaco, to Avignon.

A memorable thrill was Les Baux, in the Rhone valley, a 12th century abandoned village rediscovered in the 1960s by artists and restauranteurs. We had a three-star experience in the spectacular Oustau de Baumanière, lunching outside on the terrace on Rôti d'Agneau en Croûte and Châteauneuf de Pape. We goggled at the $80 check, *le plus grand addition* we'd ever seen at lunch. People nearby were driving Maseratis and walking whippets. We felt we were in the movies.

Taking the night train to Paris, we sat up in a compartment with two scruffy French soldiers who hadn't bathed in a week. But we were all so young and flexible; we could sit up all night, then arrive at our hotel and fall in a heap on the beds, drinking wine, laughing 'til our sides hurt.

Three years later, 1974, we tackled Iberia, staying mostly in state-run paradors, the restored convents or old mansions. One midnight in Jerez, Franco's *Guardia Civil* escorted us to our rented car; it was too late for laughter on the streets. In Portugal, the "flower revolution" had just blown through and brought down the dictator Salazar. We were taken to dinner by a Lisbon couple who had visited Pittsburgh. "Two weeks ago, before the revolution, we could not have been seen in public with Americans," they said.

As we were leaving Lisbon, Dana was anxious about the flying, particularly in a then-new, fully-loaded 747. A hostess threw herself into a bucket seat facing us, looked directly at Dana and said, "I just don't know how these things <u>ever</u> get off the ground."

Next came college years for our boys, and time for us to economize. But, in 1984, the four of us again flew off, this time to Athens for three weeks in the May sun of Greece. We climbed up to the old gods at Delphi, crossed the Corinth canal to follow the Olympic runners. There I bought Dana a gold coin that's been around her neck ever since.

While Lois and Jim took a week's cruise to the islands and Turkey, Dana and I flew to Crete. From our $8 room (with bath!) we could see across an inlet to early Christian caves, now inhabited by hippies. Re-meeting in Athens, Jim laughed: "While you were finding the authentic Greece, we were applauding the Baked Alaska." And sure enough, there was the photograph of Jim on shipboard, in a Madras jacket, applauding.

Things changed when I was diagnosed with prostate cancer three years later. I was 57. I heard the doctor, his voice coming down a long tunnel: the biopsy was <u>positive</u>. Then Dana said, "Well, Don, if you're going to do things like this, we're going to rent that house in France we've been talking about forever!"

Surgery by Patrick Walsh at Johns Hopkins eliminated the cancer. And Dana found a house in Provence through a tiny ad in The Atlantic Monthly. "HOUSE RENTAL: 1749 restored Provençal farmhouse, walled garden. Avignon/Aix area, 2 km from small, unspoiled village; near tennis/swimming; 2 bedrooms/2 baths; sleeps 6; $1,500 a month." Who could resist that?

Provence started out as our finest hour and ended as our worst. We stayed for a month just south of the Luberon mountains, near Lourmarin, which had its ruined castle and the striped awnings of the café, and beauty enough to be painted by Winston Churchill. We had many visitors: our just-married son, David, with Margaret, spent several days of their honeymoon with us; our son Hardy visited on his way to a college semester in Salamanca, Spain and Jim and Lois came.

The five of us roamed around southern France. A high was the Pont du Gard; then the Maison Carré in Nimes. We ordered coffee on the elegant main street of Aix-en-Provence, cooked chickens and drank the bad wines from a hose in the wall at the Lourmarin wine co-op.

On a Friday, Lois and Jim took the train from Marseille to Nice, to catch the plane to New York the next day. After dinner at their hotel on the Promenade des Anglais on the bay of Nice, they were returning from a stroll, crossing the big boulevard, when they were both hit by a car that just flew up on the grassy divider. Jim was thrown onto his head; Lois had a broken pelvis. An ambulance took them to the Hôpital St. Roch and *réanimation* (intensive care).

We had no telephone. Saturday afternoon, stickers appeared on our mailbox: <u>urgent</u>, <u>urgent</u>. A telegram. "Gym (sic) in coma at St. Roch. Please call. Lois." Somehow, word had gotten to our owners' caretaker, and within minutes she appeared at our door. "Your sister and husband have had a terrible accident. You must go immediately to Nice." She opened the owner's telephone that had been locked up. We called. Ten minutes later Hardy was driving us to Nice, under the same full moon of our son's wedding four weeks before. A silent, eerie ride. At the hospital the doctor said, *"Très grave, très grave."* Lois, in a ward, cried, "I don't think Jim's going to make it."

JIm was brain dead. Lois had to say when to let him go. The hospital notified the American consulate, who made arrangements for flying back and for a cremation. TWA gave Lois three seats to lie on. I had Jim's urn at my feet to turn over to his three sons at Kennedy airport.

After Jim's death, our travel changed. Lois took more tours, to Alaska, to Israel, bought a winter home in San Diego. Ten years later, she finally toured the south of France; grieving, she told us, had been replaced with some closure.

Life went on; the older boys were established in Philadelphia bond houses; our last son, Hardy, graduated from college, my business turned international. Dana and I added onto a business trip to Germany and to St. Petersburg, Russia. We stopped to see the house in Lourmarin. The Canadian owner had added a suite to the third floor and a swimming pool in the back garden. The rent tripled.

Later in the 90s, we joined friends, two couples, on a barge trip on the Canal du Midi, starting near Toulouse. The six of us crewed the unwieldy boat through some 50 locks. Ron, a former Navy officer, became our captain. Joan held too long on a line as the boat dropped in a lock; her hand dripped blood. I sank into muck up to my arms, and would still be there except for tall John lifting me out. Jane called it our trip down the river Styx.

After we both retired in 1997, we spent two winters near Nice, at Villefranche sur-Mer (recommended by the above Captain Ron) in an apartment with a stunning sea view, and the next year in St. Jean Cap Ferrat across the bay. And basically we learned how to rent apartments and grocery shop in Europe, find our way around, and enjoy, after 44 years of work, no imperatives, no must-dos. We even liked the lack of a social life. We read, Dana took French lessons and knit grand-baby blankets; I studied Beethoven quartets.

Both of these winters in France were followed by six weeks of volunteering through the International Executive Service Corps, the agency that links retired business people with needy organizations in the developing world. Although that world didn't need a retired advertising man, they did want my expertise in planning fund raising. Volunteering took us to Vilnius in Lithuania, to Istanbul, and recently, to Yerevan, Armenia, described later.

Also in here, 1998, between the trips to Villefranche and Istanbul, I started having heart problems. Nothing too terrible; I had two angioplasties, two stents, followed by medicines and rigorous exercise. And, just after 9/11 and the selling of the house, I had a small stroke; my speech felt funny enough for me to see the specialist. Yes, it was a stroke, a little more serious than a TIA, but hardly discernible; aside from an every-once-in-a-while mumble, there's been no effect. To this day, Dana has never been able to detect these, to me, funny sounds.

Like it or not, you've been swept through our 60 years of travel. Two years after Istanbul we realized what we wanted: to sell our house and live in Europe.

Lunch in Provence, 1971

– #3 –
The Big Idea

In the summer of 2001, I was painting our basement floor as we thought of selling the house, not now but a long time in the future. Steamy August brought forth a cool idea, a different one. I washed the roller and walked up the stairs. "Dana, I have an idea."

Over a beer and a pizza, I highlighted our situation. We were 72; we loved the house we had lived in for 35 years, but upkeep on its nine rooms and gardening was getting expensive and tiring. Our children were on successful paths for both homelife and career. Friends were beginning to talk a lot about Longwood, the local retirement home. Most of all, we loved traveling and we were retired.

"What if," I said, "we sold the house now, stored the furniture, went to Europe for 18 months, rented apartments in Rome, Vienna, London and Paris, then returned to an apartment in Shadyside, and three years later we go to Longwood?" That may seem overly-pithy and theatrical but it happened pretty much that way. (Shadyside is the cultural and university area.)

Dana thought a moment, and said, "Fine with me." We had visited all those cities except Vienna, but never longer than five days on any one trip. On longer stays we had rented apartments in the south of France, and visited Lithuania, Istanbul and Armenia on month-long volunteer projects. We were travelers; the modus operandi was not totally new. Now, after all my years in advertising, we both recognized we had a big idea. I wrote an eight-page plan with objectives, goals, strategies, timelines—the full court planning process—which we promptly ignored. Terribly excited, we realized it would seem adventurous to some and absurd to others. We kept quiet about it for weeks.

The two main caveats were money and health. We lost a significant share of the value of our investments in the overheated tech turndown in early 2000. Among the greedy army of Cisco owners, we carried too much risk for our age and we knew it. As for health, with two heart attacks and a stroke—all mild—I needed permission from the doctors to travel this ambitiously.

To sell the house, we contacted a real estate agent in Fox Chapel who toured the house and garden and suggested a price ten times what we paid in 1966. (Fox Chapel is the location of Teresa Heinz Kerry's farm, a far cry from our third of an acre.) Now, our homestead sported an all-glass family room, a remodeled third floor, more bathrooms, a deck, a stone wall in the garden and, *pièce de résistance*, a new fish pond.

We found a moving company and a storage facility. Moving would cost $2,100 and storage $240 a month. Our borough's engineers showed up for the requisite house check. Digging a ditch in our yard and lowering a camera, they found roots crawling into our sewer. That cost $7,500 to fix. The 75-year old knob-and-tube wiring, fine for us, had to be replaced; for this we left $3,000 to the buyers. Windows from 1925 had to be replaced.

We told our kids about the plans. David, who lived nearby, thought it was the right thing to do. Ted, our Philadelphia bachelor, thought it was exciting; Hardy, the youngest, in Baltimore, had pangs of regret. He wanted his young Grace and Teddy to be able to visit his roots. We wrote daily tasks on shirt cardboards with an earnestness we hadn't seen in years.

Over the next few months, we sold our shiny black grand piano, our long, old farm table that would never fit into an apartment, and books to the local library ($1 for hardbacks, 50 cents for paperbacks). We celebrated our last Thanksgiving and our last Christmas with all our sons' families and grandchildren in our home. Saying goodbye, we shoved old silver and never-used antique linens into their reluctant arms.

We invited neighbors and friends to a large, goodbye cocktail party right after Christmas, with much screaming, and "how could you?" Jeanne and Tom McCallum, our oldest friends, drove in from Cherry Hill, New Jersey for a surprise appearance.

On the day of the sale, three buyers vied for our house. The "winners," 30-something Lisa and Todd Ireland, wrote a love letter to our house. Lisa said it answered her dreams. We were glad they were the top bidder.

We had several days between selling and flying to Rome. Dana had found an apartment on the Internet, so we were assured a Roman bed. Friends Romaine McKean and Dotti and John Bechtol put us up while we shipped apple boxes to Rome. (Because I could not believe the prices quoted, I called competitive carriers. Romaine overheard me on the telephone. "There you go," she laughed, "with the rich and famous, living on nickels and dimes.") Eight boxes cost $800 through the U.S. Postal Service.

Before we left I talked with Al Van Dine, a good friend and my former partner. "Why don't you write a book?" he asked. "Being creative is not just what you <u>do</u>—carving pipes or playing golf—but how you live," Al said. I had bought into this many years before. We didn't plan to shrink into fetal positions. Dana and I saw ourselves as Gerald and Sara Murphy without the money. My notes say "it was important for me to <u>invent</u> something in these late years, and not focus on the medicines and the eventual retirement home."

What would be different about our trip? No concierge, no travel guide, no one to make arrangements, no middleman for language. We would stay in one place, by ourselves, for long stretches of time. We knew the economics were good; wherever we stayed would be our only rent on the planet. We liked learning a neighborhood, not exactly like Peter Mayle and his experience with recalcitrant tradesmen, but knowing the grocer, the pharmacist, the local camera shop. We would have the luxury of time to revisit, read and relate things to history. Al, the constant reader but rarely a traveler, summarized the differences between us. "I want to know everything and you want to experience it," he said.

– #4 –
Why Did We Leave?

Why did we want to change our lives so dramatically? And sell our house? The house with 35 years of memories and babies and living and working? Where we raised three boys, saw them through high school and college into jobs and marriages? And Fox Chapel...leave the pretty borough, the trees, the deck, the fish pond?

Life was fine, friends were good, we read, went to movies and lectures, parties and dinners. We did as much traveling as we could afford, had book clubs, played tennis, all the suburban middle-class life. Were we dissatisfied? Or, if not, looking for more?

One answer was simple: age. With Don's having two mild heart attacks, with the subsequent angioplasties and stents and then the added complication of a small stroke, we became aware, a little late, of time fleeting. We started wondering, as did Peggy Lee, "Is this all there is?" We weren't going to be 70 forever, as funny as that would have sounded some years ago. (My Uncle David in his 80s, always the performer, loved to proclaim, "Ah, to be seventy-one again!"...and we would double over with laughter; we were a good audience.)

Now we knew seventy wasn't all bad, but then right around the corner coming on fast would be the 80s, and that was entering strange and unknown territory. We decided we wanted a retirement home at some point, as a lot of our friends were doing. Don, more of a planner than I, and feeling more fragile, wanted the assurance of care and stability in a later life, and felt quite strongly about it. We checked out the local favorite, and it didn't look bad. But...not quite now. Later.

Another answer was our growing awareness of how much energy and money we were putting into the house; even more, the time and attention it was taking. There was the constant vigilance to gutters, termites, new sewering, here a leak, there a drip, everywhere some water, water. It seemed to dominate our every conversation, which we came to resent intensely. I knew every repairman's phone number in the area, plumbers, roof men, electricians, carpenters; I knew their wives' names, their trucks, their rates. Again, there must be <u>more</u>.

Then, there was travel. We kept trying to juggle the repairs and the budget and life's ordinaries, with the places we wanted to see. And not only just to see, but to live there, to spend time, to learn some of Europe's favorites. When our third son was in college in 1987, and Don had a bout with cancer…his intimations of mortality…we decided to do some of these things we'd always wanted. We rented a house in Provence, in southern France, for a month. Then, another year Don had a business trip to Russia and I went along. We went to California to see my brother, went to Charleston, South Carolina one Christmas, went to Rio, went to Costa Rica…fitting these trips in between our jobs and daily lives. And finding the cash to do it all made us nervous. Sometimes we took it out of capital, which we knew wasn't an answer. Ater all, retirement was coming soon; the paychecks would stop.

Another big factor was that Don, for years, had wanted to live in the city. He wanted to trade the suburbs and the trees and the deer for museums and lectures and classes. Now, I'd never lived with sidewalks. I'd grown up in Fox Chapel; I thought cities were of the devil. They were swell short term, but to actually live there? People peed on your lawn and mugged you getting out of the car. No, cities were bad things.

All these ideas: health, retirement, money, house upkeep, travel, moving out of the suburbs kept flying around in our heads, and nothing made any sense. Until Don put it all together one summer day, as in "How about selling the house, storing everything, going to Europe for two years, coming back to live in the city, then retiring to 'the Home'?" It all fell into place, in one big moment; it took me only a second to agree…and I said "<u>fine</u>!"

Many of our friends simply could not fathom what we were doing. Selling a house, yes, that was OK, but the rest of it? Not to buy another, to be, in effect, homeless? What about your "things?" "Well," we said, "we'll store everything. People do it all the time!"

We figured it wasn't the details that bothered everyone; it was the unconventionality of the plan. Selling and not buying another house, coupled with storing all our worldly goods; those were unusual ideas, just "not done." The age-old dictum of owning property is strong. Plus, many people simply don't have the desire to leave our country. "Must you sell the house? Disrupt your life so dramatically? What's the matter with traveling the U.S.? Why Europe? Why so long? Do you really want to be gone for <u>two years</u>?"

Our answers were simple. "It's time. We were going to sell anyway in a few years. We'd like to get out from under while we're still walking and fairly spry. We've always wanted to travel and learn Europe. Everybody has a dream, and this is ours." Then we'd say…"And if not now, <u>when</u>?" This really silenced everyone. And it became our mantra.

A few friends were in disbelief and/or disapproval. Most understood what we wanted to do; and some envied us. To me, our planning, and indeed the whole venture, was a triumph of optimism and hope: "It'll all work, and if something goes wrong, which I doubt, we'll fix it." When the kids were little we always used a shirt cardboard to list the plusses and minuses of any venture. And we still do. Here, the verdict was "the positives win…they outweigh the negatives." And they did, far more than we could have guessed.

– #5 –
Old People in Pittsburgh

I t's not without credentials that Dana and I are stressing age in this journal; we come by it honestly. In August 2004, The New York Times detailed a Pittsburgh demographic problem.

"To be perfectly blunt about it, Pittsburgh is getting old," says the newspaper. To paraphrase, half the workers at Duquesne Light, its electric utility, and half the nurses in the hospitals of the University of Pittsburgh Medical Center will hit the typical retirement age of 65 in the next seven years.

"And what is happening in Pittsburgh appears to be an early installment of a demographic drama unfolding across the nation," continues the article.

This phenomenon, discussed widely in terms of social security payout, is anticipated not only in the U.S. but also in Europe and Japan. With more people living longer, what will they do, even if they retire later than age 65? Everyone is not going to sell their houses and rent apartments in Europe.

The common denominator will be the increasing need for creative uses of time when the alarm clock no longer rings early in the morning, and there's no boss to set an agenda. Our way is just one of an infinite number of answers to start a pot of ideas boiling.

– #6 –
"Good Morning, Mr. Zip Zip Zip"

As a young boy, Don had his dreams of travel; they stemmed from his own personality and imagination. But I was a child who lived in books, and I was content to stay there. Now I think my taste for the foreign and the different was just latent, sitting there in the genes, waiting until the right time to surface.

My parents loved to travel, although only by car, mind you. It was the 30s, and my father distrusted planes. He said they didn't stay up. Although my brother Bobby and I were usually taken along, I remember one time crying as a four-year-old, watching them all drive off to the Chicago World's Fair, while I was left behind with my grandmother. Later there were summer vacations to the Jersey shore, to the New York World's Fair in 1939, to visit friends in New Jersey, to see family in the North Carolina mountains. In the late 1940s the family drove cross-country; my nine-year old brother John proudly announced he had put a toe in both the Atlantic and Pacific oceans. A year later Mexico surfaced for my parents; they had found it on business trips and drove down several times all the way to Mexico City, feats that still astound me. (I think that's why our first trip, Don's and mine, was to Mexico; it had a familiar feel, yet still was exotic and foreign in our imaginations. And we could afford it.)

My grandmother, however, was the one who had wandered the farthest from Pittsburgh. She had done adventurous thngs in her earlier years; she saw the building of the Panama Canal and sailed to Europe several times. She was the traveler, the energetic one. Years after she died, I discovered her diary.

In September 1918, at the age of 47, with the war in Europe in full fury and U-boats ranging the North Atlantic, my grandmother left Pittsburgh to sail out of Montreal, bound for France. Of all her trips, this was the most exciting; her diary termed it "The Great Adventure." She kept a record of her six months there as a YWCA worker, a lucky move for me as this is my sole source of information. (It's hard to believe, but the family rarely talked about this dramatic event, at least not to me. I found the diary in my mother's papers after she died. Our family didn't communicate well.)

My grandmother, Edith Harris Scott, was born in 1871 in Wales. As age was one of the many things not discussed in our house, I had to figure that date out from her obituary. The story in the Pittsburgh Press read "Aged Fox Chapel woman dies." My mother and Uncle David were outraged at the adjective. "Heavens," they said, "she was only 72 and still young, so vibrant!" To me, at 12, that was old. To me, she was Nannie, my grandmother, white-haired, pale, quietly knitting at one end of the couch in our living room. And that was what 72 was like, then.

They were remembering a younger woman, one I'd never known. The Nannie I knew had cancer and had a breast removed. And she still wasn't very well. I knew she had been a singer, and had entertained the American soldiers in France during World War I. She taught me fun songs like "Good Morning,

Mr. Zip Zip Zip (if the Camels don't get you, the Fatimas must)" and everything George M. Cohan ever wrote. Great stuff. And she had a small bronze statue I knew was connected with France. But I never asked any questions; I never knew the 'how' and 'why' of her trip, and it wasn't until I read her diary that I learned how unusual a woman she'd been.

Nannie went to France as a YWCA worker. Her group hailed from all fields: publicists and musicians, businessmen and Canteen workers, all pledging to help with the "War to end all Wars." Ironically, the war was ending before Nannie even arrived in France; they didn't get to Le Havre 'til the end of October, just days before the Armistice. Their ship, part of a convoy of destroyers, was caught in a hurricane, and the crossing took three weeks. The storms of the North Atlantic were dramatic, as Nannie recounted in her diary. "We spent one whole week being turned around…most of the time was spent heading north, and even west." On October 8, "the fury seemed to gather and concentrate in one enormous tempest, and what a night. Pandemonium reigned! The officer on the bridge told me that at 3:30 a.m. the old boat was in the trough, on its side. He never before had actually looked up to find the sea, nor felt nearer to death." Proud of her strong stomach, she wrote, "I was the only one in my group who slept through the storm and so missed all the excitement!"

First landing in Scotland, they met with the control group in London and were sorted out and distributed where necessary, according to their wishes and talents. My grandmother, a motherly, warm-hearted lady, had first wanted to be "hands on," to meet the soldiers, to talk, to comfort, to advise. It was called Street Patrol. After one shift of almost 10 hours with another worker and an English Bobby, from 5:00 p.m. to 3:00 a.m., she wrote that "walking, visiting various Y 'huts,' through a fog where I could hardly get my breath, I was dead. My mind was made up, I couldn't stand that work and was reassigned as singer and reader, which pleased me."

The troops were stationed around France: in hospitals, recovery centers and military camps, all happy to see an American. In those simpler times, before Bob Hope raised expectations of army entertainment, a quartet of portly, middle-aged singers would be warmly received and roundly applauded. She saw the armistice celebrations in Paris, and described the city as "all upset, joyful, with dancing in the streets. I walked down the Champs Élysées to the Place de la Concorde, through the crowds singing, celebrating, trying to keep from being hugged and kissed by the volatile French!"

Based in Rennes, north of Paris, she gave recitals and readings in hospitals and camps ranging from Cherbourg on the west coast, to Dijon, 100 miles south of Paris, and Amiens, 100 miles north. Most trips entailed a return to Paris, the center of relocation, then a trip out, by day or night. Singly, or in small groups, by train, army truck or car, they moved over muddy and rain-slogged France. Twice a car overturned, "throwing suitcases everywhere," but no injuries. It was a rainy winter, cold and damp, and getting meals and hotel rooms was many times left to the workers. She wrote of often finding a room in a new town only after several tries, and "cold coffee and stale bread" for a breakfast.

Colds and laryngitis, a singer's worst enemies, plagued her. Several times she related hospital stays, and the kindness of the French sisters in caring for her. The work seemed to be a mixture of officers' receptions and luncheons, interspersed with hard duty. "Spent the day singing in five wards (in the American Hospital near St. Nazaire) in both diphtheria and flu wards. I think we really brought a touch of home to the boys; they cheered up immensely." Many times she gave two programs a day, then left by train that night for a new assignment.

By February, still not in voice, she and a few others were sent south to Nice, for the warmer and curative weather. Here she found the sunshine "comforting and bone-warming" after the cold and clouds of northern France. She loved the markets with the masses of flowers in bloom, and thrilled at the ride from Nice over the mountain, the "long route" to Monte Carlo. From the snow-covered summit they "looked down on groves of lemon and orange trees; lower down still were the palm trees, the beds of pansies, daisies and cyclamen."

(Remembering her descriptions, and the later ones of Scott Fitzgerald and Gerald and Sara Murphy, Don and I spent a winter there, some 80 years later, in 1998. We had an apartment outside Nice in the port town of Villefranche, and we marveled at the soft climate, at the sun and the sea and the same flowers, planted in the public park on Valentine's Day. Truly an enchanted land.)

On returning to Paris, Nannie described a trip to Château Thierry and Rheims, both centers of heavy fighting. "The demolished villages, the partially destroyed bridges, the ruined churches," all prepared them, in part, for the destruction at Rheims. "That great old cathedral looked so helplessly pathetic, so weakened and pounded that it seemed powerless to hold up its towers."

She asked for reassignment to Germany in April, but on discovering that she would have to sign up for four months, she decided on a release. Nannie sailed for the States in June 1919. Passing through the Straits of Gibraltar, she wrote, "I could see the shores of both Spain and North Africa," and wondered if "I would ever get back to really explore Europe in quieter times."

Nannie did get back to Europe about ten years later, maybe 1930, gauging from the look of the women's costumes in a picture I have, labeled "Under Vesuvius." It shows twenty middle-aged women, with Nannie in the forefront, next to a dapper, smallish Italian-looking man…a guide?…and the familiar cone-shaped mountain in the background. Now with the Women's Overseas Service League, she had escorted a group of women to Italy. I keep on the dining room table the della Robbia candlesticks and bowl that she brought back from that trip.

In her other life, about 1900, before cancer, divorce and grand-mother-hood, Nannie had been a Pittsburgh personage, a singer with a rich contralto voice. Trained at Emerson College in Boston, she was in demand for concerts and recitals. I found in her papers several yellowed programs from various concerts, dating from 1907 to 1915, where she was featured as 'Mme. Edith Harris Scott, contralto singer." Another big thing the family never talked about was her trip to the Panama Canal area. She apparently had sailed with the YWCA, where they sang for the workers during the building of the canal. Something never mentioned. Strange, the topics ignored by one generation that are newsworthy for the next.

Edith Harris and George Scott had been married in the Gay Nineties, the era of songs like "A Bicycle Built for Two." Life was easy. When parents sent them off to buy a bedroom suite, the newlyweds came home instead with a pair of bicycles and matching bicycle suits. There were two children, Uncle David, and my mother, Margaret. Energetic and dynamic, Nannie gave concerts and church recitals. With her handsome husband, who, as I divined from family stories, had been a wealthy man's son, the two were a popular and entertaining couple.

When the inherited real estate (nine houses, I was told) had all been occupied and sold off, the fifteen years of good life that probably far exceeded their income, disappeared. My grandfather Scott went to work at the U.S. Steel Homestead works, while Nannie used her singing talents to bring in the rest of the family income, even to putting my mother through college.

We should have known each other better, as she lived with us during the Depression years. Somehow we didn't. We weren't a demonstrative family, not much hugging, but she often gave me licorice drops hidden in her bedroom, and let me play with the small bronze statue of Jeanne d'Arc that I sensed, even as a child, was important to her. A handsome piece, the statue showed the revered saint of France in full armor, arms resting on the sword dramatically posed in front. Maybe 12 inches high, it was a copy of the famous d'Epinay statue in the Cathedral at Rheims, the cathedral so tragically destroyed, the one that had, I believe, so dramatically brought home to my grandmother the senselessness and waste of war.

Her voice never regained its quality, and she never sang in public again.

– #7 –
Oom the Omnipotent

The only way I can tell this story is how I learned it…all in pieces, bit by bit, over many years. I'm not really sure of all the facts, as by the time I got curious about it almost every-one concerned had died. Probably I'll never know the real rea-sons, or the finer details, of how my family got involved with Oom. It's the kind of story you read in the papers, or see in the movies…a perfectly ordinary family runs into an out-of-the-ordi-nary situation. The event is newsworthy only in the very conven-tionality of their lives.

We first heard about Oom from my Mother in 1960 one winter evening in our suburban Pittsburgh home. Up from North Carolina to see us and her only grandchildren, David and Ted, she started reminiscing one night after dinner. The kids were in bed, we were having a drink. She asked, casually, "Have I ever told you about Oom the Omnipotent?" We laughed and said that we never heard of him. And she was off.

First, the part that I know. My parents, Karl and Margaret Fulton, smart, educated, middle-class people, were both born and raised in Pittsburgh, early in the century. They came from people who worked, went to church (well, some of them did), had families; to my mind, they basically followed the conventions, give or take a few turns.

I knew that my parents as young-marrieds had spent some of the 1920s in New York City…I never knew much about it. I knew they had loved those years…the big city, the theatres, the people, the speakeasies (yes, they were tidy drinkers)…and Mother always regretted having to leave. "In 1932, in the depths of The Depression," she repeated many times, "we had to come back to Pittsburgh." Where, I gathered, Karl had gotten a better job, or at least some job, as, after all, it was The Depression.

They had gone to New York in 1926 with my brother Bobby, a one-year-old; I wasn't born until 1929. To me, an odd part was that although there wasn't much money, they apparently had lived on an estate in Nyack, thirty miles up the Hudson. Mother had talked about a lake with swans; I'd seen pictures and had wondered about this exotic life. There was a picture of my brother, a toddler, on a big lawn with water behind him; I assume it's on the estate grounds. I knew they had lived with two other couples, and that some time later my parents moved to Jackson Heights, where I was born. But so much I never asked...why were they living so grandly? why did they live with two other couples? and what did my father, a chemical engineer out of Carnegie Tech, do for a living there? Later I did hear of a connection with 60 Wall Street and/or Cities Service; whether that was a job, I don't know.

My cousin, Nonnie, Uncle David's daughter, filled me in on the next part just recently. (I decided she knew all this because her parents had divorced and she'd had a lot of concentrated time with her mother. They would have had many more conversations than in my world where the past was hardly ever discussed.) She told me the three couples were my parents and her parents (my mother's brother David and wife Martha), then a third couple named Burke. They had all left Pittsburgh for New York...to seek their fortunes?...and lived at the Clarkstown Country Club in Nyack. My cousin had never heard the name Oom, but she knew a Dr. Bernard was head of the Club. Google told me that Pierre Bernard's other name, and the one by which he preferred to be called, was "Oom the Omnipotent."

The story my mother told that night was about Oom. She very matter-of-factly recounted one night, after a six-month stay on the estate in Nyack, when my father, Karl Fulton, was summoned into Oom's office. Here he was peremptorily ordered to leave the estate immediately, with the accusation that Karl had been dallying with Oom's lady friend. After some words, when my father protested, Oom brought out a gun and laid it on the desk, pointing it at Karl. My mother said that Karl turned around and left the room. And that was all she told us, that night in 1960. There was no hint in her voice of blame, or accusation, or disbelief, or even of scandal…she was just telling a story quite dispassionately, as if it had happened to someone else.

It's hard to believe we don't know any more. I'm sure we quizzed my mother that night; we must have. "What do you mean, 'he had a gun?'" or, just as pertinently, "Was he really 'dallying?'" However, I remember nothing other than these few facts stated here. My cousin had learned from her mother more of the living arrangements than I did, but nothing of Oom the Omnipotent. (The two sets of parents obviously had selective story-telling abilities.) The group broke up, presumably after Oom's ultimatum; my cousin's parents went to Haverstraw, New York, a small town near Nyack; the Burkes went back to Pittsburgh and my parents to Jackson Heights.

One night this summer I got a terse e-mail from Ted, our second son, the one who's more interested in family history than the others…who, for whatever reason, had remembered my stories of Oom, and on a dull night was currently researching him on Google. Over the ether came "Oom…tantric sex orgies…upstate New York." That certainly got my attention. We happened to be visiting in Chatham, Massachusetts, and my new cell phone had rung, right in the middle of a cocktail party. And on it appeared Ted's text e-mail about Oom, and 'tantric sex' linked to my Pittsburgh family. It was almost an out-of-body experience, reading that text in the middle of a definitely non-exotic Cape Cod party. My parents, from Pittsburgh…in 'tantric sex orgies'?

I've since learned, via Google, that Pierre Bernard, or Oom the Omnipotent, was a charismatic man with a long and disreputable career. He was the leader of a group, some papers called it an "ashram," that had dabbled in yoga and communal living, and was rumored to indulge in the sex practices that Ted had found in Google's newspaper reports. Somehow, in the early 20s, probably from one of his wealthy friends, Bernard amassed $200,000 to buy the estate of the late Joseph Hilton in Nyack where he formed the Clarkstown Country Club as a site for his yoga and physical exercise practices. One of the papers called Bernard the originator of yoga in the United States.

Items also mentioned were some snippets that Bernard had "socialite followers," with some from the "financial world." I learned the socialite connection referred to in the papers was Mrs. W.K. Vanderbilt and her two daughters; some scandal erupted there, hitting the newspapers in the early 1930s, several years after my parent's stay there…and I only have a guess as to the 'financial world.'

The possible orgies were long over; I knew I'd never find out what happened there. It was the connection, the 'how did they get there?' that seemed answerable. I figured a friend of my parents, a Pittsburgh broker named Alfred Kay, of the investment house, Kay, Richards, and who, my cousin told me, also lived on the estate, could have been my parent's link to the Clarksburg Country Club and Oom. Kay was about ten years older than Karl; whether they were simply friends, or Kay was a mentor to my father, I don't know the actual connection between the two men. But I've theorized how it could have happened: my father could have mentioned he was moving to New York, Kay then offering housing on a handsome estate he knew of up in Nyack. This could be a reason why, and/or how the three couples, including my parents, came to live on this estate.

This is the sum total of my knowledge, Google and all; my plot is all conjecture, and faintly anti-climatic. No gun shots, no naked ladies, nothing nearly as dramatic as an ordinary night on TV. It just opened my eyes to a new chapter in an otherwise fairly staid family history.

– #8 –
Missing the Boat
to Bremerhaven

When I was in the Army, I was stationed at Camp Kilmer in New Jersey with orders to sail to Bremerhaven in Germany. It was 1952. An enlisted man, I had been trained as a stenographer, something that I needed three beers to tell anyone then. I was with a half-dozen buddies from basic training. On the day to leave it was rainy. We got in formation with our duffel bags. The sergeant gave an order "to wear raincoats" which we took from our pistol belts. Twenty minutes later the sun peeked out and the sergeant gave another order I didn't hear: "raincoats on pistol belts."

I was standing there—oblivious is what my friends called me—in my raincoat when the same sergeant raced at me. "What's your name, soldier?" I told him. "You're scratched from orders. Report to your company commander!" He drew a fat black pencil line through my name on the sheet on a clipboard.

I picked up my duffel bag, took off my raincoat and put it on my pistol belt, and found the company commander, a captain.

"Sir, the sergeant scratched me from orders to Germany because I didn't take off my raincoat when he gave the order," I said. "Oh, get back in line where you were. He doesn't have the right to do that," said the captain. I took my former place and soon the platoon marched to a bus, which dropped us off at a train station. A train took us to the docks somewhere in northern New Jersey.

We got off the bus in roster order and marched toward a gang plank leading up to a troop ship. A sergeant was calling off last names. We were told to reply with our first name and middle initial. After going through the L's, he said "Manges." Or I thought he did. "Donald E." I responded.

"There he is," screamed a familiar voice. It was the same sergeant who took me off the clipboard. "There's the culprit. Get back in the bus. Now you're twice insubordinate." As my friends climbed the gangplank, I returned to Camp Kilmer on the bus. Alone. I was assigned to a barracks full of 40-year old corporals and other guys who, one way or another, had missed the boat.

There was nothing for me to do and no one was interested in my plight. Then I discovered that every day at 5:00 p.m. a free bus went into Manhattan. I had six weeks to learn New York City. The USO had free tickets to Broadway shows. I saw half a dozen plays and got to listen to jazz piano, nursing a beer forever, and discovered Barbara Carroll, who still plays in New York. Although the Army could ignore me, I couldn't ignore the fact that I wanted to go to Germany.

I went to the chaplain, something only "crybabies" did in 1952. I told him about the sergeant with his clipboard and how I was scratched from orders. "Well, most of the soldiers who come to me are trying to get out of going to Europe. You must be telling the truth." I was on the next boat to Bremerhaven, Germany's port in the North Sea.

I was assigned to a three star general's staff in Vaihingen, a suburb of Stuttgart, with the spit-and-polish protocol I was never good at. It peaked when I was brought in from bivouac to type a letter from the general saying goodbye to John McCloy, who was retiring as high commissioner of Germany. My general had forgotten to write him a goodbye letter. A small plane was standing by to fly the letter to Bremerhaven. On my eighth draft—he was dictating and pacing—he said "oh, for Christ's sake. Get out of here. I'm calling Mrs. Adams to come in from Stuttgart." She was a civilian secretary.

Another day I was being driven to the quartermaster to get fresh linen for the general's apartment. His driver had forgotten to cover the three stars on the license plate. Officers and enlisted men were saluting the car, not me, a private first class. With sheets on my lap, I returned every one of them.

What I wanted to do was write. I applied and soon was an editor of the Seventh Army Sentinel, a newspaper edited for the troops of the army headquarters. I spent a year writing, editing and learning how to put out a paper. But with a German production crew. The German typographer, Herr Heilman, would say to me every Tuesday, when we went to the printing plant, "free as birds on the wing." It was the only English he knew.

This was my first experience in working with, indeed living with, writers. Dave Wachsman, from Connecticut and just graduated from Yale, imitated Hemingway in his sports writing. Chris Stevens, from Montana, liked James Joyce so much he had hitchhiked across the country and sailed to Dublin to search out his haunts. At lunch we talked about who wrote the best lead, who wrote the funniest editorial. I should have paid the Army for that experience.

The Army also made me a traveler. After flying to Rome in 1953, or seeing Paris, I would never be the same.

ROME

– #9 –
"Can We Still Go To Europe, Dr. Fallert?"

By fall 2001, plans for leaving home for Rome were on track. With two heart attacks and two stents under my shirt, and three-a-week visits to cardiac rehab, I needed to find a cardiologist in Rome. By coincidence, I met an Italian-American doctor at a dinner party whose daughter was a physician in Rome. I telephoned her and she recommended Massimo Delfino, an English-speaking cardiologist who had studied at Stanford. Records were sent from Pittsburgh to Rome. I was set. (The American Embassy in Rome sent me a list of English-speaking doctors, dentists, lawyers, etc. but the names were more than a year old. Their address is on Google.)

A few days after September 11, my speech felt funny at breakfast but it was nothing Dana could hear. I drove to my general practitioner, Dan Monahan, who promptly brought in a neurologist. In less than 30 minutes I had IVs in both of my arms receiving Coumadin. It was a real but mild stroke, not just a TIA (trans-ischemic accident).

Now I was on Coumadin which involves monthly blood tests. But still the plan was "The Plan." I returned to my cardiologist and said, "can we still go to Europe, Doctor Fallert?"

"The medicine in Rome is as good as the U.S. Yes, go," said Michael Fallert.

"I know you hate this question, but we're planning. How long do you think I have?" "About 10 years," he said. And we've planned accordingly.

In Rome, we walked up the three floors to Massimo Delfino, M.D. No one was waiting. He saw Dana and me for a casual 30 minutes. Quietly affable, he had an air that said "no big deal." Opening our Pittsburgh files, he asked, "What is all this paper?" I simply needed a monthly blood test, which could be done in a laboratory. Private *laboratorios* are very common in Europe and, luckily, one just happened to be in our apartment house. I learned how to read the results, which were also sent to Dr. Delfino. My blood tested in the healthy zone our entire Roman holiday. At the end of three months, he charged us only 60 euros for two visits and three telephone calls.

Now, I needed an exercise club. One block from our apartment house was a gym called Push Up throbbing with disco music. Average age: 32. It had all the machines, weights and aerobic programs for 60 euros a month. We both signed up.

The first day at Push Up I rented a locker, then promptly forgot the number. A young man sawed off first one lock; that wasn't it, then another, to find my clothes. Was acting 72 any excuse for this? The young people working there offered more smiles than I deserved. So Push Up plus all the walking around Rome kept my vital signs on the good side with no health problems.

A friend had told me I seemed cavalier about my health problems. I disagreed, saying I tried to stay in the mean between being totally self-absorbed and dumbly nonchalant. I think we're both good at this.

– #10 –
Our Landlady of Rome

Mariola Boecklin was the owner of our apartment in Rome; she asked us to call her Maria. We met through the Internet, where her agency had advertised a "totally new apartment for rent in the Vatican area." One bedroom and bath, with a tiny balcony and a monthly rent of 2000 euros was about par for small apartments in Rome in the winter of 2002. (With the euro at $0.87, that equated to $1,740. As I'm writing this, the euro has risen to $1.28, and that same apartment would cost $2,560.) Pictures on the Internet sold us: a sunny yellow-and-white living room, a bright new bathroom and a charming shaded courtyard complete with fountains. These pictures were all we knew of our living arrangements for the next three months in Rome, but we were satisfied.

We discovered later that Maria and her husband had bought a run-down apartment in the building across the courtyard and completely restored it for their visiting children, with rentals in the off-periods. And we were her first tenants.

We took a taxi from the airport to the romantically-named *Piazza dei Martiri di Belfiori, #4,* the Place of the Martyrs of Belfiori. Christiana, the rental agent, standing beside her motor scooter, and Maria met us at the entrance. Both were chatty ladies: Maria, a handsome, energetic 60-something; Christiana, dark-haired and professional. The *portieri*, or gatekeeper, helped us with our six bags through the courtyard into *entrato* B. The elevator was tiny. Holding only three people, it took several trips to get us and our bags upstairs to our third floor apartment.

Talking, explaining, demonstrating stove and washing machine, shower and hot water heater (all fortunately in English), the women introduced us to the apartment: Christiana talked finances and quickly left. Maria stayed to help us unpack the new sheets, pillow cases, towels and kitchen necessaries from their wrappings, showing closets and drawers, setting up housekeeping right then and there. When Maria left, she explained that she lived across the courtyard and told us to call, anytime, with any questions. She also gave us a Rome city postal booklet, fifty pages of detailed street maps of the whole city which was our Bible. It was our single best resource; even when we were lost, we could figure out how to get home.

Maria grew up in the *quartieri* she lives in now; she's fiercely proud of Italy and her heritage. She also knows Rome's faults: the litter, the subway cars covered with graffiti, and most important, the disrespect for the law. But she loves the warmth and color and exuberance of Italians and, to us, she personified all of them.

She also loves the States. She and her husband Arnoldo, an engineer with Alitalia Airlines, had lived in Washington, DC for five years and came to appreciate our country and its people. She had taken full advantage of the American years: she volunteered, improved her English, drove car pools, and even did Meals on Wheels. With this background, she readily took us into her apartment and into her life.

We arrived on a Thursday. Saturday morning, Arnoldo arrived with a wooden clothes drying-rack, vital in this dryer-less country. After five minutes of chatting, he asked, "Would you like to drive with us up to our country house today, and stay the night?" Trying not to shout, "Wow," we hastily said, "Yes, we'd love it."

Looking back on it, we all just accepted each other at face value, with very little knowledge. The hour we'd spent with Maria, putting the apartment together, talking and laughing, was apparently enough to establish a mutual trust, a friendship, a recognition of common ideas and interests. (However, I do think she had sent Arnoldo over to check us out, to see if he agreed with her initial impression.)

Arnoldo is tall, handsome, well-educated and, for an Italian, quiet. His name is the Italian version of his famous great-grandfather's, the German 19th century painter, Arnold Boecklin. Neither

Don nor I had heard of him, but friends, more knowledgeable about art than we, knew his name and his work. There were several posters in our apartment showing Boecklin exhibitions in various cities of Europe, most recently in Munich 2001.

Saturday afternoon about 5:00, we met in the courtyard and sped off into the night with true Italian *brio*. Fifty minutes of fast, really fast, highway driving, and ten minutes of winding, circuitous streets brought us to Toffia, one of the many villages north of Rome. Passing a well-lighted village commons, Arnoldo carefully navigated the big car through narrow streets, up a dark, tiny alley to a dead end where we stopped. We had arrived at their house, Maria explained, but couldn't park here; we'd unload the car, then Arnoldo would back down to leave the car in the community parking.

Maria opened a door in the wall, telling us that the house was part of a complex dating from the 17th century. The little I could detect from the one street light looked like all the ancient stone dwellings we had seen exploring other small European towns, wondering, "Does anyone live in these places?"

Squeezing through the splintered wood door, we found ourselves still outside. I could see the stars above in the sky. Now we climbed a dark flight of stone steps, and Maria opened the door at the top. The lights revealed another world: a large, white-walled living room with a beamed ceiling, two fluffy, comfortable couches, oriental rugs, antique tables, a corner cabinet with shining silver, and a big fireplace on the wall between the dining room and kitchen. The two bathrooms were as modern as tomorrow.

The house had two bedrooms. Ours was down a level, the master suite above. Maria and I made up the beds with linens from an old armoire, bringing out pillows and piling on huge down quilts. "It will be pretty cold by morning," she said, and we'd need them.

Arnoldo returned and lighted the fire for grilling. Back in the kitchen we unpacked, brought out the wine and groceries. We opened the red wine, Arnoldo put on the steaks, and the night began. Don loved the *biede*, spinach-like greens that Maria sautéed lightly, then served with olive oil, salt and pepper. The steaks were rare, the bread was fresh, the wine copious. We ate, laughed, talked about kids…they had three, one girl in Rome, another a doctor in London, a boy in college living in our building. We cleaned up and went to bed.

Next morning we woke to a clear sunny day; the view from our bedroom was of fields with mountains in the distance, empty of houses and people. After breakfast, Arnoldo drove us into the hills to some of their favorite towns. In one, we went to a local museum that specialized in Etruscan artifacts. "This area north of Rome," he explained, "is famous for its Etruscan ruins; they date from about 700 B.C." The area was pretty but barren, with few trees…the soil looked stony, not much farming. Small roads wound up, down and around the mountain; interspersed were tiny towns, crumbling barns, not many cars.

Exploring nearby, we trekked up through an ancient gate into a town high on a hill; a woman passed us driving a Mercedes convertible. We could see that people were living in this tiny bit of old Italy, and living very nicely. We ate lunch here in a roadside café; I complicated things by asking for ice with my Coca-Cola…I knew, but forgot, that ice is a rarity, particularly in the small towns. The afternoon finished with a 5:00 p.m. service at their favorite small church in a town called Farfa, some worshipers in jeans and sweaters, others in fur coats on this February Sunday.

We packed up and drove back to Rome. We'd had a first weekend in Italy and we'd made good friends; we'd seen small town life that we'd never have found by ourselves, and were now ready to tackle a sophisticated Rome with its history and art and good food. And we owed it all to Maria, to luck and the Internet.

– #11 –
Scenes from a Diary

During a marathon along the Tiber, a small car slowly drove into a policeman.

Maratona

On a gray and cold Sunday—perfect for running—Rome held its *maratona*. In the newspaper, we learned the marathon ran on Lungotevere only two blocks from our apartment. (The Italians know how to name streets; it means along the Tiber.) Colorful crowds gathered; traffic was diverted; balloons abounded. Soon the world-class Kenyans came by, predictably minutes ahead of the rest. What's this—a small car speeding down Lungotevere? <u>It didn't belong there.</u> A policeman waved them to stop! But the car drove on, hitting the cop, who slid right up the hood. The woman driver jumped out, no apologies, hysterical with the cop who appeared unhurt. The last we saw, the policeman was writing down details, the driver still screaming. Rome! When the race was over with cold and dirty air blowing down the Tiber, we chose a café and a *budino.* You don't know *budino?* A scooped-out muffin filled with warm chocolate pudding, perfect after a cold marathon.

◆   ◆   ◆

An Easter Present from Pittsburgh

For an Easter present, Dotti and John Bechtol joined us from Pittsburgh. We were their excuse to see Rome again, their favorite city. John started his own law firm, now run by Dotti. Before, Dotti was CEO of a small steel fabricating company and once my advertising client. Almost a generation younger than we, they both race sports cars. We introduced them to a few new sites: The Tiberina, the small island in the river near Trastevere, Palazzo Spada and Borromini's Perspective, an ancient *trompe-l'oeil* built to appear much longer than it is. The most fun was a dinner at the restaurant Vecchia Roma, "old city" indeed. For an after-dinner game, we summarized their short Roman holiday the way we had learned from Jim Gillespie, my brother-in-law. We asked Dotti and John key questions: "the most vivid moment?", "the best surprise?", "the worst surprise?" and more. It's a way to make your travel more memorable. John's answer for the best surprise was "ask Dotti about this afternoon in the hotel." Then they left us for Paris.

◆   ◆   ◆

Do Americans See Italians as Too Cynical?

What is it like for an American living and working in Rome? Dinner with Susan and Richard, not their real names, gave us an insider's view. Introduced to us by an American friend, Susan, from Pittsburgh and former editor of a fashion magazine in Milan, was the mother of two small children. Richard, an Italian from Australia, was communications director of a large energy company. Their surprising viewpoints: although they loved Rome and its soft weather and excitement, they didn't want to raise their children in Italy. They found cynicism rampant among other parents and their children. Richard found the same at his company. For example, he said, it was understood that everyone would stay at their desks until 8:00 p.m., whether or not work was finished. The extremely close relationship between mothers and older sons, married or not, seemed odd to them. Personified by the custom of ice cream in the late afternoon between mothers and their grown children, the relationship is so common it has a word: *mammismo.*

◆　　　◆　　　◆

Stabat Mater with Mariola and Arnoldo

Landlords Mariola and Arnoldo Boecklin invited us to hear Rossini's Stabat Mater at the 500-year old Gesu cathedral. We had seen this high baroque church before; you could never forget its plaster angels falling from the ceiling into hell. Getting there, Maria showed us how to cross a six-lane *piazza* by just striding forth, left hand high. We learned never to change your pace; motorcycles judge your speed and can dart around you accordingly. Although we had come by subway, Arnoldo arrived by bicycle. Dana and I stood, appropriately, during the choral piece next to a Benedictine monk from San Diego. He explained that Stabat Mater means "standing mother" in front of the cross after Christ has been taken away.

What follows a heavy choral work better than "Rome's best pizza" and Montepulciano, one of Italy's best red wines. Maria tried to sell us on staying in Rome longer and avoiding Vienna: "Oh, those heavy Germans," she said. But we would decide later.

— #12 —
Finally Finding Moses

In 1953 I tried to find Moses, among Michelangelo's most majestic sculptures, but failed. When Dana and I went to Rome in 1971, we missed him again. In 2002, seeing Moses had become an imperative to me. Now or never. Our guide book pointed us to a church new to me, and to a new story. Moses resides in the church San Pietro in Vincoli—St. Peter in chains. The ones he had been shackled to in prison are exhibited here. (One chain was taken to Constantinople in the 5th century, the other kept in Rome, but now they're reunited in this church, located near the Colosseum.)

Although the chains are the famous relics the church is named for, we finally found Moses. Unfortunately, after this long search, both he and the church were great disappointments. The sculptures were being cleaned and the interior of the church was being restored, leaving Moses half-ignored. Scaffolding covered much of the Moses statue and the Tomb of Pope Julius II, designed for Michelangelo's client, benefactor and nemesis.

The great, bearded white marble Moses sits on his throne, challenging the viewer, projecting power and force. A historian writing in 1568 of the hair and beard of the statue, says "it seems that the chisel must have been exchanged for a brush." Because a great cleaning was underway, the setting was less than perfect, the art half-abandoned and messy. Moses, located in a side aisle and subordinate to the tableau of the tomb, doesn't command the dominant space I had expected. His head is covered with a great irony. In sculpting the head, Michelangelo referred to text describing Moses' head as covered with beams of light, mistranslated from Hebrew into "horns" in Latin. It must have been a committee because on his head are two…horns.

Michelangelo started Moses at the command—it was not really a request—of Pope Julius. But the timing was confused with that of the Sistine Chapel, which took priority. Although Moses was commissioned in 1505, it wasn't completed until 1513. Michelangelo had constant harangues with the Pope over money; the project had been budgeted at 10,000 ducats, but after nasty letters and delay on the part of Michelangelo, the final fee was raised to 16,500. To put that in perspective, however, the average worker earned 100 ducats a year in the mid-1500s. Michelangelo saved much of his fees and bought a farm near Florence.

Pope Julius's tomb was also scaled back because of money. Michelangelo first designed 40 larger-than-life statues but ended up with only six. Because of politics, the episode ended with an artist feeling out-of-sorts and underpaid and a client feeling that the work was late.

But for you, the story has a happier ending. By the spring of 2004, stains and grime have been removed from Moses; he is now shiny and clean. The tableau of the Tomb has been scrubbed, and church windows have been repositioned to permit more natural light.

– #13 –
My Market in Rome

Buying food in Rome was convenient, and for me a total delight. It was my first taste of city living, where you walk to a small market and only buy as much as you can carry. I'd seen the ubiquitous string bags famous to Paris shoppers; now it was my turn. We had a small grocery store right out the back entrance to the apartment house, where I'd get the staples of housekeeping. I had a limit of three bags a trip, an easy load for just across the street. Here also were a few favorites, the pesto and tapenade, already made up, waiting in the deli case. So good. But it was the daily (but never on Sunday) open-air market that was the real jewel, a veritable feast of food.

The market was in the mostly-unused alleyway beside our building. Starting up from scratch about 6:30 or 7:00 a.m. every morning, it was a complicated affair, with stalls and bins and electric hook-ups, a pizza oven and even a semi-permanent shed for the meat vendor. All this was brought in at dawn, winter and summer, by the individual vendors…stands set up, baskets and bins organized with signs and prices for literally hundreds of items. Then, by 4:00 in the afternoon, everything was totally gone, the space was empty again, the little street cleaned up and open for traffic.

The work involved seemed staggering to us. This combination food market and department store, so alive with the market smells and sights, the people sounds, was a moveable feast…a mind-boggling quantity of equipment and goods were brought in daily, and taken back out in eight hours.

They sold every locally grown, fresh vegetable imaginable, but also oranges and dates from North Africa, cherries from Sicily and butter from France. There were refrigerated cases of meats and dairy products. Fish was on bins of ice, sometimes in a case, sometimes not. You could get any cut of chicken, pork, veal, beef, trimmed or boned to your choice. The bins of greens, of arugula and cilantro were a treat; I'd get handfuls of each for 50 cents. Most vendors spoke only Italian, we communicated by pointing and holding up fingers...but some of them were proud of their English; one boy in particular, selling tomatoes, would call out, "Hey, American lady, you buy from me today??? Fresh here!!!"

Food was rigidly priced, everything was marked, and you bought it 'as is.' Prices were basically competitive with the super-markets, maybe a little more expensive as it was reputably fresher. Another sight that impressed me was every vendor's expensive scale, the one that weighs, gauges the price, and spits out the slip. These are common enough in the States; somehow, here in the sunshine, in a suburban Rome alley, they seemed so high tech, out of place.

Farther down the main aisle were tables of hardware gadgets, books, laundry products, drugstore necessaries. On large racks, blowing in the morning breezes, hung blouses and skirts, coats and sweaters. Some of the vendors were refreshingly casual; I was looking at a handsome knit skirt and coat one day, and the vendor not only let me take it to the apartment to try it on, but when I brought it back to buy, he took 25 euros off the price. Some days more tables sprouted up for several blocks on the street in both directions, almost filling the wide sidewalks, again with piles of new clothing, sweaters, handi-crafts, watches, trays of jewelry.

The usual noises were raucous, from the street, cars, buses; then cash registers, noises of crates coming in, people talking, vendors selling. But one day I went for the morning paper out the front gates, and the market had a new sound ringing out over the customary hubbub. I passed our café with its normal full comple-ment of espresso drinkers and sweet-cake munchers, and, round-ing the corner into the melee, I heard familiar music. It was Gene Kelly, from the movie, doing "Singin' in the Rain," coming from a radio that a vendor had hooked up. It was so bouncy and American and light-hearted, it really warmed my soul. It played for perhaps three to four minutes, then went silent. But it was enough to make a wonderful, nostalgic start to a spring day in Rome.

– #14 –
The Spanish Steps in Winter

Subj: Roman Report to the Family
Date: Wed, 27 Feb 2002
From: Donner110
To: DManges, DManges630, EManges, HilManges,
         W.Hardy.Manges

Hi kids. We're back at our scroungy cybercafe in Trastevere. With the news that…yesterday we saw the Sistine Chapel. All the books say to arrive, and we did, at the Vatican at 9:15 a.m. It had opened 30 minutes before, and we found very few people. Of course, it _is_ February, which is probably the key.

Again, as the books say to do, we walked straight to the Sistina, ignoring everything else. (In this way, you can be first into the Chapel, and you can catch all those other goodies on the way back.) It's a fair hike; you're routed through galleries, up and down stairs, outside passages, through great works and rooms. But you can't let those distract you. A few more turns left and right, and we were in the historic room that we last saw in 1971 with all the dirt and soot and grime, except nobody realized it at the time. They began to clean the ceiling in the 1980s. Now it's stunning bright colors, pink, green, blue, causing all the art historians to rewrite their rationales for how Michelangelo really liked those dark, dun colors. And, it looks so much more exuberant, more truly Italian than before.

To the seats around the room they have added clear plastic slanting backs that ease your neck in the steady looking-up at the ceiling. We had read up on it the previous night, and could identify many of the monumental figures and stories, and felt much closer to the great work. One of Michelangelo's big tasks was to keep things in proportion as they would appear from the floor.

Today, we rediscovered the Spanish Steps, still there, still full of teens, even out of season. We went to the top, now a bigger hike than it used to be. Then, with Maria leading us, we went back down to the Condotti, the great shopping street right across the *piazza* at the bottom of the Steps, to the Anglo Book Store, where we browsed for an hour, buying David's recommendation, "Guns, Germs and Steel." We also got a child's book on learning Italian, as that's our speed.

So, consider yourself updated. The Japanese cherry trees in our street are a-bloom in late February. Gorgeous.

– #15 –
50 Years
Between Sistine Chapels

I first saw Rome in 1953 on leave from the Army in Stuttgart. It was March. I was leaving long leather coats and briefcases, stolid faces, cold winds and white skies. It was a trip of firsts: palm trees, an airplane flight over the Alps, a stopover in Nice where Rex Harrison waited languidly in the airport. When our Pan Am flight arrived in Roma, I found bright sun, flowers blooming in window boxes, burnt umber buildings in the late afternoon light, and, in my imagination, a busty soprano leaning from a window singing Puccini. It was Italy, it was…<u>Europe</u>!

When in Rome, we did what the tourists do: some buddies and I quickly got ourselves to St. Peters, where we dutifully took pictures of each other. Despite the research, I couldn't comprehend the scale of St. Peters nor the technology of the 1500s. I walked up to Michelangelo's Pieta; in 1953 it stood on the floor near the entrance. I ran my hands around the smooth, cool marble, unheard of today. The scale of the figures was even smaller than I had read, more tender.

But now it is 50 years later. Security today calls for a thick, bulletproof glass barrier between you and the Pieta after it was vandalized decades ago.

To find the Sistine Chapel we wound our way through the mazes and through the Raphael rooms, through the little wooden door frame and there was the chapel! I still have the art book with photographs of the colors we didn't realize then were <u>dirty</u>. Nor did a critic in 1952, describing the Sibyl of Libya: "The color is extremely delicate, rose and purple in the flesh, orange in the robe, and silver-gray in the garment…" Regarding the Expulsion From Eden, she writes "the indefinite colors (violet, blue fading off into white and dark green) contribute to the atmosphere of impending doom." Today, those subtle colors are bright greens, blues, purples and reds as Michelangelo painted them.

The downside, of course, to the Sistine Chapel, is the pain in your neck. Ideally, arrive around 8:30 in the morning and take one of the seats around the wall. Have a book to explain the amazing work Michelangelo created in 1508 on his scaffolding while he remembered the perspective from the floor below. The painting of the ceiling, which took four years, has been described in the book "Michelangelo and the Pope's Ceiling," replete with haranguing and late payments from Pope Julius III. But the proper words for this soaring work are beyond the limits of this memoirist.

– #16 –
Pompeii

On our first trip out of Rome to see the ruins at Pompeii, we took the train to Naples…and we got on the wrong train. It went to Naples, all right, it just took three hours instead of two. So we had a lot of time to see spring in southern Italy: bits of ancient columns intermixed with flowering fruit trees; the curling clusters of wisteria, the ruined aqueducts among the green fields.

Naples, sprawling on its beautiful bay, was totally urban with busy streets, cars, pedestrians, trucks and horrendous traffic. After checking into our hotel, high on a hill, we set out to explore. We walked down, down toward the water, and found a restorative café in a large square, Piazza dei Martiri, the same Martyrs of our street in Rome.

And it was not the Naples we expected. It was an elegant shopping street, with all the prestige of Hermès and Cartier. Suddenly everyone was very well dressed, simply but expensively. There were charming townhouses, smart flower shops, dress shops, all the accouterments of the good life. We never did see that Neapolitan scene (probably apocryphal) of the narrow streets teeming with people and hung high with laundry.

"We have two things we want to do," Don said to Salvatore, as we got into his cab the next morning: "To see Pompeii, and to tour the archeological museum here in Naples." All three of us had to refer to our yellow *Langenscheidt* Dictionaries for our stilted sentences.

After some bargaining, we made a deal: for 80 euros he was ours for two days. He'd drive us to Pompeii, where we had lined up a tour of the *'scavi,'* wait two hours, drive us back to Naples; the next day he would take us to the big museum here, wait, then drive us down to Sorrento and Capri and the famous Amalfi Drive. He could go, we'd stay the night and come back by train. A trip with luxury not typical of us, but such a comfortable one!

Pompeii was big, fascinating, and, surprisingly to us, still under excavation. Our guide vividly narrated the big blow. My notes quote him:

> In August 79 A.D., the top 200 feet of Mt. Vesuvius blew off. Gases killed many right in their tracks. It was midday; bread was found on tables and in ovens, coins were left on a bar. Several feet of ash preserved the many bodies. The city lay undiscovered until the 1600s, with excavation beginning 100 years later. A magnificent city plan, complete with paved streets and graffiti. Many houses were big and luxurious with atria and baths with vaulted ceilings.

As we walked through with the guide, the overarching feeling was that life then, roughly 2000 years ago, was not too different from today, give or take a few inventions. Our favorite was a comfortable, easy-living home termed the House of the Faun, named for the famous and graceful bronze statuette found there. This restoration of a wealthy man's house showed the floor plan built around an open courtyard, with rooms opening off each side, just as in California or Florida houses of today. Much, but not all, of the town has been excavated, uncovering streets with public baths, bakeries, an amphitheater, extravagant villas and ordinary homes, a large forum and a market place, so much of it like small towns in Italy today.

People lay as they were caught by the fine pumice ash of the volcano. In 1868, an archeologist, Guiseppe Fiorello, devised the ingenious method of making the amazingly true-to-life replicas of the bodies; they are really plaster casts of the <u>void</u> formed by the body as it lay (and slowly disintegrated) in the ash. These hollows hardened with time and stayed intact, undiscovered, through the centuries. Fiorello poured liquid plaster of Paris into the cavities, forming accurate and detailed copies of the victims. You can see these often poignant copies in the big Naples Museum, one, particularly, of a dying mother and child.

Thousands of amphorae, statues and everyday artifacts have been discovered through the ages in Pompeii; many of them we saw piled up in storerooms at the excavations, seemingly ignored. The Museo Archeologica in Naples houses the extraordinary relics: finely-wrought silver dishes and combs, glassware, beautiful mosaics and frescoes. The mosaics were true works of art, with tiny, delicately-made tiles arranged in spectacular designs wonderfully preserved, the colors fresh and true. In a *sala secreti* was Pompeiian erotica for adults only. Don's favorite was the coupling of a man and a goat; the goat is smiling.

That afternoon Salvatore aimed his taxi along the famous Amalfi Drive, hanging over the sea. The drive was brilliant, houses everywhere clinging to the cliffs, the blue Mediterranean below. It was almost a carbon copy of the lower Corniche, my favorite on the Côte d'Azur of France. From my journal: "I know everyone is in love with Italy, but to me, the Amalfi just looked a little ragged compared to the views from my bus ride along the French coast from Nice up to Monaco." Maybe I just missed Amalfi's best!

We had lunch with Salvatore, seaside. Checking his yellow phrase book, he smiled, "I'm ver-ee pleased to meet you." He was a nice kid, doing all the right things, earning money to buy a cab, going to school, studying English. I hope it all worked for him.

Capri was tantalizingly close, but we got lazy and opted for an overnight instead in Sorrento, with memories of Italian tenors in our ears straining with "Come Back to Sorrento." Wisteria dominated the town square where we drank beer in a café and shared our thin-crusted Neapolitan pizza with the pigeons.

Ancient dust mixed with springtime and the south of Italy. "It doesn't get any better at 72," Don said.

– #17 –
Visiting Europe
With Kids

Pantheon

On the train to Naples, near us sat a young American father and his son about 10, quietly speaking English. "Where are you from?" I asked. "We're from Montana," said the father, perhaps in his 40s. "We come to Italy every spring." That's all we spoke, but it was enough to pique our curiosity. Was he a teacher or history buff? What drove this interest?

The next year, in the American Church in Paris, we met another young father, this time from Tyler, Texas: a lawyer, with two of his four children, aged eleven and thirteen. "Every year, either my wife or I bring two of our children to Europe. To make history more exciting and vivid. They've become really educated, much better than I was at their age," he said.

– #18 –
Waiting on Lungotevere

Ponte Sisto

Subj: Impressions from Rome
Date: March 5, 2002
To: WSGarrett
From: MBoecklin

Dear Bill...I am writing on our landlady's hotmail (and computer) as we're too lazy today to bus down to our Trastevere cybercafe. Here are just a few recent impressions from Rome.

Spring came around February 20 with the blooming Japanese cherry trees. All beside our building, and in front of our café, Giolitti, which the travel guides say has Rome's best *gelato*. The plane trees are now greening up to soften some of Rome's winter gray.

Judging by what you see on the street, many Romans, however, are reluctant to give up their winter coats and over-the-shoulder foulards. One warm day we saw a woman in gloves and a wool hat. For us, it's been degrees of spring. On Sunday, everyone gathered in the sunny-side-of-the-street cafés, over those long lunches when the food has been long gone, and no rush on the check.

We should have been studying Italian rather than going to our wonderful neighborhood parties. People here in Rome hear us stumbling and then offer their few words of English, often the same words we know in Italian. Last night I went to the dictionary before going out to buy some ball point pens. Dictionary said the word is…hang on, you'll never guess…*penne*. Of course. I bought three *penne*, shaped just like the pasta.

A recent night was a traveler's high. We had been busy touring sights, finishing up at our favorite place in Trastevere to e-mail, until 8:30 p.m. We waited on Lungotevere, along the Tiber, for a bus. (We've thought we should have a word like that in Pittsburgh, say, Lungallegheny.) It got colder and colder and the wait longer and longer.

Finally our bus came. We went straight to a restaurant in our *quartieri* that has no name and no menu and is always crowded…and ordered Pasta Carbonara. *Grande!* House *vino rosso*. Very ordinary and just the thing. Beyond *al dente*. Only 12 tables inside, but 30 on the sidewalk with gas heaters and young folks…lots of conversation and waving of hands and arms in the air.

Yesterday was our first unpleasantness. Set out to see Moses by Michelangelo, whom twice I've tried to find, in 1953 and 1971, missing him both times. I took the subway, but got disoriented, walked forever, got tired, and settled for Santa Maria Maggiore, a church under construction from the 5th century until the 13th.

Gives new meaning to "adding on." Big! Beautiful tiles and inlaid marble floors. So another day for Moses.

Early May we go for a week to Orvieto where our landlady's sister owns a horse farm; we get an *apartemento* in her villa. Then to Venice for four days, and on to Vienna for three months, where we're assured 24-hour cable TV and Internet. What more could anyone want?

Don

− #19 −
Speaking Italian After You've Said "Ciao" and "Pizza"

When we arrived at our Rome apartment, we were met by Maria Boecklin, our landlady, and Christiana, the real estate agent. They spoke only English, which, it turned out, set our expectations too high. We've been learning tourist talk a long time, enough to learn "the central heating doesn't work" in Greek. And, if you've had Latin, you can guess a lot from reading.

All that means nothing. It's the sounds. Here are a few must-learns, published in the back of the "DK Eyewitness Book on Rome," or most any travel book.

Where is	*Dov'e* (dove-ay)
Good morning	*Buon giorno* (bwone jorn-oh)
Thank you	*Grazie* (three syllables—grah-tsee—eh)
Please	*Per favore* (pear fav-or-eh)
Good evening	*Buona sera* (bwone-na say-ra)
Goodbye	*Arrivederci* (but you already knew this)
Do you speak English?	*Parla Inglese?*
I don't understand	*Non capisco*
Left	*A sinistra* (think sinister)
Right	*A destra* (think dextrous)
That's fine	*Va bene* (excepting crises, you'll say it most of the day
For everything	*Ciao* (chow can be goodbye or hi)

We also learned the numbers from one to ten, but any serious negotiations demanded a calculator and the English language. To learn a little Italian, we used "Italian For Beginners," a child's illustrated book that comes with a CD, published by www.usborne.com. By the end you'll be able to say *"Puo parlare piu lentamente, per favore,"*—"could you speak more slowly, please?" Rick Steves' books also have language sections.

Nobody tells you the most basic thing: you <u>must</u> always pronounce the Italian vowels the same way, the Italian way: a = ah; e = ay; i = ee; o = short o, not oh-oo; u = oo, not yew.

And unless someone has just hit your front fender, smile! It goes a long way toward communicating, and keeps Americans from looking so dour or commanding. Use plenty of arm and hand movements the way Italians do; otherwise, relax. Italian is music, whether or not you play an instrument.

Here, however, is the street truth to our communicating in any urgent situation, say the post office. You're talking through a grill, and your opposite is looking down, making sounds that do not sound human. We learned *"scusi, non parlo l'Italiano. Parla Inglese?"* ("I'm sorry, I don't speak Italian. Do you speak English?") The least excusable but certainly understandable gesture for a stressful movement is holding both arms out wide and looking helpless. Someone always comes from the crowd to help, as in the woman who came to us as soon as we carried a large package into the Rome post office.

What's our favorite phrase in Italian? *"Dolce Far Niente."* The sweetness of doing nothing. You'll never find an Anglo-Saxon saying that!

– #20 –
Halt! Welcome to
The American Academy in Rome

For many years I had heard The American Academy was a place for sequestering American writers and artists. One afternoon, I walked there from our apartment. We were in I Pratti, or the fields, northwest of the Vatican. I crossed the Tiber twice, moving south through the old city and then again to Trastevere, the quarter heavy with students and home to one of the oldest churches, Santa Maria de Trastevere. I followed my map carefully. What's this? I had to walk up steep steps, asking strangers questions as I rose. The map didn't indicate the changes in levels and heights I had to reach.

The climb, however, was worth the effort. I was on the Janiculum hill. Finally, I arrived at the commanding views of Rome, and then the high iron fences of the Academy.

A sentry in the guardhouse told me to stop, then buzzed me in through the locked gate. I entered the imposing atrium of the grand house, built by American philanthropists in the 1910s, and walked around looking at paintings. From the beginning, the purpose of the Academy was to offer a hideaway for American writers and artists to absorb the culture and history of Rome. As I wandered, an American woman who identified herself as a writer said, "Tea is being served across the atrium." There I found cookies and tea and a comfortable room furnished with leather sofas, 19th century landscapes and some international newspapers. I certainly felt at home in Rome.

Suddenly, another woman walked up to me and asked me to leave, please. "This space is not open to the public," she said. "You are not allowed in!"

I backed out of the room and walked around the atrium to another gallery showing paintings by Chuck Close, the American painter. It's sort of a compelling, warts-and-all pointillism. I was dismayed by the treatment of an institution that purports to promote the American image, and comes off as a policeman's whistle. I realized I was there only months after 9/11/01 and security had to be tightened all over the world. How do we combine security with a welcoming attitude?

I returned, however, to the Academy several times with friends to see the arresting views of Rome from the Janiculum hill and the charming neighborhood of Trastevere. Among many other things, the theaters that play American films' *version originale* were located there, as well as our favorite cybercafe.

When you visit, spend some time at Santa Maria in Trastevere, the church founded in 217 A.D. Twenty-two granite columns taken from Roman ruins support the structure; beautiful mosaics were added a <u>thousand</u> years later. In front of the church is the big *piazza* with Sabatini's restaurant where we had dinner with Jim and Lois, giggling in 1971. Since Dana hadn't felt well after dinner, I walked her around the graceful *piazza* in the full moonlight. Then 42, we were now 72. In 30 years, a lot of water had washed down that Tiber.

– #21 –
Arrividerci, Roma

I n late April 2002, nearing the end of our three-month stay in
Rome, we had packed seven apple cartons of clothes and
books. Dana had bought heavy wrapping paper at a cybercafe in Trastevere along with wide, thick Scotch tape, so that the
boxes were well secured.

Our most arduous shipping event was organizing and sending stuff to three cities: three boxes destined for Pittsburgh, two
for Vienna (our next rental) and two boxes of winter clothes to
London. Did Eisenhower have tougher problems with the
Normandy invasion? Arnoldo lent us his dolly to transport the
boxes from our third floor apartment to ground level, on the
nervous three-man elevator. In two trips, I rolled the seven boxes
from the third floor to the street. After a wave and a shout, we

had a taxi. The boxes and the dolly fit into the trunk of the back seat, and off we drove to La Poste.

The 15-euro taxi pulled into "INTL PACCHI." Out came the dolly and the seven boxes. To our pleasant surprise, no line; our best post-office experience. (Some of our most stressful moments over 18 months had been at the post office, talking through the grill, with lack of language and anxious people behind us, but not today.) Total cost was $260, far less than the $850 from Pittsburgh to Rome. Maybe we were learning. Christiana, the in-charge real estate agent, came to settle the utility bill for our three-month stay. The bad news was the electricity: 387 euros, equivalent to around $350! It should have been far less. We screamed; she looked for reasons. We had Scotch-taped the water heater switch so that the heat was permanently <u>on</u> for three months.

How did we feel about Rome? We hated to leave but there were unseen adventures over the mountains to the north. We had learned to cope and enjoy, not always equal partners. We had solved most of the practical things of life: buying food, finding cybercafes, learning to use maps and subways and trams, communicating with family and friends.

We had landlords who gave us the keys to their own apartment when they were out of town. They explained the Metro, showed us where to buy important things like a cell phone. They invited us to their country home, took us to church, provided us with an apartment in Paris a year later and helped arrange a week on an Umbrian farm.

We had seen the daffodils of Rome arrive the middle of February, several months earlier than in Pittsburgh, followed by the flowering trees and the rhododendrons. We had sat on park benches, sun on our faces, warmed by only light jackets.

We had enjoyed most of the things tourists must see in Rome, and returned many times: The Pantheon from first century A.D.; Capitoline Hill with Michelangelo's stairway; Livia's underground dining room from early A.D., looking like an

Impressionistic fresco; walking along the Tiber with the proud, straight-backed Romans; licking the *gelati* cones in the late afternoons in Giolitti, Rome's best *gelateria* and in our building. We had learned to dance amidst the daunting traffic. We had a yellow-and-white apartment with a terrace (well, yes, it was tiny) off the homey kitchen.

We had seen the destruction that Vesuvius had wrought and the artifacts collected in the Naples museum; we'd hung over the cliffs of the Amalfi Drive and admired the blooming wisteria of Sorrento.

We had learned to live and work together in very small places, to enjoy the style, the tempo and looks of Italians. We had made some friends. We were there so long we had guests—from Antibes and from Pittsburgh. But there's no place like Rome.

– #22 –
Small Favorites of Rome

– The Isola di Tiborina, the little island in the Tiber just under the Garibaldi bridge at Trastevere, where we *anziani* walk and enjoy the sun, the young sleep and study.

– My favorite church, among the many, was Santa Maria della Vittoria, off the Veneto not far from the Barbarini *piazza*. Here is Bernini's famous sculpture, The Ecstasy of St. Teresa. In a small chapel at the front designed to look like a theatre, St. Teresa is watched by marble patrons in a marble-draperied box...on-lookers with stunned, awe-stricken faces.

– And the small church itself is a jewel. It's all in subtle, striated tones of beige marble, totally Baroque, with curlicues and cherubs everywhere.

– Motorcycles abound; mostly small Vespas, they whiz deftly through the bewildering maze of cars, buses, taxis. Many young women are driving, smartly dressed in black, in skirts, pants, high-heels...and helmets.

– The time I forgot my sunglasses in a sidewalk café on Cola di Rienzi: when I remembered and returned an hour later, I found them on an overhanging tree, right where someone had carefully placed them.

– Most bus rides pass breaktakingly world-famous buildings that are pictures out of countless history books. Our most-traveled route whirled around Castel Sant' Angelo, passing Mussolini's Via della Conciliazione where, if we looked fast enough, we could catch sight of St. Peter's Square and Church down at the end. Just an ordinary bus ride in Rome.

–   The Borghese Gardens are worth the many rules encountered...if only for famous sculptures; my favorite was the reclining nude of Pauline Borghese by Canova. Pauline, Napoleon's sister, who apparently married well, lies on a couch; the indentations of the body on the marble couch cushions struck me as the height of expertise.

–   The sidewalk cafés from 4:30-8:00 p.m. were filled with Italy searching for sweets. We saw little wine, no beer, but a lot of ice cream and cake and coffee...teenagers, *anziani,* workmen, housewives...all socializing in the hours before dinner at 9:00 p.m.

–   Livia's Garden, in the Museo Nazionale Romano, near the Piazza Republica: the actual frescoes, excavated from Livia and Augustus' palace, from about 100 A.D., and supposed to be her summer dining room, show a garden of spring trees in bloom, fruit trees, flowers, bushes, all in soothing blues and greens, a few red touches. The garden retreats into the background, the cool greenery giving a definite feeling of space and distance, and an artist's perspective a millenium before Giotto's famed murals in Assisi.

–   The little walking bridge, Ponte Sisto, that spanned the Tiber, between Trastevere and the Via Giulia: perfect in proportion, it had three distinctive large, circular holes put in centuries ago to help during flood times.

–   Parking is totally inventive in Rome. The Smart car, by Daimler-Chrysler, is a common sight; so small, its length equals the width of ordinary cars, so it's often found parked straight into the curb. You see bigger cars on sidewalks, too...double, even triple parking. A prolonged horn on a suburban street means a car is trapped; usually within minutes a driver comes running to help…and it's all done with no recriminations. It's just Italy.

—   We had the luck of arriving in Italy January 2002, just as the euro became legal. So as everybody was fumbling for the right coin, we weren't obvious as inept Americans in the super-markets.

—   The little electric minibus #116 that travels the small crowded streets of the historic center: depending on traffic, it was about a 60-minute round trip from the wall of the Borghese Gardens at the top of the Veneto, down that winding street of cafés to Piazza Barbarini and the Bernini fountain, over to the Spanish Steps; it nears the Piazza Populo, passes the Pantheon and Piazza Navona with its three Bernini fountains and blocks-ful of cafés; drives along the river on the charming Via Guilia under the unfinished Michelangelo bridge and archway, designed to link the Farnese Palazzo and its gardens with the family's country house, Villa Faresina, across the river. The mini-bus circles back up, goes through the Borghese Gardens to wait again at the top of the Veneto.

—   And a wonderful April sight: the plane trees, with their long, spring-green tendrils lopping, unpruned, over both sides of Lungotevere, the river road, provide a quieting canopy for the traffic. Closer to the river, another row of trees has long branches leaning down, almost touching the water.

– #23 –
You Can't Get to Orvieto Through Cassino

After three months in Rome, we left for Orvieto. Well, Vienna was really the final destination but Maria, our landlady, convinced us we should stay at her sister's farm near Orvieto on the way, just a few hours north of Rome. We were leaving with all our world-traveler goods: six bags including a laptop, not an average lightweight purse.

In the Rome station there was confusion about which *binario* (track) to take. A uniformed man in the Information booth, seeing our agonized expressions, offered help in English and directed us to track 19. We got a cart and dragged the bags and ourselves to 19, second class, and found two seats. An hour later while admiring the farm land still being worked since Etruscans' time, Dana offered our tickets to the conductor.

"You're not going to Orvieto; you're going to Cassino…in the south," he said more with an arm wave than with words.

We were headed the wrong way. So we dragged the bags and got off at the next stop, a hamlet of a dozen houses. Standing too near the tracks, we were waved to move by the stationmaster just in time for an express train that whizzed by only inches from our luggage. But then came a train back to Roma.

Seeing ourselves with a third eye, we laughed ruefully. We were, after all, *anziani*, the ancient ones, and the looks from fellow passengers only confirmed it.

As seat mates gave us the sign, Orvieto finally appeared. Two of them helped pull bags down from the racks as we waddled to the door. The stop was very short; as I slid down the steps on top of our bags, the door kept shutting, Dana pushing the button to keep it from closing on me. We were clear of the train just seconds before it moved on.

Anziani indeed! We found a taxi to our Villa Mercede, a practicing convent that rents a few rooms. It was starting to rain. Of course. The brother who greeted us in his long brown robe had no record of our reservation. We had a piece of paper from the travel agency, but the brother had notified them "no room" after we left Rome. What to do? People standing around sympathized and translated, when another, more businesslike Padre Franco arrived. Sent by heaven, he rented us his *apartmento* with kitchen, with great views of a soccer field and tennis court. One condition: out by 9:00 a.m! Dana, ever curious, played with the stove and triggered a clicking sound we couldn't turn off. All we could do was punch a breaker and sneak into sheets damp and reminiscent of summer camp. The convent was quiet like nothing in Rome, a precursor to sleep.

Before 9:00 a.m. we were out, leaving bags in the hallway (Turkish carpets on well-waxed floors), the electricity turned back on, and no more clicking. We had some rolls and coffee at a cafeteria, then wandered the town. Horizontal bands of white travertine and blue-gray basalt define the exterior of the Romanesque-Gothic Duomo. Arresting! With construction beginning in 1290, one of Italy's greatest cathedrals stands sentry to the large plain *piazza*. Surprisingly, its front entrance features bronze doors from the 1960s.

Turning from God to *mammon*, we walked down the street and found Dana some smart shoes (there are no unsmart shoes in Italy) for walking. Two hundred euros to Sergio Rossi!

We had invited Pittsburgh friends Bob and Sally Worsing to stay with us on the farm. Bob is the architect who designed an addition to our house in 1970; he and Sally Stone recently made a second marriage. She runs a community music program at Duquesne University. Both are adventurous, travel at the drop of a euro and love Italy. Wearing her new shoes, Dana and I strolled back to the Duomo and there sat Bob and Sally in a café. Their flight and the car rental had worked. With their arrival our good fortune traffic light had turned from red (on the train) to green.

Bob had rented a big Opel. We called Chiara and got directions to the farm near Monte Gabbione. Through the windshield: nice rolling hills, few houses. Driving through the gate, there came Chiara, sister of our Roman landlady, Mariola. Chiara, with a breezy manner, recently retired as a corporate communications officer. Now she and her husband Giovanni breed horses and rent a separate two bedroom apartment in their Umbrian farmhouse. (Umbria is hilly, much less developed and to the East of Tuscany. Our guide book calls it "Tuscany's gentler sister.")

The apartment was comfortable with good beds, renting for 650 euros a week. Since today was our 45th anniversary, the four of us celebrated at a *"typico Tuscani"* restaurant nearby. The drive was tortuous around the mountains and certainly curtailed any celebrating with wine. We slept under blankets hearing an occasional whinny from a horse or the barking of a dog.

The next morning we walked the countryside, the rain leaving mud that played havoc with Dana's <u>new shoes</u>. The only building nearby was a handsome old brick house, abandoned by an owner who left magazines on the living room sofa. All else was trees, bushes, streams. Arriving home, Sally, a horse lover, snuggled up to Chiara's horse named Lucy.

The next day, a Sunday, was Sally's 62nd birthday. Chiara recommended a celebration at La Torrette near the town of Chiesa. We got the last table amidst a big party after a young girl's first communion. In her all-white dress, she brought us a piece of white cake with chocolate icing. The guests were effusive; the views from the restaurant rural and idyllic.

The week went fast: Sally made spaghetti; we visited Deruda, a town where ceramics are made; Dana and Sally tried truffles at a nearby pizza place one night, yelping with satisfaction. Both Bob and I, in the Army in Germany in the 1950s, spoke pidgin Deutsch. Since the Italian owner of the pizza parlor had worked in Germany, bad German became the currency of communication for ordering pizza. Chiara gave us a bottle of good local wine and directed us to the vineyard that would sell us more. We found it, owned by an Austrian who had moved south for his wife's health. For only five euros a bottle, we had a pleasant merlot-like red.

Driving around, we happened upon a medieval celebration in Assisi. We found the Basilica di San Francesco where Giotto created 28 frescoed panels of the life of St. Francis. This was for me one of the art highlights of 18 months. I had studied the frescoes in college, but it wasn't until I saw them *in situ* that I appreciated how modern and impressionistic they seemed. That night we stayed in the Hotel Umbria where we found CNN, unusual for us, and with good news, too: Cisco, our angel/devil Nasdaq stock, was up for the day.

In Assisi we celebrated Ascension Day. Bleachers had been set up on the cobbled street, with the men in tights and the women in long, sparkling gowns. It was the Middle Ages. A parade with drums and trumpets passed the reviewing stand at their city hall. For us, discovering the hill towns late in life instead of as juniors in college seemed just right.

The Waters of Venice
Prologue

Venice is water. It's the beauty of Venice, and its enemy. The waters of the Aegean Sea surround and nurture the ancient city, all the while slowly, minutely, swallowing it up. Somehow, Venice, a cluster of tiny islands in the sea, still survives, with its centuries-old history and drama still intact.

Venice is water. You eat by waterside; your expensive hotel room overlooks the water. You travel by water; food and furniture arrive by water. Boats are everywhere: *vaporettos*, motor launches, romantic gondolas for hire, freight boats, row boats. High noon on the canals is all hustle and bustle; it's a watery Fifth Avenue in New York City, a State Street in Chicago.

You arrive in Venice by causeway over water; the Grand Canal greets you right out of the train station. At water's edge a roomy *vaporetto*, a waterbus, waits. It starts up and heads toward the heart of the city. It moves slowly, sturdily. If a local, it will stop at alternate sides of the Canal, taking 45-60 minutes to reach the Lido at the end of the island.

Your boat passes the famed striped poles and the semi-ruined *grand palaces*. You see the high-water marks of past floods on the buildings, the supporting timbers that look half-rotten. The boat makes the turn at the Rialto bridge, the real heart of the city; then the Grand Canal widens as it flows into the Canale della Giudecca, the vistas open up. Here are the famous domes of San Salute on one side, San Marco on the other, islands in the distance. It's all sea and sky and history.

Finding San Marco

Our first morning in Venice Don and I came out of our tiny *pensione* into a beautiful spring day. A block away was the train station, and right in front was the Grand Canal, water rippling in the sunshine, complete with a dock and a waiting *vaporetto*.

(*Vaporettos* are smallish ferry-boats, with seats in the center but a lot of standing room around the edges.) We hopped on, discovering it was a local that stopped at alternating sides of the canal, a bus tour without the guide and the microphone.

Both sides of the canal had picture-postcard views. We lumbered slowly past empty ruined buildings, past elegant *palazzos* with moored motor launches. The canal itself had everything, from heavy boats filled with plywood sheets and concrete blocks to fast boats driven by businessmen in suits and ties. We saw a gondolier with striped shirt poling the traditional curved-prow boat, impressing a tourist family.

It probably was an hour before the boat chugged slowly to the last stop…"everybody off"…called the Lido. We'd read about the Lido beach for years; it was famous as a European playground in the high-living 20s and 30s, particularly for Cole Porter and his troop of friends. But this was different. Not a sign of a beach. We were in a small village that looked like any Italian town…remarkable only for being ordinary. It had cafés and pharmacies and dress shops, a startling change from the Venice we'd just left.

After the obligatory café-and-sweet break, we walked a mile through the village, through a grassy, tree-lined park…and found the famous beach empty, only one man walking his dog. High noon in Italy is siesta time. No Cole Porter and Linda Lee, or Noel Coward or Elsa Maxwell, those wandering, pleasure-seeking personalities of the 30s. However, the elegant flowery boulevard was lined with the seaside mansions and estates that we expected; but they looked old…not charming or money-old, but imposing and slightly crumbling-old. It was another era.

Arriving back at our hotel, we realized we hadn't seen the enormous San Marco Cathedral. It surely was on the Grand Canal; did we just miss it? We checked with the hotel clerk. Yes, it was there; we'd just been looking the wrong way, at the imposing, also enormous, San Salute cathedral on the other side of the Canal; we never saw the world-famous landmark of Venice.

If you choose to walk from Santa Lucia…a wonderful name for the train station…you're on a 12-foot wide *allée*, flanked by shops, restaurants, hotels, even a cybercafe. As you explore further, most of the tourists disappear, the streets become narrow passageways of domesticity, with doorways, curtained windows, children playing. The street names are high up on the wall. Side canals appear, fingers of water, with small bridges arching between the tiny specks of land. It's all bigger than you realize.

Night or day, people are everywhere, predominately the young…late-teens and twenties of all nationalities. Cybercafes, hotels, souvenir shops, the ubiquitous tee-shirt vendors, all this is Venice. Here too are museums. Our favorite was the Peggy Guggenheim, right on the Grand Canal. An art aficionado and heiress to the Guggenheim fortune, she bought paintings and sculptures through the 20s and 30s, finally housing them in a *palazzo* in Venice after WW II. Waterside, you're greeted by a dramatic red steel work, closely followed by a wonderful Murani sculpture that has raised a few eyebrows in its day. Inside is an eclectic array of modern art through the decades, housed on several floors of the palace. A café overlooks the tree-shaded courtyard with more statuary, and touchingly, a small graveyard of Guggenheim pets.

One twilight, searching out the famous Cathedral di San Marco, we walked up through the side streets from our hotel. We followed the high, faintly marked, almost hidden arrow signs through the maze of winding, twisty narrow walkways. Turning a last corner, we suddenly emerged into a vast *piazza,* enveloped by mist from the sea, the bulk of the San Marco looming up right beside us. We walked past the Cathedral, gigantic and shadowy and Byzantine, across the immense open space to the arcades of shops and cafés with tables of white linens gleaming through the mist.

Two competing orchestras were playing, violins and waltzes from one, light guitar jazz from the other across the *piazza.* It was early for an Italian dinner, maybe 8:30 p.m. A few people were there, mainly tourists. We joined them, listened to the music, savoring the wine and the ambience. Dusk came; we watched San Marco retreat into the fog and the *piazza* grow dark. Some dim lights came on in the arcades, most of the tables remained empty. The tourists disappeared and the bands packed up their instruments. We walked across the *piazza* to the water's edge and caught the next *vaporetto* back to the hotel.

The next day we went back to tour both the San Marco and the Doge's Palace, situated on the same big *piazza* on the water side of the Cathedral. Lighter in feel than San Marco, the Palace was founded in the ninth century and was given its Gothic airiness some 500 years later, according to the "DK Travel Guide," by "perching its bulk (of pink Veronese marble) on top of loggias and arcades." Inside are the bare, familiar rooms of the Italian Renaissance, the wide porches to catch the cool air of night, the imposing stairways, the ballroom for state receptions.

Touring the Cathedral was a different walk; it was Byzantine, not Italian, a myriad of dusty hallways and chapels and dim lighting. We tourists went through in single-file groups, fairly rigorously patrolled…and it was all basically disappointing. I remember no furnishings, no light, just dusty dark rooms and corridors. Then I realized it wasn't the interior of San Marco that the artists loved; it was the exciting, exotic, Eastern architecture, it was the facade of the huge building and its *piazza* that has been photographed and painted for centuries. Yes, that's the classic picture of Venice…the marvelous Byzantine San Marco with its familiar domes, the pigeons in the *piazza,* beside the Grand Canal.

Epilogue

We ended our four days in Venice, and as we settled down in the train up to Vienna on our first class seats (finally!) we realized some truths. We hadn't seen the Academia, one of the largest troves of Venetian art. We didn't search out some of the famous houses and palaces, the ones in every Venice photograph. We didn't go to the sister islands of Murano, noted for its glass, and

Burano, another fascinating town. Or Harry's Bar, famous in the 20s. We'd missed a great part of that fabulous, exotic city, and we knew why.

The first excuses were basic tiredness and the lack of time; we could have seen more had we not needed the necessary lie-down hours. Four days was not enough for us to do it all; we should have given it much more time.

The bigger reason was that we simply hadn't done our home-work. As much as we'd based the move from Rome to Austria around northern Italy and Venice, we didn't read and plan and organize this visit as we had others in the past. We didn't think it through. I think we just forgot about planning. We had been so spoiled by the expanse of time in Rome, where we could visit a famous landmark and leave, to return at our leisure, or not, as we pleased. We just got too casual, and the price we paid was Venice.

– #25 –
Coping With Italian Trains

This story is how <u>not</u> to travel in Italy. Traveling by train in Italy is not simple, at least for those of us who don't know the language or the different Italian customs. We figured we could handle most of the pitfalls; however, we kept finding a bundle of new ones, most of them our fault. As dumb as most of our mistakes were, I don't think they're terribly unusual for foreigners.

Now, we knew about getting tickets ahead of time, not waiting until the train station to buy them. We used a local travel agent…they usually speak enough English, and they're everywhere. And the fee is small and definitely worth it. Without the language, it's just too hard at the station, speaking through the little hole in the glass barrier that's between you and the ticket-seller, surrounded by the hustle and bustle of all Italy.

When we went to Naples and Pompeii about a month after we got to Rome, the first thing we did was get on the wrong train. It was going to Naples, all right, and at the correct time, which was what fooled us. It turns out those tricky Italians had <u>two</u> trains leaving for Naples at 11:18 a.m.; one was the faster Eurostar we had booked, the other was a crowded local, stopping all the way south. Of course, our train had a designation we should have looked at, like E for Eurostar, or something simple. But that's one of the things you tend to forget…you see a train marked Naples, you get on it. Or at least we do. And we saw a lot of small Italian towns that day.

It's hard enough just finding the right train, even when you've got the right track, because they can put two trains, heading out, on the same *binario*. Also, it would help if Italy would number the trains, but they don't. In the States, or in most of Europe, your ticket has the train number and the destination, both of which are put up on the big announcement board. In Italy, they don't do that. What they do is put up the name of the destination train <u>station</u>, not the city.

We discovered this coming back from Naples, when no train to Rome was listed on the board. In our case, it wasn't even the Rome station not listed, which we might have recognized as Rome's *Termini*. It was marked with the Milan station, as our train was going on north with just a stop in Rome. It never occurred to us that Rome wasn't the end of the line…Rome, the capital of the country? Just a pit-stop? It's as if they put up South Station for a Boston destination, instead of the city name, and you want to get off in New York. The natives can figure it out, but the travelers and tourists can't…you just have to find out in advance how the train will be listed.

Another constant was the difficulty in getting off at the right place. Coming back into Naples from Sorrento, aiming for the big central station there, and seeing we were underground, hearing the announcement of Napoli and coming to a stop, we joined the mass of people getting off, only to be told "Non, non, the <u>next</u> station." We were close, but still a mile out…it looked like downtown Naples to us. The probable answer: have the proper destination written on a card, in Italian, ahead of time.

Now, our problems in going by train from Rome to Vienna, the second city on the itinerary, were again our fault, not Italy's. We had too much planned for this transition through Italy, too many destinations, and far too much luggage. The reason we chose the train was logical, but only to us. First, we were meeting friends for a week in Orvieto, just an hour out of Rome, and we knew they would have a car, and who needs two cars? From there we would leave them, have four days in Venice, and <u>then</u> travel on to Vienna. And even though we had shipped most of our stuff on, we, of course, had too much to carry; we always have too much to carry. When you travel by train, those bags and suitcases are yours to carry, to hoist above the seats, to stagger out with at your destination. Sometimes there are carts, or porters to help;

usually they disappear by the time we ancient ones, the *anziani,* disembark. So, yes, a car would have been far better, even considering those wild Italian drivers.

Getting to Orvieto alone was a disaster, as Don recounts elsewhere. But we survived, and as planned, we met our friends there the next day. After our week of exploring Umbria and eating and laughing, now it's time for our next train. Bob is driving south, and they bring us back to our by-now-familiar Orvieto train station. Our train to Venice arrives. We know there's not much time at this stop. We start to sling the bags in, only to be met by crowds of people, mostly young, standing in the entrance. It's Saturday afternoon and all Italy is traveling. Not enough seats. Not enough room to even crowd through and look for a seat. We push onto the train, waving good-by to our friends, who are shaking their heads in disbelief.

As we sat, panting, on our luggage in the doorway, we had another moment of "We're too old for this, this is going to kill us," and "You suppose we'll have to drive everywhere?…or not travel at all?" We got seats in about an hour, and finished up the trip with time to think how to do this better.

The bags were a given; we were stuck with them. But we repacked, keeping a small bag of necessaries for the next four days, then stashed the rest of them in the train station when we got to Venice. (That freed us for the walk to our hotel, which unfortunately was a necessity as there wasn't a cab in sight.)

Then we exchanged our Vienna tickets for first class; there you have a seat in the first class car, and a lot of the hassles don't occur…such as the crowded Saturday trains. Somehow, despite our reading and preparing for the big venture, we still had the mindset of fifty years ago, when all the knowledgeable travelers were going second class.

We've realized that none of these problems are earth shaking. Most of them come from our not thinking through all the permutations of moving about…probably also from a lifetime habit of saving money, of not even realizing that spending an extra dollar could make everything simple. That might have been the biggest epiphany of the whole trip, and one we really internalized: if throwing money at a big problem would make it disappear, do it. Don't even hesitate. <u>Do it</u>.

And it worked. We had a quiet, restful, air-conditioned trip up to Vienna the next week. The train wound through the Tyrolean Alps, with the steep crags so dramatically close to the tracks. We passed into quiet farm land in Austria, through the suburbs of Vienna, and finally into Westbahnhof where we were met as promised. Those Austrians. Wonderfully organized, neat, precise, Germanic, efficient. We loved Italy and the Italians, but now we were ready for another world. It was a good time to see Vienna.

VIENNA

Outside Grim,
Inside a ★★★★ Hotel

We arrived in Vienna late on a May evening. Alfred Krammer, our landlord, whom we knew only by Internet, had arranged to have us picked up at the Westbahnhof, the main train station in Vienna. The driver was a taciturn, androgynous character, a woman dressed in a man's suit and tie, who muscled us and our many bags into a late-model van and took us efficiently through the city. It was clear that Vienna was smaller than Rome; there were few people at the station on a Saturday night and the streets were mostly empty. As we expected, it seemed a neat and orderly city.

At our dark apartment house, we met Alfred, a thin, blond, 40-ish man with a good sense of humor and cable know-how. Inside, a curving three-story winding staircase reminded us of scenes in the 1940s movies where the Nazi storm troopers raced up to haul out some poor innocent. In the courtyard below, garbage cans banged around…not an auspicious beginning.

Alfred opened the heavy door to…a surprise: light birch woodwork, wonderful kitchen appliances in a granite and birch kitchen, followed by more granite and glass in a sparkling bathroom; merino blankets were on the large bed. An entry hall with the ubiquitous, tiny toilet room greeted us at the front door; next came a dining area and kitchen, beside it a large, shining, spotlighted bathroom; then a combination bedroom and living room joined a smaller bedroom/study farther on. Alfred said he would connect our iBook to the Internet with his high-speed cable. As grim as it was outside, inside it was a four-star hotel.

The next morning, we looked at each other and said, "But where <u>are</u> we?" We walked down our street, imposingly named Darwingasse, found the food store, a little ratty with drooping carrots and spotted apples, but close, just in the next block, found the Baroque Augarten park a little farther on, then we took to the map. The heart of Vienna, the Stephansdom district, was ten minutes away; the tram stopped a half-block from our apartment, right in front of the shop called Katzenwelt, literally Cat's World, a big store catering to the cat-lovers of Vienna. The two-car-long tram delivered us to the big Schwedenplatz, bustling, crowded with sightseers, children, family groups. We followed a line forming at a booth and bought two travel passes good for a month on subway, tram and bus. We were legal, and ready for all Vienna!

Our first day was a Sunday, blue-skied and sunny. Walking through the *platz*, we discovered the ancient St. Stephen's cathedral, the Stephansdom. The 12th century church, whose age and grace were accentuated by the surrounding post-modern, high-rise buildings, dominated the square. It was on the Kaerntnerstrasse, a wide, car-free, strolling street with every imaginable shop, restaurant and café. Here we were greeted by magicians, singers, balloon-makers and clever street entertainers. We heard all languages, with plenty of English from, we assumed, American and British tourists.

Moving through the crowds along the pedestrian street, we found ourselves at the Ringstrasse, an even wider, tree-lined boulevard encircling the old city. The Ring took the place of the original, protective, Vienna city walls. Many cultural venues are on the Ring: The Kunsthistorische (the big art museum); the MAK, center for applied arts, with furniture, fabrics, silver, ceramics through the centuries; the Natural History Museum. The Opera is near. A few blocks on was the cinema, Burg Kino, that played English-speaking movies, and today…"What luck," we said, "it's 'The Third Man!'"

Our first day here, and we fall into the famous Oscar-winning film, plotted and filmed in the post-war Vienna of the 1940s, with Orson Welles starring and directing. The stark lighting of the city shots and the dramatic camera moves, particularly of the scene high up in the Ferris wheel between him and Joseph Cotton, showed Welles at his director's best. Vienna, war-torn and depressed in the film, didn't fare as well. "I hope Vienna is going to look better than what the movie showed," Dana remarked as we emerged into the daylight. I laughed, "It's been 50 years, don't we all look better?" (We subsequently learned that "The Third Man" plays <u>every</u> Sunday throughout the year, and is on all the tourist schedules.)

A quick check of our neighborhood the next morning showed it was more downscale than our Rome *quartieri*. The buildings were of a uniform gray concrete, dirty, unkempt. Our own apartment building had the same appearance; we reached our second floor apartment (remember it was, however, four-star!) through a wide, basement-like hall where a few weary bicycles were stored. Several doors from our apartment house was a bar with girls standing in the door, beckoning. Nearby, schnitzel and beer, billiards, cafés, shabby entrances. It was a diverse area, with many Muslim women covered except for their faces, some color-fully-robed Africans. "We're not in the Pittsburgh suburbs any more," I said; "Well," Dana replied, "we found the new and different we were looking for."

And we didn't know the half of it. Our first clue came a few weeks later, reading (or rather catching key words here and there) a local paper. Those words were *"prostituierte," "erwurgen,"* and *"Heinestrasse,"* a street one block from the apartment. We were in a café at the time, and asked the waitress what *"erwurgen"* meant: she put her long napkin around her neck and pulled it tight. We got it.

A morning walk to our post office was only ten minutes along tree-lined streets of small businesses, travel agencies, a few bars advertising go-go girls. School kids were punching each other down the street as I passed a doorway to a small hotel. Out of the entrance came a woman, short, fleshy, maybe five feet tall, with tousled, bleached blonde hair and covered in pink makeup, Pepto-Bismol pink, from forehead to half-bare bosom. As she started to take my arm, I remembered *"Nein, nein danke"* and she pulled back. I thought it would be funny to say "Not here with the children," but by the time I had worked out *"Nicht hier mit dem kinder"* she had retreated into the hotel. Makes "Bye, honey, I'm going to mail a letter" a new game of post office.

But the Augarten Park was only two blocks away, in the other direction, and we spent a lot of the hot summer there. It was green, with broad lawns for sunning or soccer, gravel paths shaded by leafy trees, an apiary <u>and</u> an aviary, kids and dogs running. Trees and bushes were formal, clipped in the Baroque manner. The park was big, perhaps 12 blocks by 8 blocks. We'd see groups of men strolling arm in arm; more often, the single male out for a walk, hands clasped behind his back, a common pose of England's Prince Philip. Once, I watched Muslim women in long gabardine coats and head scarves playing volleyball in the park.

Here also were two large *"flakturm"* left by the Nazis in World War II: heavy, six-story concrete housings for anti-aircraft guns and hundreds of military. Our guidebook said they were so structurally dense that to dynamite them would bring down nearby apartment houses.

Mozart and Beethoven had played concerts in the Augarten, perhaps in the small palace that later became a factory for exquisite china, and is now a museum. Hidden in a far corner of the park, we found a contemporary art gallery with its café nestled under the trees. Here I learned about the Viennese *windbeutel:* a pastry, with meringue and whipped cream, equal to any French creation.

Another park, Vienna's famous Prater, lay a 10-minute trolley ride from our apartment. It had, in addition to the big Ferris wheel, a miniature railway, a racetrack and trotting stadium, a golf course, a church and, my favorite pavilion, now a restaurant called the Lusthaus.

When we weren't in Vienna's parks, or the Old City, or on the Ring (our three favorites), we were looking for more. A flyer on the street advertised *Festwochen* (Party Weeks, my Army German was clicking in) and I telephoned for a schedule. Checking out the happenings from mid-May to mid-July, I found theater, opera, music groups producing works in Russian, Ukrainian, Polish, Italian, French, Spanish, English and German. Not unsophisticated and not cheap. Some plays and operas were priced from 70 to 100 euros a seat.

We subway-ed out to the Volksoper to see a production of "La Traviata"; we took the tram to a theatre off the Ring. Several experimental evenings from London were lined up for the summer, some good, some not, all interesting. One was a theatre group called "The Shout": a cast of six actors stood silently in a row on the stage, periodically uttering in-your-face confrontations like "Five people in this theatre will have cancer three months from now." Another was the rock singer Marianne Faithfull, former wife of Mick Jagger, making a singing comeback. Since we were more the Rosemary Clooney type with tastes closer to jazz, we were not overcome. The theatre, however, was crowded with appreciative 30- and 40-year olds; they were mainly on the first floor designed for standing, with several bars for drinking and mingling. We chose the second floor and the seats.

– #27 –
A Little Viennese History

Of the several dates important to Vienna, nothing quite matches 1683, when the Austrians withstood a final assault by the Turks. Constantinople, the powerhouse of the region, had been trying for years, if not centuries, to conquer this important city; the Austrian victory saved Vienna, and probably all of central Europe, from Islam.

The Habsburgs had been in power over much of Europe for centuries, consolidating through intermarriages links with Spain, France, Germany and Austria. Two hundred years later, Vienna was secure enough that the Emperor Franz Joseph (whose last name, if Emperors were ordinary people, would have been Habsburg) demolished those encircling walls. Thus began Vienna's most ambitious and magnificent era of building, completed in the 1890s. The walls were replaced with a grand ring of boulevards, sidewalks and parks, and laced with museums, cathedrals, the Parliament, the Opera house, concert halls, grand cafés and restaurants that still amaze visitors and residents alike.

Inside the Ring was the old city; at its center was the Hofburg, a rambling series of magnificent palaces added onto by each generation of Habsburgs over 500 years. Emperor Franz Joseph, the last of these rulers, built, in the late 1800s, an astounding palace of huge marbled hallways and stairs, centuries-old armor collections, and 8th century B.C. artifacts from Ephesus in Turkey. (In 1999, we toured that ancient city and learned that Austria was funding the current excavations.)

In our three months in Vienna, Dana and I spent much time on the Ring, in the grand *Kunsthistoriches* Museum, in the Natural History Museum, with a dinosaur given by Pittsburgh's Andrew Carnegie, and in the MAK. This, the Museum of Applied Arts, was Dana's favorite, with a stunning display of Thonet chairs.

Lunch, one windy day at the Landtmann, the grand old café from a century ago, nearly took us, and the wildly flapping umbrellas, into another world. (Their sausages tried to do the same thing.) And several times we simply took trams around the Ring, just to see the sights.

We kept struggling to define the difference between the Latin personality and the Germanic. How's this example? On a jar of Austrian preserves: "This konfiture is finished 27 March, 2004 at 10:56." A most precise people.

– #28 –
In Budapest, "Language-Lucky and Geographically Promiscuous"

Our plan in Vienna was to see a little bit of "the East"—Mitteleuropa.

Working through a travel agency near our apartment, one owned by an Israeli family whose bread and butter business was arranging trips to Israel—we chose first Budapest, and then, separately, Prague, both by train.

We left Vienna by train in early June, slowly edging East through nicely-planned suburbs, with new plants located between stuccoed houses and apartment buildings. Then the view morphed into manicured Austrian farms which became less manicured as we came into Hungary.

Compared with Vienna, Budapest at first looked poor and ragged to me. Our hotel, K&K (for *kunstliche und koenigliche,* the slogan of the Habsburgs, close to "arty and kingly") was nicely contemporary in its theme of orange and yellow. K&K is just a few doors from the Opera House, gloriously Baroque, which, along with the wide boulevards and smart shops, began to change our perceptions about Budapest.

One shop said a lot about a certain way of life here, an English shop for men's sporting goods. With guns, fishing rods, covert hunting trousers, and expensive boots and saddles, the image of a 19th century English gentleman still reigns.

Budapest could be the destination for certain bargains. While a month's supply of Plavix, one of my heart's favorites, cost 100 euros in Vienna, it was only half that in Hungary. To buy these, I discovered an *apotheke* or pharmacy nearby, all polished paneling with a library-like railing around the second floor.

We became confused in forints, the Hungarian currency which traded 240 to the euro in 2002. At an ATM machine, we got lost in our zeroes and took out 150,000 forints instead of 15,000. Fortunately, the forints would work next week in Prague.

A block from our hotel, on the wide Andrassy Utca, were more trendy shops and outdoor cafés. The Hungarian language is difficult to read; all we learned was that *"utca"* means street. Many people, however, speak English. A columnist in the International Herald Tribune nailed Americans who travel: *"language-lucky and geographically promiscuous."* When, for example, Swedes sell to Italians or Poles buy from Spaniards, everybody speaks English. And when our power is resented, those resentments are expressed in English.

One balmy night we sat in a huge square with a 50-piece orchestra playing Offenbach in one corner and a jazz guitar playing Jobim in another.

Another day, a bus tour took us to the Castle Hill overlooking the Danube. Massive spaces and monumental buildings characterized the view from the hill (which paralleled, interestingly, the view of Pittsburgh from Mt. Washington). I couldn't help contrasting the development of Budapest with similar cities in the States. In Hungary, Greece and Rome were the models for construction in the 1700s and 1800s; in America in the 1900s the rivers were used for transporting coal and sand, function over beauty. In the burgeoning industrial 1800s we placed railroads along river beds to deliver goods efficiently to factories, a practice we're just now dealing with in the "rails to trails" movement.

Dana summarized our stay in Budapest with an e-mail to a childhood friend:

> Great walking streets in Budapest, cafés everywhere, shops, very hot in June. A building's cement can be peeling, but when you look into the courtyard there's glass and brass and stainless steel. When they spend money, they do it well. Last night, we ate in one of the new "in" restaurants, a roof terrace, great food and wine, and it was the equivalent of $35 for two. And yes, it's in two parts: Buda on the west of the Danube

and Pest, where we are, on the East. Castles, Turkish influ-
ences in buildings, Habsburgs until 1918, then it all fell apart.
Now 10 million Hungarians with two million in Budapest.
Enough facts for today?

– #29 –
Heavy Pain in Vienna

A new and dramatic disease attacked me in Vienna, and it started with just a backache. As I had carried a heavy load of groceries up the stairs to our apartment a few days before, I assumed sore muscles and forgot about it. It kept hurting; I fooled around with aspirin, then Ibuprofen, but nothing seemed to help. It was really getting painful to move, or just to breath, but it took several increasingly sleepless nights, with pain spreading around my upper body, before I finally realized I should see a doctor. When you're normally healthy, you can be really dumb.

By now it's Sunday, a week after I'd started hurting. A doctor. Who?…well, one who spoke English. Then what? Don remembered Alfred, our nice landlord. He recommended a big Vienna city hospital, the Allegemeines Krankenhaus, and called a cab. We had a little trouble with the language signing in, but I got it across that I was really in pain.

Half an hour later, I was in a treatment room with two technicians. As one was connecting the leads for an EKG (when you're 72 they start by assuming heart problems), she touched something on my back that made me yelp. A dermatologist was called, he took scrapings, examined them by microscope, and pronounced it to be "Shingles!" All that pain was caused by two tiny spots on my back and two on the rib cage. He gave me three prescriptions…one for pain, another for the magic bullet of the antibiotic, then a salve. He said it would probably be a mild case.

Getting the prescriptions filled wasn't easy. As it was Sunday, all pharmacies were closed. However, the hospital explained that, by law, there would be one pharmacy open in every district, and they gave us the address of the one closest to our apartment. When we got there, we were greeted by an empty street and a pharmacy closed tight with a stark, heavy sheet-metal facade. But a helpful teenager passing by made us understand that if we rang a buzzer, someone would open it up. And sure enough, a small panel opened, like the old American speakeasies, to show the face of a smiling, uniformed woman. She spoke English, took my three pieces of paper and returned with the medicines that cost 225 euros, in cash.

The pain pill took a few hours to kick in, but in two days the pain was gone. I continued the antibiotic as directed, quit the pain pill in three days, never used the salve. As the doctor said, it was a mild case and I was lucky. For the two examinations, two different doctors and some lab work, the total bill was 76 euros. They wouldn't take payment at the time, but insisted that they would bill me in the States. I received it at home about a month later and paid with a check in dollars, which was accepted.

All we knew about shingles was its connection to chicken pox. (The family story was that my grandmother came down with shingles as my brother and I erupted with chicken pox.) But we had gotten firsthand knowledge of it several years ago when a good friend had a terrible case. She was in excruciating pain all one summer, even with the medicine; she couldn't stand to be touched, or even to wear clothes. Her clever husband fashioned a cage, made of some wire, that could support a sheet as a kind of covering…to let her at least get out into the fresh air. It sounded God-awful.

After my own bout with it, I e-mailed her, asking how many spots she'd had. She replied that the spots had been "uncountable, some were as big as quarters," and that two years later, she still could hurt. I had four little spots…you could hardly see them…that screamed the worst pain I'd ever had.

A Post Script: I've since learned that an antibiotic is not prescribed for shingles, or at least not in the States to the people I know who have had the disease. I <u>thought</u> that was what had cured me in Vienna, but I don't remember the name of it and may be wrong. But, whatever it was, it worked well.

– #30 –
He Lived in Six Different Countries and Never Left Home

We couldn't get the excitement glands going for Prague, and we still have trouble. I'll write and you decide. We relied a lot on John Allison, the young friend of our family who met his Parisian wife, Cecile, there in the early 90s. To them, Prague was Paris in the 20s. The Soviet regime was freeing up Czechoslovakia; poet/president Havel was making international headlines. John was covered by U.S. media as if he were Hemingway. In fact, he was an editor of the English language paper, Prognosis (pun intended).

For our first night, John recommended dinner at *U Zlate Hrusky* (The Pear Tree) near the castle above the river. It was raining. A taxi took us across the river, up the hill, down a little road to a house with the famous pear tree. Charming. A courteous man received us, directing us upstairs to a paneled room with only two couples. After 15 minutes, our waiter, the only waiter, brought the wine list; I chose a Czech white wine. It took 20 minutes for the waiter's 15-year-old son to bring us an *amuse bouche*, liverwurst with butter and bread. We wait. Wait. Finally the boy brought us an unopened bottle to examine. Yes! Yes! That's it. Ready to order? Yes! Dana ventured into veal medallions with shrimp, pear, orange and coconut shavings; I, salmon and potatoes. Neither the veal nor the salmon tasted like anything we recognized. The 60 euros bill (in crowns) was reasonable but we felt abused.

We taxied back across the river. The exchange rate was 240 crowns to the euro. The bill was 500 crowns and I had only 250. No credit cards. To our hotel desk I ran to change euros to crowns and gave the taxi driver a bill.

"You just gave him 100 <u>euros</u>," said the hotel clerk," who had followed us out. I raced back, caught the driver. Sheepishly, he returned the 100 euro note and I paid him the 500 crowns I owed him. We got to the room. Now Dana couldn't find 5,000 crowns, until she discovered them rolled up in a jacket pocket. Why weren't <u>we</u> on those tours where someone else takes care of all this?

The next day we had more "authentic Czech food." I tried goose and circles of bread dumplings with deep-fried potatoes. We two, Czech food and I, were not developing a good relationship.

What was fun was meeting Ladislav Verecky, a feature writer for the big Prague daily and a good friend of John's. He stayed with John and Cecile while writing a feature on Jaromir Jagr, the ice hockey star who played for the Pittsburgh Penguins and now owns a bar in Prague.

"Tell me about your family living through the 20th century," I said.

"Good question" said Ladislav. "My father, 88, has lived in six different countries and never moved: The Austrian Hungarian Empire, the Ukraine, Sudetenland, Hungary, Czechoslovakia and now, the Czech Republic." It's not often that an assumption made in a question pays such dividends. "My father was a bookkeeper in the Hungarian Army and then worked as an accountant when he got out. And he's still living," said Ladislav.

"How is the economy now?" I asked. "Well, let me tell you a story," said Ladislav. "Many people are doing much better since the Soviets left." Then he related an anecdote more colorful than typical. He had joined a Prague group flying to Las Vegas.

"I went with a Czech heavy hitter who left $90,000 in a taxi at Kennedy airport. He ran back, found the cab <u>and</u> the money. Gave the driver a $200 tip." How much had Prague changed since the Soviets left? That story was Ladislav's best answer.

We were never sure why we didn't connect with Prague, because it's a beautiful city untouched by World War II.

– #31 –
Breakfast at Stephanie's

The Hotel Stephanie in Vienna served a big, enticing breakfast buffet, and we ate there every Thursday morning. We had found this jewel early in our stay, on our way to the old city, down about three tram stops on Taborstrasse. Open to the public, the buffet was in a formal dining room just through the lobby of the hotel. It was an enormous room, almost ballroom size, with two long tables of the buffet centered under two large crystal chandeliers.

The white-linened tables were filled with gleaming silver steamers, plates, flatware, carafes of coffee, and the breakfast of your dreams. Every nationality was represented; you had your choice. There were the cheeses and salted fish of northern Europe, the bacon and eggs, jellies and preserves of England, milk and cream for the cereal and toast of Americans, bagels and lox and cream cheese and sausages for Germans, butter from Denmark, *crème fraiche* and *croissantes* and *omelettes* of France, Russian *blintzes* and sour cream, pancakes and pastries and juices and fresh fruit from the rest of the world. As Gershwin sang, "Who could ask for anything more?"

It was hot, into the 90s, that summer in Vienna. Mornings were cooler. Out on the terrace of this small, elegant hotel, a step from the main dining room, it was shady or sunny, as you wished, under the tall leafy trees; there were cool fountain sounds from the adjoining courtyard. We'd load up plates and retire to this open, tree-shaded terrace with the morning Herald Tribune; we'd go back for seconds, it was heavenly. We ate ourselves silly, we drank coffee, we read the paper, went back for more coffee, it was 22 euros of perfection. The buffet closed about 10:30 a.m. and they would sweep us last stragglers out into big, bustling Taborstrasse, waddling on to our day.

Early every Thursday morning, as sure as the sunrise, our pretty, blonde landlady, Barbara Krammer, appeared at the door, holding the week's supply of freshly laundered and ironed sheets and towels. Always with a helper, she was there to change the linens and supervise the cleaning. She'd ring the bell somewhere between 8:00 and 8:30 a.m.; after a few "*Guten Tag's*" we'd leave for the Hotel Stephanie…and return three hours later to a sparkling clean apartment, newly scrubbed and polished with Germanic efficiency. The Krammers advertised it as a ★★★★hotel, and they were pretty close.

We had learned her family owned the apartment building, and were surprised at her involvement with the cleaning…definitely grateful, however. I think she mainly did the linens, or maybe she only carried them in. She and Alfred had bought (or were given, I don't know which) three apartments in this building that they turned into 'luxe' rentals, as they termed it. It was a separate business, called Vienna City Apartments.

Alfred, a computer whiz, devised the web site where we found the apartment. (I had asked Google for 'rental apartments in Vienna, Austria', and up bubbled VCA.) It was all in English, very professional and informative, with good pictures and descriptions, and aimed, they told us later, primarily at Americans. We were the customers the Krammers wanted; the reasons why, we never discussed. I do know they had a bias against the 'East,' which we took to mean the Balkans or any of the old Soviet states. Whether it was personal distrust, or financial, I don't know.

We had two apartments to choose from, that night in May when we first came into Vienna. One was third floor, we took the other right beneath it on the second floor. They were both quite similar, both in size and charm and in 'luxe.' Maybe a tiny difference in the color in the blond kitchen cabinetry…we chose the lighter color. Nothing more different than that. However, the contrast between these handsome apartment interiors and the dingy…in our imaginations, bullet-studded…halls and stairways, was dramatic. I can only assume they couldn't convince the father to clean the building exterior, to improve the public areas; or, more likely, nobody cared. (That's a European trait we've noticed before; they live behind walls, the outsides aren't as important.)

We got to know their family that summer. Right away, Alfred got our laptop up and running, connecting it to the Internet. He puttered about the three apartments on weekends, fixing, repairing, and would wind up at our place, usually with one or more of the children. They had three: Florian, a handsome, shy boy of 12; then Julia, maybe 7, and little Matteus, 3. They were all cute and very well-behaved, but mainly silent, speaking only German. Alfred loved to talk to us…he was totally fluent in colloquial English…and he came over often.

Barbara had less command of English than he, but could handle a conversation fairly easily. She was a pretty 30-something, with a thin, cute body always encased in a tight T-shirt and shorts this hot summer. We saw her primarily on cleaning day, when she and the helper stayed for two hours at our place, going on to the other two apartments that day. We'd chat for a while, but we always left them to work, and only saw the finished product of a clean and shiny kitchen, bathroom and bedroom. They're a neat and tidy people, those Austrians.

We four went to dinner one hot night at the smart little café/art gallery we'd discovered in the Augarten. We ate outside on a deck overlooking large painted iron sculptures that were carefully lighted and placed among the trees. Alfred was an interesting combination of dreamer and environmental engineer; he spoke English like a native, as he'd gone to college and worked in the States. He had an idea for a business and talked to Don endlessly about his plans. (One day he inexplicably brought over, and left with us for two months, an expensive Sony laptop; I never knew why. Maybe it was thanks for the many conversations. Don and I used it to e-mail each other between the rooms.)

Barbara was the organized partner; life was totally in order for her family, and her role was to continue the status quo. But she had a nice humor and I know she was a good balance for Alfred. We had told them our plans of returning to Europe in the fall, and she invited us to Alfred's big birthday party in October. (Don's foot operation precluded that jaunt.)

When I remember Barbara and Alfred, they're mixed up in my mind with the breakfasts at the Hotel Stephanie. Both the hotel breakfast buffet and the Krammers let us see a touch of class; they gave us a view of the nice life in Austria, of elegant living in our somewhat downscale part of Vienna.

– #32 –
Tafelspitz and *Palatschinken*

In Vienna, it wasn't too often we got to meet people. We knew only our young landlords, Alfred and Barbara Krammer, until we got an e-mail from a friend in Fox Chapel, Verne Koch. He and his wife Mary Ann wanted us to meet Dr. Krexner, who, several years before, had helped their niece, in Vienna on a tour, through a broken leg. Verne sent us their telephone number, and we called them for dinner.

Again, that old devil language was a problem, and telephones always make it worse. I had my Army German, Dr. Krexner a little English. But I got through it, explaining who we were, and set up a date for the following Thursday at 7:00 p.m., to meet at our apartment. Wednesday night, 7:00 p.m., our buzzer rang just as we were sitting down to our supper. I went down, and there were the Krexners, casually dressed, both of them standing in the July heat at our outside entrance. Dana got there as I was uneasily trying to explain that the date was for tomorrow…it seems to go better when the ladies can meet each other. But, finally, the Krexners understood, and said they would return the next night. Perhaps they just wanted to meet us first, to check us out before they committed an evening, a not-illogical thought.

Dr. Krexner (his first name would remain "Doctor," but *die Frau* was Marthe) was a tall, rangy, retired physician in his early 80s, friendly but reserved. Marthe was 70-something, warmer; we found out over dinner that she spent three days a week caring for a grandchild. They lived probably fifteen minutes from us, in a nicer area out of our "red light" district, and had walked over, both nights.

Thursday night, we joined them in front of our apartment house, and we walked a block, through the waves of heat emanating from the sidewalk, to a tram on Taborstrasse for our tenminute ride downtown. The Doctor had chosen a restaurant on Kaerntnerstrasse, the wide pedestrian street that leads from St. Stephen's Church down to the Ringstrasse.

This summer night the street was packed with apartmentdwellers seeking fresh air. The mimes, the clowns, the jugglers, the shoppers were in full array, a festive, friendly atmosphere. The restaurant, obviously a favorite of the Doctor's, was dark, not air conditioned, and decorated with the heads of long-dead deer. Most of the diners were at tables outside in the breezes, but the Doctor strode past them into the breathless heat and gloom of the dining room. I think we were the only people inside.

But there, in a hot but roomy booth, we had a good time. Dr. Krexner and I added to the temperature by ordering *tafelspitz,* an Austrian specialty meant for the dead of winter: boiled beef with boiled potatoes, hot but really good, demanding a great amount of horseradish. Dana's favorite was the dessert, another Austrian dish: the heavily-named *palatschinken,* which turned out to be a light crepe filled with ice cream, wonderful for a steamy night.

As our conversation was at first on the level of two-year-olds, we could only exchange the basics. But both the Doctor and I had brought our respective dictionaries with us...God knows they were needed. And we all improved; we could converse. They were interesting, up on politics and history. We ran through the Koch family visits, and heard a certain sadness as they spoke of their son, also a doctor, unmarried, with a child.

They were good people and liked Americans. It wasn't until we started talking about the Habsburgs, however, that they really became animated. They both spoke of the Emperor Franz Josef (who died in 1916) and his beautiful wife, Sisi, as family, with the same feeling as for a relative. Sisi's anorexia, her beauty, her constant traveling were problems to be discussed. (Sisi had been assassinated in Switzerland in 1898.) Yes, a while ago, but unfortunate, we all thought. We had a small breakthrough here; we were on their sentimental turf. Franz Josef and Sisi still live in the heart of Vienna.

– #33 –
Riding High in Vienna

One 90-degree day, Don and I decided to find some breezes at the Prater, Vienna's biggest amusement park. The Prater is just like parks we knew at home, with the same rides for the kids, the lagoons with couples rowing little boats, countless gift and food shops. We'd taken the tram out there several times to ride bikes through the heavily-treed park; we'd even seen horsemen trotting on their paths beside the bicycle way. But we'd never tried anything else. Today we were aiming for the Ferris wheel, the 240' high wheel made famous to our generation in the 1949 movie, "The Third Man." We knew we couldn't leave Vienna without at least seeing it, and, if it was still running, we'd go for it.

Totally different from its slimmer, faster sisters in the States, with their open, swinging gondolas usually built for two, this wheel was a ponderous, heavy-beamed affair straight out of the Industrial Revolution. The compartments were as big as buses, each holding about 20 people. We bought our tickets, waited, watching the next car slowly, slowly move toward us. This was when we realized that the views would probably be the only excitement. And we were right.

Finally it was our turn; we filed in. Enormous and slow-moving, the wheel took about 25 minutes for one complete revolution. Its very construction obstructed the views from the inner side, leaving the passengers to crowd over to the other windows in order to see anything at all. Obviously, there was no sensation of speed, and even little of height, the cars were so big. But it still was a ride into the past, one that we both had remembered for some 50 years. We felt we were following in the footsteps of the Hollywood great.

And then it was over, we were off. And sad to say, aside from the fact that we'd actually been on this relic from memory, it was a non-event. But we were right about the view; to see the city and terrain from on high, with so much green summer beauty in and around the city and on the hills to the east, and the Donau River (Danube to the English-speaking world) in the distance, those were memorable sights.

The other part of our view from the top was the park itself, which was big and raucous, replete with carnival booths and rides, little kids with their parents, teenagers, all out for a fun afternoon. And from up high we saw a small roller coaster ride nearby; feeling frisky, we decided to try it. We hadn't been on one in years, but it looked cute and certainly tame enough.

As we went up the first slow ascent, we knew this had been a bad idea. It was much bigger than we thought, much higher, faster, curvier...and it almost killed us. I think roller coasters are different now. In quieter times, they simply went up and down and around...some were higher and faster than others. Not a big deal. Now the engineers and designers of these new tracks are out to provide more screams and thrills per ride; I think they're succeeding. Now the curves are much twistier and more sinuous, constantly throwing us, and our heads, from side to side as we hurtled onward. The speed was the same as memory. It was the twisting that hurt.

The ride couldn't have lasted more than a minute or two, it seemed endless. I saved my glasses only with a desperate lunge; Don's somehow stayed on. We both tried to scrunch as far down as possible, fighting for the lowest possible position in the small car. It was that tensing against certain disaster, fighting it every second, that put our bodies, necks and muscles into such shock. Relaxing, just going with it, would probably have been much better. But that's after the fact; who can think rationally in the face of certain death?

When it finally ended we staggered off, quivering, somewhat surprised that we were still alive and breathing and moving fairly normally. The little café right at the exit (maybe it had been put there just for us and other *anziani)* restored and rejuvenated us.

We recuperated with wine and a Viennese pastry and, in minutes, even started to feel pride in our exploit. But we certainly weren't going to try it again.

Sitting there, watching even the teenagers emerge with white faces, for the first time we could see what our kids meant in telling us we were <u>too</u> <u>old</u> for this nonsense…that we should act our age, and not go wandering around doing strange things. But we also knew the other side of that coin. If we had listened to them, we wouldn't be here in Vienna in the first place. No, the plusses still outweighed the minuses. Think what we would have missed.

– #34 –
Critical Falls

The night before I turned 73, I dreamed a joke. Remembering it the next morning was extraordinary for me. I was in Vienna, and our friends' health problems must have been lurking somewhere under my bed, like Thurber's. I dreamed there was a retirement community in Arizona called Critical Falls. I thought of the names of streets.

The next morning I wrote them down, but of course I couldn't help embellishing them a little: Twisted Ankle Avenue, Wounded Knee Pass, Broken Shoulder Boulevard, Curving Spine Way,

Fallen Arches—you'll think of more. The local bar is called Hip Joint and the counseling office is Mined Wanders. This kind of thing is common in advertising agencies but I had never dreamed an assignment before. I think my mind was disoriented because I had bitten into a dumpling the day before in Budapest; it was really a ball of fat.

There's nothing funny about critical falls after you've reached that certain age. Dana fell over a curb in St. Jean Cap Ferrat and cried. I sprawled on the sidewalk after stepping into a hole at night in Paris. As we walked through the cities we learned to shout, like some batty British retired colonel, "change of level." But still, you can't ignore a good dream.

– #35 –
Wheeling Through Museums

We discovered, years ago when the kids were little, a handy gadget that would get us through museums without aching bodies and screaming feet. It was at the big Carnegie International in Pittsburgh, the showing of contemporary art that runs every three years; this was probably the first time we'd gone *en famille*. We were five: the two of us and the kids, Ted and Dave, aged seven and nine, and Hardy, the three-month-old.

For whatever reason, we'd never thought of doing anything but slogging through the marble halls, trying to absorb as much as we could in spite of a creeping tiredness. At one point that day I was carrying the baby, lagging behind the brothers who were speeding through, when I saw, behind a folding screen, a wheelchair. With a cry of discovery that alerted the troops, I fell into it…and museums have been a source of gaiety and light ever since.

Now that I know about the world of wheels, life has become so simple. Museums are interesting <u>and</u> fun. And I've learned and retained a lot more from a museum than before. It truly makes a visit more accessible, faster, and much more enjoyable. I've used them as many times as I could get someone to push me, which isn't always a given.

After our initial Carnegie expedition on wheels, we tried it several other times: I remember a Picasso exhibit at MoMA in New York, and something at the big Philadelphia Museum of Art…all worked perfectly. Our next foreign wheelchair event was Paris, 1971 at the old Jeu de Paume where the Impressionists were then housed. In former days I had felt that only the truly exhausted sightseer, or at the very least a new mother, deserved such a gift. I thought I should at least look tired and frail when asking for one. But now, I was older, women's lib was coming in, and I decided it was none of their business. If I wanted *"une chaise, monsieur, s'il vous plait,"* I could ask for one. And, without so much as that waggling finger of disapproval, the guard found me my rolling chair. I was empowered.

Off we went, Don pushing. I'm loving every minute. We wheeled to the Van Goghs, paused, then read carefully about Renoir and Mary Cassatt and Pisarro, lingering, savoring, comfort oozing from every pore. Or at least from mine…Don was still on duty. Looking for the Monet series of paintings of light on the Rouen Cathedral, we realized they were up a level. We found the imposing stairs, Don wheeled me to the side of the steps, I hopped out, and we ran up, hoping that nobody saw. We wandered through the Monets and more. Ready to go, we saw *la chaise* dutifully waiting at the foot of the staircase. Here we switched, and I pushed Don around the last half of the first floor, assuming nobody knew, or cared. Even for the pusher, it's not a bad way to see a museum.

Our next trip was to Spain, which was full of paradors and beach time and flamenco dancers, but we saw only one museum, the magnificent Prado in Madrid. Here at the admissions desk I brazenly asked for the wheelchair, and waited, standing straight and tall, with no pretense of frailty. There must have been an elevator, because I remember wheeling myself onto the second floor, as by now Don was bored with this routine. Whipping merrily down a long gallery, I was caught up short when I saw a young man with an eight-inch sole on one shoe, gallantly limping through the paintings. Now there was guilt. I drove into the next room and ditched the chair in a small hallway, and walked on. And it was several years, maybe decades, before I tried this gambit again.

This last jaunt in Vienna, we were now definitely of legal wheelchair age, and we were at the vast art museum there, the Kunsthistoriches. This time the roles had reversed. I was pushing Don, who was facing a painful, soon-to-be bunionectomy. We did trade at one point, but he needed it more. The whole outing didn't last long; the several level changes, really only two steps, were enough to stop a wheelchair cold. Plus, the elevators were so artfully hidden that we gave up. And Don limped home.

A postscript to the story: now that we've reached the age of really needing a chair, I find myself loath to ask for it, unless I'm dying. It was one thing at the age of forty-two to show myself to the museum crowd as exhausted and foot-sore, but as a 70-something, my pride seems to get in the way. Now I trade a (potentially) comfortable museum trip for the heroic but totally false, statement: "Heavens, I don't need that. I'm OK, I love to walk through museums!"

– #36 –
Hauptallee and *Heurige*

On a really hot July 7, Dana and I celebrated my 73rd birthday with two authentic Austrian customs. The first was to ride bicycles in the Prater. Taking the tram to Vienna's famous amusement park, we ignored the giant Ferris wheel; we'd done that before. Now we rented bikes, and spent the morning wheeling among the cool trees and flower gardens, in and out of the bicycle paths along the Hauptallee, the central avenue in the park.

To ride a bike through the Prater is almost to visit another era, one truly Austrian. In 1766 the Emperor Joseph II gave to the public his original hunting grounds which became a "funfair" and amusement park a century later. It comprised the woods and area between the Danube and its canal. The Hauptallee is a grand avenue, and is now primarily for bicycles. It's the orderliness, the politeness, the surprising number of oldsters, and a general lack of speeding, rowdy teenagers that makes it seem so civilized. Bikes are everywhere around the fairgrounds, but it's on the wide, wide paved path, the Hauptallee, that you see them en masse.

Boulevard-size in width, it's lined with tall leafy chestnut trees, and runs for three miles through the park. It's a real sight on a sunny day in summer: decorous senior ladies, some well-skirted, some in pants, pedaling along in the slow lane; lovers, arm in arm even though on the bikes; gentlemen with neat goatees and green Alpine hats; laughing young girls riding fast in the passing lane. The occasional horse and rider clopped decorously down the assigned trails that border each side of the bikeways.

Our second local outing was planned for the afternoon. We'd read of *Heurige*, and sought our landlord's advice, as in "Where's a good one?" A *Heuriger* is a special inn, designated by law to sell wine made from grapes grown only on the owner's property. Alfred recommended a favorite in Grinzing, a leafy suburb of Vienna, that we could get to by subway. In fact, you may enjoy rolling your tongue around these place names on our route: Schwedenplatz, Heiligenstadt, Pfaarplatz. (Dickens said German names are so long they can march down the street.)

In Grinzing are houses rather than apartments, trees hundreds of years old; it's *ein Dorf*, a real village. Now a sleepy suburb of Vienna, Grinzing in the 1600s was repeatedly sacked by the Turks, and later by Napoleon in 1809. Beethoven is reputed to have lived in this *Heuriger, Mayer am Pfaarplatz,* while working on his Ninth Symphony. In a large courtyard, shaded by a loggia of vines, we found it to be a basic German beer-garden, with plump waitresses in dirndls, men in the authentic, but hot, leather pants, Japanese tourists, and tables full of hungry, hearty eaters.

A terribly inefficient cafeteria was set up inside a small house, with no real line, just people reaching for the food behind and around you. The food was pretty ordinary; it was only the atmosphere, the experience that was special. I had lentils and spinach with cheese, more Italian than Austrian, Dana had something forgettable. We found seats at a crowded table in the courtyard. No surprise that the peasant-dressed waitresses brought pitchers of a bubbly white Riesling from homegrown vines. It was a family crowd, with little kids running around, all ages and dress. The night was cool, the wine was good, and we stayed until dark.

Two musicians, older than we, in the inevitable *lederhosen*, wandered among tables with accordion and bass singing "Ein, Zwei, G'Suffa" kinds of drinking songs. It took me back to my 1952 Stuttgart army days, when an Army roommate, Dave Wachsman, after a Saturday night of these songs, would throw wide the shutters on our barracks (which, painted pink, I could never reconcile with reality) and yell "FUCK the Army!" My birthday night in *Mayer am Pfarrplatz* was an older reality, and a lot quieter. After all, this is Vienna, today, and I'm 73.

– #37 –
Thrilled

There's a funny thing about travel. We go to great expenditures of time and money to get to foreign locales or maybe just to the next state. We talk to friends about their trips, look at pictures, go to lectures, read magazines. But often what affects our travel outcomes depends upon other, more elusive factors.

The Mood You're In. Maybe you've had some bad oysters and you're dyspeptic, or it's raining, or someone in your group has to go to the bathroom at the wrong time. A lot of things extraneous to your enjoying, say, the Pantheon in Rome can happen to make you wish you were home. In this mood you can become extremely critical of the Pantheon, developing strong opinions where none existed the day before and, further, you're not fun to be with. In this mood, you'll be like Emerson, who said he had seen the world from his armchair in Concord.

Your Expectations are Unduly High. You've probably been waiting to see the Louvre since you were 14, hearing your parents talking about it in exultant tones. Sometimes a feeling of independence sets in, maybe against your parents. After rave reviews from friends and your reading, you just turn into the curmudgeon. The solution to this, of course, is to know nothing about what you expect to see on your trips. Arriving on the rue de Rivoli, you say "The Louvre. What's that?" This way, expectations will be around your shoes. You'll whip through it saying things like "I can't believe those gates are from Persia. I never *heard* of them!"

You Can Be Thrilled Only So Long. This happens especially when you are viewing scenery for spells too long, and/or you have a friend who won't stop exclaiming over: a) the light in Rome as the sun sets; b) the ninth tapestry late in the afternoon in an already-dark museum; or c) someone directs your attention to one too many quaint cafés on the left bank. The reaction you'll find yourself expressing will be something like "if we have to _____ today I'm going to jump off the roof." If you find yourself in the <u>State of Being Unduly Overthrilled</u> but must make nice for your group, you probably need ear phones and that airline mask. A good book will also do the trick or you can fake that sinus condition that sends you to bed.

– #38 –
Factoids From Austria

Subj: Factoids from Austria
Date: June 3, 2002
From: CDana51
To: Friends

We asked our travel agent on the next street (she's an Israeli, speaks very good English) about the prostitutes we see in the neighborhood. She said they're mainly young, 15-16, from the east, Bucharest, the Balkans, earning money for drugs and home; she said they're harmless. And two doors down from our building a café opened, with girls sitting there at high noon, and those tasteful red lights shining. Such excitement. However, for whatever reason, we feel totally safe; life here, in spite of all of the above, is so ordinary, with women pushing baby strollers, men carrying groceries home, the trams clanking along.

Today was my first apartment crisis. Don had gone into the city, forgetting his key, and then I left too fast on a run to the grocery store. When the door closed, I knew both sets of keys were inside. Couldn't believe it. No concierge, obviously, nothing. A kindly neighbor (neither of us had a pertinent word of the other's language, but somehow we communicated) called a locksmith. And two hours later, for 120 euros, I got back in. (Another example of the "geezer syndrome"…sad.) One funny thing; he wouldn't let me look while he unlocked it, said it was against the law. I dutifully turned my back; he jiggled something, broke nothing. It took only two minutes, but a big budget screw-up. Probably should have called Alfred, the nice landlord, but I couldn't bear to bring him out through the hot Friday afternoon rush-hour traffic…for something so dumb.

Our news is that maybe reality has crept in. Don has some bone growth in his foot, another bunion, and it <u>hurts</u>. He's bought sandals and now looks totally European in socks and sandals, and feels a lot more comfortable. But I think the knife is in the future, at some point. Meaning operation. And I had a fast case of shingles! But not to worry; we're basically fine. I'm just reporting.

Our apartment here has a washer and a <u>dryer</u>! Almost unheard of in Mitteleuropa. All the appliances are sparkly new with bells and whistles, but they take forever. The shortest time I can find on the dishwasher is 79 minutes, the washing machine takes 109 minutes, and the dryer lives a life of its own. It times by dampness, in German yet! Hi-tech stuff—very European. They beat everything to death and then will say that dryers are bad—they ruin the clothes. But I'm not complaining…I love these machines.

The old city, ten minutes away by tram, is total charm. It's really a mixture of the old and the new, with a tall, new, shiny glass and steel building, the Haas Haus, right across the *platz* from the Stephansdom, the thousand year-old cathedral of St. Stephen. We never get tired of the winding streets, the *kaffees*, some tiny, some big, restaurants, the great shops and old churches in these ancient parts of these ancient cities. The biggest pedestrian street here is the Kaerntnerstrasse; it's wide and crammed with people and all of the above shops. They're such bustling places. And on hot nights, they bustle til midnight. The most elegant street is named Graben, which translates as "graves;" it has the expensive shops, of the Armani and Cartier ilk. Too bad we're not buying.

The famous Schoenbrunn Palace, out in the country, is the direct antecedent of Heinz Hall in Pittsburgh, just a tad bigger; it's full of red velvet and white walls with a lot of gold/gilt work. Magnificently repaired, restored, refurnished and refurbished, everything glistened. And that's just the summer residence of the

Habsburgs. Their town palace, the Hofburg, right in the center of Vienna, is even more magnificent, with more grandeur and luxury and red velvet, made even bigger by each succeeding emperor through the centuries.

Wandering the old streets on a Saturday morning, we got into a "vegan" food fair…right across the pedestrian street from the high-end shops. Funny combination. Booths were set up telling, and unfortunately, showing, the dangers of eating meat, with God-awful pictures of how pigs are slaughtered, chickens, cattle etc. Terrible looking stuff. You don't ever want to look a steak in the eye again.

That's all the news that's fit to print for the moment. Bye and love, Dana

– #39 –
Missing the Opera,
the Sachertorte and the Lippizaners

B
ecause we were in Vienna in the summer, because we were late or because we were just lazy, we missed a lot of Tourist Vienna. It was too hot for the elegant Lippizaner stallions at the Spanish Riding School. Pictures show an interior riding ring built by the Habsburgs in 1729. The school itself goes back to 1572. But for us, *verschlossen*...closed.

To further embarrass ourselves we didn't eat *Sachertorte* at the Hotel Sacher. A big commercial enterprise, it's all set up for you to mail a cake to Aunt Maude. The cake has a layer of apricot jam under smooth, dense chocolate, but we were never starving for dessert when near the Sacher.

And, we didn't get to the Opera. Some people go to Vienna *just* for the Opera, but not us. It, too, was *verschlossen* in the summer. We did take a tour and it's bigger than your Opera House. With much Baroque gilt and handsome red upholstery, Strauss waltzes play in your mind as soon as you enter.

But we saw much of Vienna through the eyes of our D-K guide book plus the reading we did. Here are some of our vivid memories. *Kunst*, German for art, and the Kunsthistorisches Museum, deliver their promises. It was built from the 1870s through the 1890s to house the art collected by the Habsburgs. Walking up a huge butterscotch marble staircase, you see:

- A golden salt cellar designed by Benvenuto Cellini in the 1500s that will make you want to throw yours out.
- "The Artist's studio" by Vermeer from 1665 with a painting being made of a standing model, full of the play of light.
- A Pieter Bruegel painting from 1565 called Hunters in the Snow. Forget those villagers romping in their codpieces; it was too cold.

- A killer sculpture—Egyptian King Thutmosis III—from 1460 B.C., both smiling and solemn, not easy to do.
- A marshmallow and chocolate-colored café amidst the marble staircase for that carbohydrate breakdown around 4:00 in the afternoon.

In 1695 the Habsburgs became a little suffocated in their Hofburg city palace—and looked for grounds outside the city to build a hunting lodge. However, nothing was simple; it took 50 years to finish the Schoenbrunn palace. No one has ever been able to count the number of rooms or the generations who died applying stucco and gilt. It is magnificent and can't be separated from its gardens. On a hill catching the breezes is a summer house called "Gloriette." Short strolls will bring you to the royal zoo, the coach museum, fake Roman ruins and a greenhouse for palms.

In the heart of the city lies the Hofburg, a series of connected palaces built over 500 years. You'll see the china, furniture and even shaving bowl used by Emperor Franz Joseph, the last Habsburg left when his empire crumbled in 1916. Another palace is a museum for recently-excavated artifacts from Ephesus in Turkey from early B.C. Another exhibits armor for men and horses, plus a suit of gold armor for Spain's King Philip. Just for show. Then you must take a break for Viennese pastries at the Café Demel, just down the street from the Hofburg. If you like good Austrian names, you'll like the imperial patent on the shopfront: *Kunstliche und Koenigliche Hof-Zuckerbaecker* (or as we say in English, the arty and kingly royal sugar-baker). Founded in 1785, its decorating would fulfill the fondest dreams of L.B. Mayer, the king of Hollywood in the 1940s. The cocoa and robin's egg blue ceiling looked good enough to eat. Dana and I went full out *mit schlag*, the whipped cream, with chocolate cupped between meringues and more *schlag* on top.

After that we saw some of the best architecture in Vienna built around the turn of the century. A rebellion had set in against the curlycues and Baroque ribbons, resulting in plainer facades.

Some of the more familiar ones are the Majolica House, with a ceramic facade and the Secession Building with a gold filigree dome. Some of the best furniture and applied arts are in the Museum of Applied Arts with, for example, rectangular Biedermeier furniture or the display of Thonet chairs.

One of the most unusual apartment houses you'll see anywhere was built not at the turn of the century but in 1985 by architect Friedensreich Hundertwasser. It's called Hundertwasser Haus. He set out to reverse the trends toward "international" design by planting trees on terraces all over the building, by embedding ceramic plates in the building, by using humor and curving lines instead of straight ones. It's a playful projection of one man's imagination.

After all those steps we fell into the Landtmann coffee house on the Ring on a sunny day with strong winds blowing umbrellas left and right. Our guide book says Sigmund Freud relaxed here between patients. For me, lunch was a foot-long sausage, sauerkraut, mashed potatoes, great mustard and a beer. That, plus a tram ride home around the Ring and you've pretty much finished Vienna for the day.

– #40 –
Thonet in Vienna

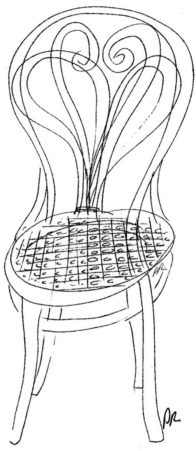

One of my favorite sights in all of Vienna was in the MAK, the big Austrian Museum of Applied Arts on the Ringstrasse. It's a fascinating tour for those who like the decorative arts: furniture, silver, materials and design through the centuries and through the different tastes of emperors. At first dedicated to Austrian art and industry, the Museum had expanded to include Islamic and East Asian art and Renaissance jewelry.

We had waded through the Biedermeier room and the *Wiener Werkstatte* room (Vienna Workshop) interesting in its own right.

Turn-of-the-century, the Werkstatte was founded by Josef Hoffman as an arts and crafts studio, producing furniture, jewelry, even book-binding with the same artistic care given to the fine arts of painting and sculpture.

On the second floor we came to an exhibit of Thonet chairs, smallish, bentwood, of the middle 1800s, copied everywhere, and still manufactured today. The chairs were handsome; their display fascinating. Running the length of a large, darkish room, about 40 by 30 feet, were two sheer curtains, leaving a large empty center aisle. Lined up behind each curtain were perhaps 25 original Thonets, dramatically lit from behind by strong lamps placed low on the side wall. The corresponding silhouette of each chair was delicately etched on the curtain. Walking down the center aisle, you could see the outlines of each chair, or you could also go behind the curtain and see the actual piece. Arranged chronologically, the earlier chairs had simpler designs; the later ones were more ornate and complicated. It was an ingenious exhibit.

Michael Thonet and his sons perfected assembly-line production of bending steamed, laminated wood. The 50 chairs here in the MAK spanned Thonet's productive years. He lived from 1796 to 1871, pioneering laminated bentwood techniques in the 1830s. The company produced furniture that was practical and inexpensive, with high-quality workmanship.

The collection showed varied designs mainly in beech: small side chairs and large armchairs, all incorporating different facets of bentwood design. Although they looked deceivingly delicate, they were strongly built and could support some serious weight.

We left Thonet and the *Werkstatte* movement for that day. As with most museums, no matter how fascinating, our interest would last only as long as our feet, reason enough for those wonderful cafés with enough caffeine and sugar to restore and reinvigorate the exhausted. But we came back several times during the summer, proving that museums are best in small doses, taken with black coffee and a fat, gooey pastry.

– #41 –
Dark Days in Vienna

I t was mid-July, and we had tickets home for Pittsburgh on August 2. When you've stayed away six months, you don't just walk out the door. Or at least, <u>we</u> don't. We have to make lists, lose the lists, then get all irritated and take a nap. We had the big picture down cold, the Big Plan, but meanwhile we were faced with bunion surgery, finding a place to stay, returning summer clothes to Pittsburgh and sending winter stuff to a friend in London. Most importantly, we still had six boxes of clothes and books here to deal with.

The best news was the resolution to the "where to stay?" question. Josie Wiley, an old friend from Fox Chapel, had e-mailed us to use their house to recoup from surgery; she and Don would be on Cape Cod all summer, not returning till late September. Their house featured a huge deck where I could sit with my foot up, and air conditioning when August was intolerable. We were beyond grateful.

My "stuff" had become my *bête noire*. I had six pairs of slacks, including a dark wool pair I'd never worn, plus jeans, a blue blazer, two pairs of shoes, a winter raincoat, far too much underwear, six sweaters; I hadn't used half of it all. We had CDs, books, a CD player, a tape player and everything you pick up traveling: museum brochures, maps, art books, and the tchotchkes you want to give your children, grandchildren and friends. (My most regrettable take-home was carrying a heavy antique box from Vilnius, Lithuania that I thought I had to have; patterned on an old roll-top desk, it was small, but still bigger than a breadbox.)

Then the dark set in, in July yet! The Yugoslavian tenants below screamed at 11:30 p.m. and 5:30 a.m. The Internet server went down. Not sleeping well, I actually wrote: "This trip too ambitious given heart problems and stroke, I'm forgetting words; should be doing speech exercises. We tried too much,

Dana tired. Gloomy, black. Maybe we should settle down in Pittsburgh, forget England and France." Alfred tried to help; he said the server would be up in a few hours. He also called the Yugoslavian family, telling them the police would come if they continued yelling.

We looked ahead; found more negative ions. Dana would like to just "sit for a while with my eyes crossed, no more museums or palaces, in the winter sun." She likes the idea of Kiawah, near Charleston, South Carolina where we vacationed one year. I wanted a place to type the notes for the book. Nothing was resolved. She went shopping for more presents, and I went looking for antique prints. Of course.

A couple of cooler nights and better sleep, and we snapped out of our gloom. Dana repeated her formula for what makes this trip work: "Optimism and denial, have to keep remembering it. Concentrate on the good stuff, ignore the bad."

– #42 –
Small Favorites of Vienna

A *preface here. We didn't do justice to Vienna; it's a beautiful, fascinating, full-of-history city, but there were just too many negatives for us, mainly health-connected. Don arrived with a cold, his foot started to hurt, which led to an operation when we got home. He felt he was forgetting names of things and people, his speech felt slurred; it worried him. He wasn't sleeping, we had noisy neighbors, it was a hot summer, into the 90s, with no air-conditioning...I got shingles and we were both tired. However...in spite of all that, we found some favorite things to remember; not as many as in Rome, or as we were to find in Paris, but all in all, Vienna had charms.*

—   A favorite restaurant was a lunch cafeteria on the Ring near the Museum Kunsthistoriche called The Art of Life. Their beer, the food, the shaded outdoor tables were so welcome after a morning at the art museum, or the MAK just down the Ring.

—   The Habsburg palaces, both the city Hofburg and country Schoenbrunn, are large, ornate, and beautifully maintained...and the visitor is permitted to wander through the rooms, and the centuries, as he pleases. In particular, the armor collection at the Hofburg is dramatic. Well preserved, these heavy relics of warfare have their own place in history. We learned they weren't often used, but were primarily for show, one famously made of silver.

—   An all-summer favorite was the Naschmarkt, the enormous and permanent open-air market in Vienna. Vast aisles of every kind of vegetable, fruit, meat, all in separate stalls with individual owners, are fascinating to wander. The smallest products had their own stalls; one shop sold only olives, from every country imaginable.

—   On a side street from the Naschmarkt was another restaurant we loved: the Running Sushi. Diners paid 10 euros at the door, and sat at a rectangular counter…an open kitchen was at the far end. On the interior of the counter was a circular running belt that held small plates of food continuously replenished from the kitchen. Whatever went by that looked good, you just picked up the plates…the empties were quietly removed by waiters. There were all kinds of sushi and its friends, wasabi and pickled ginger and sauces; then soups and rolls, and coleslaw and applesauce and desserts. A lot of fun and great food.

—   Right next to the Stephanie Hotel on Taborstrasse was a small women's shop that sold only cotton and linen separates, mainly white…cool and charming purchases in a steamy Vienna summer.

—   A tiny but totally up-to-the-minute Apple Shop on a side street: the owner agreed to rent me a brand-new copy machine to attach to my Mac iBook for 30 euros. She gave me this with only my Pennsylvania driver's license as security…a relaxed attitude we wouldn't find in France.

—   The turn-of-the-century architecture of Otto Wagner's famous Majolikahaus, with its facade of colorful, floral patterns in glazed ceramic. Then, from a hundred years later, 1985, is the even more dramatic Hundertwasserhaus, by the architect Hundertwasser. Tired of what he called "soulless modern architecture," he built a large apartment complex of irregular heights, bands of color (pinks, blues, yellows), all sizes of windows, and rooftops planted with trees and bushes. An unbelievable sight, yet attractive and in great demand. Both these houses are on city tours.

– Vienna is one of the four world cities that has a United Nations complex, along with New York, Geneva and Nairobi. 4,000 employees from 100 countries work here in such international organizations as the UN Industrial Development, and the International Atomic Energy Agency. Called UNO City, it's on an island in the Danube and can be reached by U-bahn; the tour is fascinating but tiring.

– #43 –
Auf Wiedersehen, Wien
Hello, Pittsburgh

I arose at 5:45 a.m. military style, showered, shaved, got into the clothes laid out the night before. It was efficient wearing the winter wool blazer, but not ideal for Vienna in a heat wave on July 31. We left two sets of keys on the kitchen table. Our one-named driver, Schmerek, came at 6:15 and helped carry down my two heavy, wheeled canvas bags plus Dana's big wheeled bag; I had my ample over-the shoulder containing the cache of drugs; Dana, her usual charge of the blue laptop. All this was to satisfy our HMO, who had decreed a return to the States every six months.

It was a tough trip, Vienna to London to Chicago's O'Hare, then a six-hour layover for Pittsburgh. Hungry, we ordered sausage pizzas at Wolfgang Puck's, the California *wunderkind*. Half an hour before flight time, Dana, always flying with a nervous stomach, said "I don't think I can get on that plane." She was serious.

American Airlines nicely rescheduled us for the next morning, for some reason at no cost. We found a Hilton in our terminal, right across the street, a wheelchair to take Dana and our four bags through the 90-degree weather, and a room for the night. We scuttled across and checked in; Dana was asleep in five minutes. Dressing the next morning, she said, "Flying nerves and a sausage pizza don't mix." But she felt better as I kept reminding her to "just brea-the."

Our son, David, had been scheduled to pick us up at the Pittsburgh airport the preceding night, but now at mid-day he was busy trading bonds. We rented a car and drove to the Wiley's house in our old neighborhood. We've known Don and Josie since the early 1970s over a tennis net, a drink, or a piano. (Dana and I both play and/or sing for our supper, as a friend says.)

After six months away, downtown Pittsburgh looked grand. The city was green, nicer than Piazza dei Martiri or Darwingasse; and Fox Chapel was even more green after a summer of rain. Grandkids Alexandra and Scott looked and acted older, David and Margaret were tanned and happy. David was now in charge of the trading of all bonds, not just municipals, at Mellon Bank. Margaret's consulting work with foundations was thriving. And they had a new, mixed-breed puppy named Louis, as in XIV.

What were our impressions in the States after six months in Europe? The buzz in Puck's and the Hilton breakfast room, people talking out loud and laughing. That's different. The very body language was more assertive, maybe aggressive, the very bodies pudgier. Movements of the service people in hotel, airport, and restaurant seemed extra brisk to us.

At O'Hare, an airport attendant near the baggage, a tall, black man in jacket and tie, whispered to me, "Do you like the Chicago Bears"? His counterparts in Rome or Vienna would not do that. The public spaces were also noisier from the air conditioning...Windy City indeed. The water pressure seemed stronger. I had a general impression that Things Worked. People acted confidently.

We settled into the Wiley's four-bedroom house, three more than we'd seen for six months. Soon, we had to attend to the seniors' top priority: Healthcare. But first, we planned our Eastern Hegira: seeing our two other sons, Ted in Philadelphia and Hardy in Baltimore; old friends Jeanne and Tom McCallum in Cherry Hill, New Jersey, and my sister Lois in Fairfield, Connecticut.

Since we had sold our cars when we left the States, we went out and bought a used car that wouldn't mind being stored for a year: a 1999 Chevy Prizm for $9,000. We asked our neighborhood mechanic to look it over; he gave us a 'thumbs up.'

We arrived at Hardy and Hilary's house in northern Baltimore. Hardy's a bond trader and after-hours father, and

Hilary, a part-time physical therapist and full-time mother. They both manage four-year-old Grace and younger brother Teddy beautifully. Grace likes to change ballet dresses at least three times a day, and Teddy prefers holsters with guns and Bob the Builder. Gender appropriate. That hot weekend Ted came down from Philadelphia with a new girlfriend, David and Margaret drove in with Alexandra and Scott. We went out for a delightful dinner near the Inner Harbor. No slouches at technology here; Margaret, sitting beside me, e-mailed "hello" to Dana's cell phone on my other side. Our family has fun together, a really wonderful thing.

Then we went to Tom and Jeanne's beach house in Stone Harbor, New Jersey. Thirty years ago they had bought a small, two-bedroom house from her parents only two blocks from the ocean, and recently turned an attic into two more breezy bed-rooms and a bath. Their house serves as a "family room" for neighbors who drop in, have a cookie or just chat…almost any hour of the day and night. They love it. Their children, Katie and TF, come from Philadelphia most weekends, often with friends. We answered questions about Rome and Vienna and made plans for Jeanne and Tom to visit us in Paris the next spring.

In Connecticut, we found my sister, Lois, in yet a new real estate configuration, a new condo just down the street from her old one. While Dana and I go to Europe and spend money, Lois buys new condominiums, making $100,000 a move. She's been plagued with replacing hips and now deals with stenosis, but gutsily keeps going. Lois has three sons, all creative, all living in Connecticut.

After seeing family and friends, we set about dealing with the upcoming bunionectomy, the Comedy Channel of Surgery. With nothing funny about a bunion…ask an owner…somehow mention of an -ectomy brings guffaws. I had a conference with William Bowman, my foot surgeon, who surprised me with news: recuperation and therapy might take three months! This being mid-August, so much for our September 19 tickets to London.

– #44 –
Doctor's Orders

This operation was planned for Don's left foot, which had been in soft, very soft sandals for six weeks, as he hobbled through Vienna's cobblestones. He'd had the other foot done 30 years earlier, not a big whoop. Back at work in three days, soft shoes, nothing to it. But, what did we know? Something had happened in the intervening years in addition to age. This time it was a big whoop. Dr. Bowman wanted him to be off his feet for four weeks (four, count 'em) then another six weeks before a check-up and final dismissal. Making it into November before we could find London, much less the Queen.

◆   ◆   ◆

Let's just cut to the chase, pun intended, and say the surgery was complicated. A titanium bar with four titanium screws had to be inserted in my foot. With this I received one long, soft, modular boot and the news that I should sit for at least four weeks with my foot high while I lounged on the deck reading Don Wiley's excellent collection of WWII history.

In September I recuperated further in Rockport, Massachusetts in Hilary's family's 1950s modern house with a big rock on the oceanfront, the rock where Hardy and Hilary were married in 1996. With salt air and rest, and Dana's patience, I slowly started walking again, much like a two-year old.

◆   ◆   ◆

The Rockport house was right on the water, on one of the hundreds of little coves on that charming, heavily-indented coastline. A small summer house, it was perfect for two people…and the views included watching our 70-something neighbor swimming across the inlet every morning.

I drove, Don hobbled, and we explored Cape Ann. Gloucester, the port setting of "The Perfect Storm," was five miles away. And so was Magnolia, another quaint shore town. We heard all the sea stories and talked to neighbors and leisurely drove around this part of New England. We trained into Boston to the Kennedy Library, beautifully sited on the Charles River. We watched sunsets in Rockport, now minus the summer tourists. Being New Jersey and Carolina shore people, neither Don nor I knew much of this area and its true charms. With so much American history, and so oriented to the sea, Rockport was a total change from the ancient, urban Europe of our past year.

◆   ◆   ◆

Back in Pittsburgh, friends Harry and Janie Thompson invited us for a weekend in their country house an hour east of Pittsburgh, in Ligonier, a small, not un-chic town founded by the Mellon family. Janie and Harry had bought a stunning house designed by Marcel Breuer, built in the early 1950s. There we were part of a big Mexican dinner party with gleaming Margaritas. The guests included Margot and Frank Reynolds, Pittsburgh friends also from the 1950s, who had long ago moved to exurbia.

Soon we settled into a small, serviceable suite in the local Holiday Inn. Dana negotiated a good price for 30 days for a one-bedroom with pullman kitchen. Although it was small, Dana invited 12 friends in for coffee one morning, with much laughter and squeezing together.

◆   ◆   ◆

After Don's doctor said we could leave in November, we had a lot to do:

—   First, to lock in new plane tickets for our six weeks in London. (We got money back in the exchange; November flying is half as expensive as September's.)

—   Second on the list was to find a London apartment, some-thing much harder to do. (Obviously, we should have been look-ing for one all along, but the immediate problems kept intruding.)

—   Finally, the last penalty for our wanderlust: where would we light for the holidays in Pittsburgh, before the next stop in Paris? Here Beth and Don Smith came to the rescue, offering their pretty Fox Chapel house while they wintered in Florida.

We could find just one affordable place in London, and it was short by a week. We discovered it through the Yale Alumni Magazine classified ads; the owner was most disappointed that neither Don nor I had gone to Yale. But she rented it to us anyway, saying it was small and serviceable, and that we could go to a hotel for the last week. Somehow, we knew this was going to be different from Rome.

◆   ◆   ◆

My toe hurried its healing, enjoying a weekly session with the physical therapist, and Dr. Bowman OK'd a November departure. We knew we wouldn't have sunny weather, but we would have a sparkling Christmas in London.

LONDON

– #45 –
Venturing Into
the City of London

Although we had lived in Rome and Vienna for most of 2002, we didn't really live in <u>the city</u> until we got to London. Actually, it was the financial district called 'The City,' where Dana and I would stay until Christmas. Our two-room flat was on Fetter Lane, near Chancery, where councilors had worked in the Middle Ages. Fleet Street, the focus of London's newspaper business, was a block away. Owned by an American woman from Virginia, our Lilliputian flat was $3,000 for five weeks. It did have a good view from our living room: a green giving onto the Gothic pile of King's College Library, which compensated a little for the cramped space…and I came to like it.

It was the location? Despite our being in the business district with office buildings that cleared out on weekends, it just became home. I found a neighborhood gym on Leather Lane, a middle ages market street only 10 minutes up Fetter Lane. Its name was a nice touch for London: L.A. Fitness. The market was convenient, just up the street, on the way to the gym. We thought of our location as spokes radiating from our flat anywhere. When you walked south, you met the Thames; 20 minutes east, St. Paul's Cathedral; 15 minutes west, the theatre district; going north we'd find the British Museum. All by walking, or buses and the Underground if we needed them. For a couple of 70-somethings from Pittsburgh, we had finally arrived in…The City.

Let me tell you my <u>gaffe</u> in looking for apartments in the first place. We were still deciding whether to take this one when we arrived in London, and wanted to see another possibility. Maria, our much-vaunted landlady from Rome, had a brother, Stefano, with some interesting connections: In Paris was Sophie, his cute girlfriend, and in London, a former wife. He was eager for her to rent her house in Belgravia.

From Pittsburgh, I had called London. An English ring. An accented "hello?" "Hello, Sophie," I said. "No, this is not Sophie, Sophie is in Rome. This is Anna." (Not her real name.) I had called the former <u>wife</u> in London by the girlfriend's name. Not cool. So I pulled it together and asked about her apartment for rent.

"You must see it," she said. "We have some rooms." Uh, oh. So, on arrival, we looked at a small, charming house with a small garden in one of London's fanciest neighborhoods. We would watch TV with her, eat breakfast with her. For us, it wouldn't work. So, back to our Virginia contact and Fetter Lane.

"Cities" can conjure up images as different as love and hate. On one end, we have friends who arrange their travels to <u>avoid</u> cities…who, in America or Europe, go out of their way to bypass the traffic, the subways, the museums. On the other end we have the opinion of Dana's friend, Andie, who lives in Nice.

"You know," she said, "I think cities are made by Man and should be judged differently. I think Monte Carlo was <u>meant</u> to look like that. Monaco is pure stone, concrete, steel and glass filling every square meter of land and many cubic meters of air. There's a place for cities." For me, Andie had made her case for urbanity, and New York is America's best example. The culture and history of civilizations are stored in museums and libraries in cities, not in the country.

Londoners, however, know how to mix their stone and concrete with greens…grass, bushes, trees and flowers…with chances to sit down, rest, ruminate. And how does the Christmas season in London change all this? Bleak, rainy, chilled, puddles of water everywhere, that's true. But our Christmas in London was crowds that bustled, extravagant trees that glistened with silver and gold bunting. On Thanksgiving Day, with no one to share a turkey, we spent the day at Harrod's. Although not committed shoppers, we went to buy Christmas presents for grandchildren: I snuck away to the Oyster Bar for six of their freshest with a glass of champagne.

A wonderful part of a London Christmas is the singing and music. We went one late afternoon to Evensong at St. Paul's for a quiet service with soft voices singing early music. At St. Martin of the Fields, we enjoyed a magnificent Bach Oratorio, followed by a crowded grill room in the basement serving hearty drinks. On a side trip to Oxford, to escape the cold and wet, we ended up with children's caroling at a service in the historic Christ Church College with a Christopher Wren steeple.

More modern was an evening at the Old Vic with Elaine Stritch, who performed a very funny monologue she wrote with John Lahr about her days in musical comedy. She loves to roar, "Here's to the Ladies Who Lunch." We also heard Jane Monheit, a New York jazz singer at the Royal Festival Hall.

Back in London in another convivial setting, carolers entertained us when we had tea at the Ritz. When our waiter arrived, Dana said, "Please bring us the highest tea you have." It was high and it was hot. The tiered, silver cake tray was loaded with calories, the table cloth was half an inch thick, and sprightly songs like Joy to the World wafted from the black-tie and long-gowned singers. We munched on scones with whipped cream, dropping strawberry jam on our jackets. Looking at the American tourists around us, we felt very British.

Again, in our neighborhood, we just walked down across Fleet Street into London's oldest Gothic church, the Temple Church, from 1196, on ground given to the Knights returning from the Crusades. It has the very thin columns I compare to the legs of a finely-bred race horse. For me it was laced with the enormous energy spent trying to unseat the Muslims in their own homeland. (Has a familiar ring now in the 21st century.)

A five-minute walk from our apartment led us to the house of Dr. Samuel Johnson, who wrote the first English dictionary. I loved his third floor office with a long table where clerks in the mid-1700s would research and write the first dictionary to include definitions; before Dr. Johnson, it was only synonyms.

The room reminded me a little of my third-floor office in Pittsburgh, although the output might have varied.

We lunched with two young women from Pittsburgh, now living in London. Both are property owners, one in Hampstead, one near Sloan Square (yuppies there are called Sloan Rangers). We learned that a 2-3 room apartment could cost $1,000,000 and London housing costs sit at the top of charts published by The Economist magazine. But here's a difference. In a real estate office we saw an advertisement for an elegant house. The price wasn't exactly news, something around 1.3 million pounds, but the age? The deed went back to 964 A.D.

All, however, was not posh. Many evenings we stayed home with the telly, which reprised old black and white footage of World War II. To the British television viewer, both World War I and World War II seem ever present, much more common than in the States. People our age, who were early teenagers in the 1940s, were sent to the English countryside or to America to escape the bombings. Londoners hid in the Underground during the air raids. (Dana's friend, Andie, was sent from her home in London to ride out the war in Connecticut.)

Although Dana and I had two short visits to London before, we had never been to the British Museum, and I looked forward to seeing the newly-covered Great Court. The famous Reading Room where Karl Marx worked for many years resonated for me, while Dana became excited over early British life. I spent the most time on some massive and ancient things: Persian stone gates and other artifacts Egyptian, Greek or Roman. And I got to examine the Rosetta Stone for the first time with its Greek and Egyptian hieroglyphics and Demotics (the language of the priests)…which broke the code for the Egyptian birds and symbols.

My most memorable museum surprise was learning of the Synopsis of the Science Museum. Commanding the space of several large rooms, it serves, in effect, as an index, summarizing the entire museum that you will walk through. Has any other museum done this? A friend once told me that I like to see the whole before its parts, and in this case, he's right.

One art technique from the Renaissance was totally new to me. For grand paintings and for large woven hangings, full size layouts were made. The National Gallery had a showing of Underdrawings (also called cartoons) as works of art in their own right, including a large one by Michelangelo. The main design elements of a painting were sometimes laced with pin-holes, then powdered, producing the same lines on the under-neath canvas or tapestry.

We had a personal touch on a graphics show at the Victoria and Albert. American friends from college, Mei Lou and Lou Klein (he taught at the Royal Academy of Art for many years) had worked as graphic designers in London since the 1960s. This show featured Lou's design of a stubby pencil as its logo, or "Oscar," for which he received an honorary award.

On December 21, it was time to leave. While we sat in our apartment house lobby, waiting for our driver to deliver us to Heathrow, we played "highs" and "lows" of London, a game we often do that reinforces the plusses and minuses of a trip. Dana's best was actually seeing, and linking up the history to names and faces, to place names she had read since childhood: Fleet Street, Chancery Lane, The Temple Bar, The Strand, Lincoln's Inn Fields, High Holborn…and she loved Samuel Johnson's house and Sir John Soane's Museum. The big minus, of course, was the weather…so many gray days, so little sun. A surprise to us both was our difficulty understanding the English spoken on the street! My favorites were the museums, the restored Reading Room at the British Museum, and the theatres…they show London at its best!

– #46 –
The British Museum
Has Lost Its Charm

know it's sacrilege; everyone loves the Cotswolds and British manor houses and pubs and Beefeaters and the royals and on and on. It's not politically correct to be negative about Britain, the mother country, indeed the birthplace for everyone on my mother's side of the family, and half of my father's, who are all either from Wales or Scotland, including those who made the obligatory two-generation-stop in Belfast on the way over. So it really should be my cup of tea. (Another bond; I just remembered my Welsh grandmother taught me to like cambric tea as a child. It's mostly milk and sugar with a little tea, sweet and good. I drank it that way for years.)

Now, we knew we were seeing London from a disadvantage. It was November and the sun never shone, which isn't news, but it was cold and rainy...and our one trip out of the city was to Oxford on a chilly, drizzly day, with no blooming gardens or other English charms to enchant. We knew we weren't giving it our best attentions; were we tired? Six weeks isn't enough time?! Maybe it was the apartment we settled into, all we could afford; it was tiny, more than tiny, it was minute and mean, with a kitchen to match. Then lastly, London was in Britain, which, for me, is high on the list of non-thrilling countries. (For me, Europe is the Mediterranean, with the sun, the colors, the art; but that's another story.)

But I did keep trying to love this London, which I know is a fantastic, exciting, happening city, with its theatres, history, art, shopping, politics. It also has the familiarity stemming from our own American educations, with the pages we absorbed of English history and customs and literature; even the street names were old friends. I did enjoy being able to read the newspapers and talk with strangers, particularly to ask them when to get off the subway.

However, just because there's a common language doesn't mean you're going to understand them...the dialects will kill you. We heard them on TV a lot, where consonants are left off, and something happens to the TH. As in: "I gah-uh go see my muvva and favva soon." It came as a surprise; there are many more regional dialects here in England, in far less territory, than in the States.

God knows I tried. We gave London the best we had. We walked, we explored, we took buses and trains and tubes; cabs were only for when I had on fancy shoes. London is filled with so much of yesterday and today, that history just oozes from the pavements; that probably was the most interesting to me. (But, for that heart-pounding excitement of seeing Rome or Paris or Athens, I never found it in London.)

Now, we did take in some spectacular and interesting sights, although mostly touristic: the British Museum and its Reading Room, the Tower of London with its gory past and the crown jewels, Westminster Abbey, Parliament, Buckingham Palace. Then we went modern to the London Eye, the new Millenium, high-tech Ferris wheel overlooking the Thames; also a few plays, and one high-rise, high-price restaurant, the Oxo Tower, for my birth-day…complete with high-heels and a cab.

The British Museum was an easy twenty-minute walk from the apartment, just up to Holborn and over to Bloomsbury. It's gray, but imposing, with an enormous covered court in the center hold-ing the famous Reading Room and a café at the rear of the court full of caffeine and sugar and chairs. On our first expedition there, Don went to the Greco-Roman floor, I went upstairs to see early life in Britain. And there, prominently displayed, I found the Sutton Hoo treasures.

"And who is that?" you ask. In 1938 in Suffolk, on an estate named Sutton Hoo, the owner, a Mrs. Pretty, allowed a local archeologist to dig into some fifteen mounds, or hillocks, on her property. The pictures show that these mounds weren't gently rolling into some ordinary hill and dale. Fifteen of them, on fairly flat pasture land, rose up into high, distinct, unnatural lumps of earth, surprisingly uninvestigated for centuries.

The contents of the mounds were termed the most important archeological discovery in all England, on a par with Stonehenge. It was so historically important that leading scientists were brought in from London, replacing the locals. They uncovered pieces of a burial boat dating from the seventh century A.D.; it was a Saxon ship, estimated to be about 18' long, together with rusted swords, gold coins, an elaborate belt buckle. However, neither personal objects or any traces of a body were ever discovered, which made it not a grave, but a 'cenotaph,' defined as a tomb-like monument to a personage buried elsewhere. These pieces, plus the discovery of an iron helmet covered with sheets of tin bronze, helped to place the ruins as Anglo-Saxon in craftsmanship. The experts have traced ownership to Raedwald, King of the Angles in early 600 A.D.

The British Museum was Don's favorite...a much smaller museum, Sir John Soane's, was mine. This original home of the 1700s architect consists of three attached houses turned into a showplace for his eclectic collection of paintings. On Lincoln's Inn's Fields, a patch of green park off Holborn and not far from our apartment, it is small, easy to navigate, and definitely worth a detour. Soane was of the Regency period, the era of George III and IV, and of our American Revolution. The few rooms furnished in the Regency style show the formal fabrics and furniture of the times: a living room with walls and period furniture all in yellow satin, a breakfast room where Benjamin Franklin ate, a small bed-room. On a lower level are more modern works not of the Soane's collection. The building shows itself as several floors of an inter-esting warren of small rooms and connecting hallways, with tiny interior bridges and balconies overlooking lower floors and rooms.

But the stars of the museum are the Hogarth paintings from Sir John's original collection...and the ingenious manner in which they're hung. In a small room, maybe 15' x 15', high-ceilinged and well-lit by a skylight, you can see, among others, The Rake's Progress displayed on multiple hinged panels, double-sided, on three walls, floor to ceiling. This method allows for 6-8 paintings to occupy the same space; thus a tiny room can substitute for the larger galleries needed for works more conventionally hung. A guard escorts the viewer in, and manipulates the panels...with the down-side being the lack of time to really inspect and enjoy Hogarth's earthy views of 17th century London.

The British Airways Millenium Eye isn't 'Old England;' it's a tourist attraction and definitely new, but stunning to see. Built for the London Millenium celebrations and termed an 'observation wheel,' it's a high-tech beauty located on the south bank of the Thames across from the Parliament buildings. The gleaming, delicately-spoked steel structure stands 443' high with 32 glass capsules; on a clear day, they say, you have a 25-mile view in all directions. It moves slowly and continuously; the exit and entrance ramps are cleverly placed to allow a pod to empty, moving all the while, then it slowly continues on while the next group enters, carefully 'minding the gap.'

Another must-see, modern but still historic, is Harrod's, the famous store in Knightsbridge. Every city has its enormous, quality, sophisticated emporium, but Harrod's really is top of the line, with prices to match. I looked at a sweater hanging on an out-of-the-way rack. Cashmere, of course, a cardigan, nice buttons, an unusual shade of green-blue. It was 590 pounds. With the pound then at about $1.60, that's just under $1,000 for that little baby; today, closer to $1200! We spent the entire Thanksgiving Day at Harrods, ogling, wandering, tasting; it was a wonderful place for a holiday in a land with no Indians or turkey with cranberry sauce. We finished the day with a high, elegant tea in their big dining room.

Every department at Harrod's was special and pricey. The gentlemen's wear sported soft, exquisite woolens, the ladies' had both classic tailored and designer mod. The antiques, both in furniture and in *objets*, were handsome, dated from all periods, and were even more expensive. The food hall had an oyster bar that captured Don; I went upstairs looking for the *crêpes*, one of my favorite dishes. (The *crêperie* was elusive...and repeating that French word to various and unknowing English sales people, I'd heard every rendition, some pretty funny, by the time I found it up on the third floor. But it was worth the struggle...*crêpes* make a wonderful lunch.)

In my searches, I came across the memorial to Diana and Dodi in a large central stairway. It was part of a magnificent, many-floored homage to Egypt; in one brass-covered hallway stands a huge statue of King Tut presiding over all. (You remember that Dodi's father is Egyptian and owned Harrod's at the time of the accident.) Portraits of the ill-fated couple, together with some mementos, specifically the 'last glass' of champagne with the lip-prints still intact, are part of the display. I bet the Queen loves it.

Our apartment was one street to the west of the City of London, the famous financial district; we were between Fleet Street and Holborn. In the daytime, the streets teemed with lawyers, bankers and businessmen and women; nighttime, with only a few sandwich and luncheon shops, it was empty. Both genders wore long, black wool coats, walked fast, looked smart. I liked the area...again, crammed so full of history. The City, London's oldest part, built on the site of the original Roman settlement, is famous for St. Paul's Cathedral, Dr. Samuel Johnson's house, and farther down the river, the Tower of London and the famous Tower Bridge.

Fleet Street, a main artery alive with cars and the colorful, double-decker buses, and for years the generic name for the English press, was just a block from our apartment. In its annual November Show, the Lord Mayor's coach rolled right past us the day after we arrived. Impressively gold and drawn by white horses, it was straight out of the fairy tales of childhood. Across Fleet Street, toward the Thames, is the ancient Temple Church from the 1100s. Constructed in the round, it pre-dates the Gothic and cruciform influences of Christianity. It was built for the Knights Templar, and is one of the few surviving round churches in the country. It's in a small, charming area, with cobbled streets sloping down to the river, restored townhouses, black-gowned law students.

St. Paul's Cathedral, just to the east, is definitely imposing and spectacularly Baroque; its landmark dome is second biggest in the world after St. Peters in Rome. One chilly day, after an afternoon of wild contemporary art at the Tate Modern on the south bank, we walked over a pedestrian bridge and went to a calming 5:00 p.m. Vespers service. Several blocks behind the big church, and just past the remains of the old London wall, is the London

Museum, which specializes in life-size displays of ordinary Londoners living from prehistory to today.

Fleet Street to the west becomes the Strand, another famous London name, with its theatres, Covent Garden and our cyber-cafe where we e-mailed regularly. We learned the buses that went down Fleet to the Strand; one turned left over the Waterloo Bridge, with a stop right at the steps leading down to the National Theatre. Here we saw "The Coast of Utopia," a new, and to us, totally unfathomable, play by Tom Stoppard. It was part of a trilogy set in Russia of the 1840s, with a cast of 70 actors, none of whom we could tell apart. We decided it was something to read, not to watch. We had tickets for only the first three-hour part. The stout-of-heart enthusiasts stayed for the 3:00 and the 8:00 performances of the other two parts. We had always, up until then, loved Stoppard's work; I don't think it was exported to New York.

We saw a few more plays. One high was Elaine Stritch at the Old Vic; she had just brought her funny monologue to London from a Broadway run. She tells her life, sings, does a step or two, dressed in tights and a man's shirt; she has good legs. Another night, we split up, Don taking in "The Lion King," which he basically liked for the inventive costumes and staging. I went to see a little-known, but clever two-man play of modern life in Ireland called "Stones in his Pockets"…two actors playing a villageful of characters, with Irish gloom and sadness and humor. A collective gasp came from the audience when we learned of the watery suicide of a character, and realized the meaning and the poignancy of the title.

I won't go further into prices in London, only to say it lives up to its reputation as one of the most expensive cities in the world. We had gotten our apartment, not from the Internet this time, but through a classified ad in an Ivy League magazine. The best we could find, it was one bedroom at $3,000 for only five weeks, which entailed a hotel for the last five days of our stay.

This last hotel came from the London Internet on Portobello Road, that interesting street full of good and bad antique shops, old and new; you can find any-and-everything if you have enough patience, cash and clear skies. Escaping a heavy, sudden rain...ah, yes, English weather...we'd dashed into a pub and found it equipped, surprisingly, with computers and Internet access. The hotel we reserved there for our last week wasn't bad; it was just an ordinary tourist haven. Still it was more bare bones living for $200/night, definitely shooting the budget.

We did find luxury this last week...Christmas came to London! The great shopping areas of Carnaby Row...and Oxford and Bond Streets...were ablaze with sparkling lights and shoppers and tinsel, all the evocative stuff of the holidays. The affluent areas of big cities are special at these times: Fifth Avenue in New York, with the enormous twinkling Rockefeller Plaza Christmas tree; the Santa's workshop windows at Kaufmann's department store in Pittsburgh; the people, the hustle and bustle, all generate a contagious and marvelous excitement. And London probably does it best. We loved that part.

But now it was time to leave. Tired and traveled out, we packed up and cabbed out to Heathrow Airport. At our gate we were met by a flight rep who offered us $1,000 <u>each</u> if we'd give up our seats for a flight the next day! We couldn't believe we were passing up this largesse, but, without a moment's hesitation, we turned it down. It was too hard, we had a wedding the next day, there was too much luggage already checked. All we wanted was to get on that plane and go home. You <u>can</u> have too much of a good thing.

PARIS

– #47 –
Two Letters to Alexandra and Scott

*A*lexandra and Scott are our grandchildren, 12 and 10 at this writing, who live in Fox Chapel in Pittsburgh. With the Iraq war just starting, David and Margaret canceled Alex's promised trip to Paris after her 12th birthday. But by July, confidence returned and she came with her Uncle Ted, a delightful whirlwind we describe elsewhere.

From: manges.dana@wandaoo.fr
Date: Mon, 14 Apr 2003 17:56
To: DMangesxxx@xxx.com
Subject: The Big Letter—Part I

Dear Alex and Scotty,
This is Grandpa at our new Paris address. I'll try to write what you may be interested in and maybe slide in a few things for your parents, too. Sorry indeed you won't be here this summer, Alex, but we want to do it some other time. Here's what you would see if you were here in our apartment.

Paris, with more than 10 million souls, is divided into 20 *arrondissements* or districts which are organized like a snail's shell, with the first one starting in the middle of the city. We're in the 15th, in the southwest of Paris. It takes two different Metro lines and about a half an hour for us to get to the first, on the Ile de la Cité where Notre Dame lies.

We live on the third floor of an apartment house with eight floors, five entrances and hundreds of people. As you enter from the street you see a garden on the left; on the right are cherry trees now blooming, tulips and flowering bushes. The building has a full time *"gardien,"* who's in charge of the building, sees that the garbage is emptied and the floors are kept clean, brings the mail to our door. A good man, Monsieur Ledru, and all we can do is smile and say *"bon jour."*

In our apartment, you enter into a generous hallway with an antique armoire, a closet on feet that used to hold the armor. From there you see a small kitchen with a little table and best, a garbage chute just like our laundry chute at home. We have a large living room which incorporates a bedroom where a wall was deleted. The star of the room is a shining chest from the

1700s, decorated with brass that belongs to Sophie, the owner, who lives in Rome. We've been dealing a lot with Sophie because the washing machine in the bathroom just conked out, in French, *"il ne marche pas."*

There's a separate bedroom (you can't always assume this) with big windows facing the morning sun where we hang the clothes to dry. France doesn't have many dryers.

In our building are shops for wine and organic foods. Close by are a *boulangerie* (you can't find a bad bakery) and a cheese shop. My favorites are a store for custom puzzles and another for miniature cars. Five minutes away are two movie theaters with at least one picture in English.

On early Sunday, Tuesday and Thursday mornings, a market magically appears on our street. The night before, a crew puts up awnings and stalls for the merchants: for vegetables, fruits, fresh fish on ice, fresh and smoked meats, and space for a man who makes crêpes (very thin pancakes with either cheese, ham or eggs, or sweet with chocolate or fruit. You'd love them and they cost less than a dollar). Nearby are jeans, shoes, antique tables and chests, coats, masks from Africa, fresh flowers, mattresses and beds, rugs, and a cook who creates *paella,* a Spanish stew, in an immense, three-foot vat.

Immediately after the market closes at 2:00 in the afternoon, the cleaning crews move in with industrial-size vacuums and brooms. They sweep the leftover boxes and broken lettuce leaves and then hose down the sidewalk. Twice a day the curbs run with water and men return with more brooms. By 4:30 it's totally clean and empty.

Kids look very much like you and are dressed pretty much the same. The "French touch" means there's often one little thing that's offbeat. A white teenage boy had his hair in corn rows; on others you'll see a huge red scarf or a purple hat or yellow shoes. They flaunt their individuality more than Americans.

What do they do? On the streets they're sometimes on rollerblades. On Friday nights around 11:00, an army of all ages, some teens, come rollerblading down our street, which has been closed to cars. They whiz and fly for about 20 minutes, arms and legs akimbo but few fall. Occasionally you'll see bicycles or just plain runners. This happens not just on the street, which must be done with care, but in, for example, the park a short walk away. It's big enough to have a few French touches: two man-made hills, one with rocks for kids to climb and one with a vineyard where adults can pick grapes in the fall. It also has a big pond for sailing large toy sailboats.

You need parks in a big city, so different from your suburbs, because there are many people so densely packed. When I walk around and look up, I see six to eight stories on average. Every now and then, there's a three-story house saved from the 1800s when Paris wasn't so huge.

Since Dani just brought dinner (at 9:00 p.m. we also eat late) I must sign off on Part 1. "More coming right after this commercial."

Love from Grandpa,

From: manges.dana@wanadoo.fr
Date: Tue. 15 Apr 2003 14:49:28
To: DMangesxxx@xxx.com
Subject: The Big Letter—Part II

It's now Tuesday afternoon, sunny, low 60s. We hear the 70s are coming to Chicago so Pittsburgh can't be too far behind.

The first letter took you through our apartment building, the street and neighborhood, and what kids like you do. I told you two movie theaters are within a 10-minute walk. Each one has at least one V.O. movie—"version originale"—usually an American movie with French subtitles.

Everything happens a little bit later here. I see mothers or fathers walking their kids to school about 8:30 in the morning. You don't begin to think about lunch until 1:00 p.m. Office workers stay until 6:00 or 7:00 p.m. when the subways are jammed.

It's also fun on the streets from 6:00 to 8:00 p.m; people shopping for food, coming home from work, kids playing ball or skating. At a restaurant at 8:00 p.m., you'll see only the waiters eating. The real crowd comes around 9:00 p.m.

Last Friday, Dani and I went across the city on a subway to see a movie about Thelonius Monk, the jazz pianist and composer from the 1950s, a black and white documentary. Your parents will know about him. It's called "Straight, No Chaser."

After coming home and getting a short rest, we went on another bus to the right bank of Seine (we are on the left bank) to the Champs Élysées (Scotty, see if you can say it) and to a theater. There we met two women, one from London and one from Paris, and listened to a symphony by Cesar Franck with a big chorus. I liked the first but not so much the chorus. I know this is not your thing but it gives you a feel for the details.

About our transportation: Most of the day, the subway you want arrives quickly, in three to four minutes. It has about five cars so that the train exactly matches the length of the platforms. During busy hours people hang from straps, but there's plenty of seats when not busy, which leads me to how the day is different here.

On the subways there's often a musician, typically playing an accordion or a guitar. They like "Lady of Spain" or "Mame." Recently, a train we were entering had stopped. The conductor was arguing with a woman who had just pulled an emergency cord. What happened? A saxophone player was in her face. The woman and the conductor both screamed at each other, then it was over, and the train proceeded.

It's fun looking at the Metro map and figuring out how you get there from here. Where the lines meet is where you change. To reach your destination, it can take two or three lines.

In addition to trains, there are buses; sometimes we can take a train one way and a bus to return. Each bus has a TV monitor that shows the stop coming up, also announced over the loud-speaker.

We have a monthly pass with our pictures on them; a little ticket is sucked through the machine. All of this costs 46 euros a month, a bargain for us.

Many of the streets in Paris are wider than both lanes of a free-way, with sidewalks on each side as wide as streets in America. This all happened when Baron Haussmann ordered a new grand plan for Paris in the late 1800s. Many small buildings were torn down and grand boulevards cut through.

In the really old parts of the city, however, streets are still narrow and squirrely. The city goes back to when the Romans were here in 300 and 400 A.D. We were in the Cluny Museum recently, built on the ruins of a Roman bath with high ceilings and big rooms for steam and cold baths. (This was when the American Indians were inventing the burial mound.)

Paris at night takes on a whole new personality. The Eiffel Tower, Notre Dame cathedral, the famous big bridges, the Louvre (ask your Mom how to say it) all sparkle with lights. Paris is a low city. In the 1960s, Paris tried a skyscraper, La Tour Montparnasse, and didn't like it. It has 60 stories, as tall as the U.S. Steel Building in Pittsburgh. "Tour" means tower.

The newspapers are playing up the bad feelings between the United States and France about the Iraq War. And we hear about "freedom fries" instead of French fries. The French don't agree with the Bush Administration not going through the United Nations and aren't wild about our attacking Iraq alone. They built the Iraqi telephone system and have more business ties to Iraq than we do. For us, it was an issue only once. We were having a French conversation group at the American Church. A Chinese man and a Brazilian both argued strongly against the U.S., but the language was so mixed up that no one could agree or disagree.

At the Internet cafés, we had some surrealist, dreamlike experiences. Muslim teenagers were playing war games, sitting next to us, screaming excitedly to each other in Arabic. With the war in Iraq starting up, "war games" in Arabic didn't seem too funny to us.

How do the French treat us? Extremely nice, they would treat you nicely too. The war, between governments, has not gotten personal with us. The French, incidentally, are extremely polite to each other (unless there's a saxophone in your face). *"Pardon,"* *"excusez moi," "bonjour, madame,"* are all built into everyday language and used constantly. You must say hello and goodbye in every shop you enter.

On TV, they have the dumbest shows imaginable (not unlike our daytime TV). Here, a combination of dancing, 1940s singers, games and girls in too much makeup and not enough underwear. One game show host likes lime green shirts. The news, however, is delivered by very classy people who speak directly to the camera quietly and with great focus. Not like Tom Brokaw standing and addressing a room. Much news, of course, has been from Iraq and there we notice more emphasis being given to the Iraqi people than American TV would do.

Since we have only French TV, our news is different except every morning on our doorstep is an International Herald Tribune, published by the New York Times. So that's how we get our news. Only once did we buy the Sunday New York Times; it cost $13.

I can see Scotty has left the room by now and Alex has her head in her hands, saying "when's he going to stop?"

Now. I wish we were with you for Easter. Huge fancy Easter cakes are in the store windows in Paris. Have a good holiday, and write something, even if it's only about the Easter Bunny.

Love from Grandpa and Dani

Romantic Tales of
Southern France

The Hotel Welcome is a little jewel in Villefranche. It looks like the hotel in a long-ago Jacques Tati movie, or the French scenes on placemats. Orange-pink in color, six stories tall, one-room-and-a-hall wide, the Hotel Welcome sits on the blue Mediterranean, on a waterfront consisting of locals, tourists, cafés, Sunday markets and French charm. When I left Don for his wife-free week in a February Paris, anticipating his fun exploring the city, my goals were simple. I wanted the sun of Villefranche at the Hotel Welcome, and I wanted to take the bus ride along the water up to Menton to see the *Fête du Citron*.

The Welcome has been renovated since we found it a few winters ago on the Côte d'Azur, and now belies its postcard exterior with a spiffy new metal and glass reception area and a modem attachment in every room. My small room, one of the three singles, is on the top with a wall of glass opening to a deck overlooking the water. The fishing boats have put out, leaving a few small pleasure boats in the bay; on the waterfront an artist catches it all on paper. The little jitneybus waits to take passengers up the mountain to the Middle Corniche, the cafés are a-bustle, the fountain in the *place* sings its tune.

As colorful as the *Fête du Citron* is, it may run second to the views from my city bus that winds its way along the coast. To me, the visitor, the ride is spectacular; the bored regulars read their papers. From Villefranche, just out of Nice, to Menton at the Italian border, is perhaps a 75-minute ride, over bridges, through tunnels, under mountainous crags dwarfing the road. Houses of every size and color cling to the mountains, defying gravity. Each town has its bay, its harbour; some have bigger yachts than others, most have a beach, all have fishing boats. Always along the coast, this ride has the best of the whole Côte d'Azur: bustling Villefranche, then sleepy Beaulieu, next comes Eze, with its two locations, one *sur-mer*, the other high on the mountain; then Monaco's beach suburb of Cap d'Ail, followed by Monte Carlo and the enormous pink condominiums, traffic jams and famous yachts of Monaco; St. Martin, famous resort of years past, and finally, Menton, just a croissant away from Italy.

There in Menton, beautifully, totally French, is the Lemon Festival, *le Fête du Citron.* The name says it all. They take an idea, a theme, and make 10-15 foot-high figures, completely covering them with oranges and lemons. Arranged on the grassy areas, or among the flowers in the park, the figures are colorful and imaginative. One time it was the French comic-book hero Asterix, this year Alice in Wonderland.

And, it's all portrayed in citrus fruit. You walk among the displays, and you still can't believe it. It's kitsch, it's corny, it's French; I love it. Alice, her dress, her face, her sash, are constructed of lemons and oranges; the Cheshire Cat, the Mad Hatter, the famous storybook characters, all done the same. Laid among the flower beds in swirling designs are combinations of the bright fruit interspersed with cyclamen and pansies of all colors. The grounds are crowded with children decorously wandering the paths, oldsters sitting on the side benches, warming in the sun.

Always in the same park, the fair is closer to the mountains than to the sea; the lower Alps rise up just over the High Corniche to form a background to the colorful figures. The *Fête du Citron* is a marvelous, inventive festival, and on a sunny day in February, it can make the heart sing.

A Post Script on Reality

At one point I started wondering about the thousands, maybe it's millions, of oranges and lemons used in this colorful Lemon Festival, realizing I'd never seen any citrus groves, even back in the hinterlands as we'd drive around exploring. I asked an official-looking someone at the park in Menton about this, and he told me, *"Oh, non, Madame, tous les fruits viennent d'Espagne, pas ici."* There's nothing local; the fruit all comes from Spain!

Les Amis in Nice

The next goal in my week's trip was to see Andie Ginsborg. We had met Andie and her husband Bernard a few years ago in our very pink apartment building in St. Jean Cap Ferrat, a village across the bay from Villefranche in the south of France. Coming down to the pool one winter morning to find some sunshine, we found Andie, a tiny lady, sitting on the tiles, leaning back again the wall, reading. I had my tapes of "Pride and Prejudice," and we talked about Jane Austen. And everything and nothing. Later we met her husband; to us, they were fascinating on several levels. They were both sparklingly bright and interesting retired professors, and at 75 they lived here for nine months of the year without a car, taking buses into Nice for lectures, plays and concerts.

The Ginsborgs had bought, 12 years before, a tiny apartment in this improbably tinted condominium and now spend the cool months of the year in France, returning to their home in Edinburgh, Scotland for the summer. As Brits, they had taken intensive French lessons their first winter there, and can now speak like natives. The four of us became friends; we spent some dinner hours with them, some walks on the *sentier* (the path around the entire peninsula), maybe a total of three or four visits before we left for home.

That was winter 1999. The following Christmas I got a long, fascinating letter from Andie. She told me she'd re-read Jane Austen's "Pride and Prejudice" with a renewed interest in the novel, and went on to discuss it. Her letter wasn't pedantic, she was just talking, writing her thoughts on the novel's construction, the characters, the author's intentions and skills, the times Jane Austen lived in. But it was a tour de force. Her language was simple, lucid, the writing as perceptive as any book review; it was the kind of letter I rarely receive (or send, I might add).

When I returned to Villefranche, I called them. Both of them hale and hearty still, Andie said she'd meet me at the Welcome, and we'd walk on the *sentier.* I hadn't seen her for five years. We're both a little older, grayer, she's had a hip replacement…but she's exactly the same to me: quick, smart, funny. We took up right where we'd left off, not so much catching-up on the new, but diving right into feelings, personalities, beliefs, the stuff of good friends. I felt, as I always had, as if I'd known her forever.

They still go back to Edinburgh for the warm months, for family and friends, and return to France in the fall. They've since moved into Nice to a bigger apartment because, as Andie said, "the buses out to Cap Ferrat had become slightly erratic." Still swimmers, they're near enough to the Mediterranean for a daily dip in the sea. "It's quite close, you know," said Andie, "only a ten minute walk." They're both now nearing 80.

The *Sentier* of Cap Ferrat

A *sentier* is a walking path; the one here is perhaps a two-to-three mile trek outlining the small peninsula of Cap Ferrat which juts southwest from the coast between Nice and Monaco. (Our wise-beyond-his-years young French friend, Renaud Calaque, told us that Napoleon had decreed that a path should define the coastline of all France.)

Tiny Cap Ferrat is a land of milk and honey. And lots of money. Protected by the lower Alps, its soft winter climate, coupled with blue skies and orange trees, has attracted the rich and famous for more than two hundred years. Leopold of Belgium settled here over a century ago, as did the heiress Eugenie Rothschild, together with countless European and Arab royalty. Today it's Paul Allen of Microsoft, for one; many other big dollars, euros and dinars are hidden behind high-walled and beautifully gardened estates. But for the rest of us, we have St. Jean Cap Ferrat, a tiny fishing village down by the sea, where ordinary life exists in cafés and little apartments and grocery stores.

The *sentier* starts here on the edge of St. Jean. The path emerges from the small park and carves a trail below private lands hilly and well treed. Walking on, you are quickly beside the blue water and white-caps of the *rade*, the bay of Villefranche. To your left and above are the steep and wooded properties of the estates. An occasional jogger lopes by; you see a sun-bather on the rocks below. The dirt path here is sometimes level, sometimes over rocks, or between trees, but always in view of Villefranche across the bay.

Periodically you catch sight of the mansions on high and see old, overgrown paths down to the water. These are from the days when royalty and their guests would hike down to swim in the sea, off concrete platforms now crumbling and forgotten. The area is evocative of faded glory, of Scott Fitzgerald novels, old photographs and movies of the twenties; it's easy to picture women in the bathing shoes and tight-fitting, woolen suits of the era, men with underwear tops to their suits, walking down these winding paths to the water. Or maybe, they're running along, secure in their wealth and their privacy, ready to plunge skinny-dipping-naked into the warm Mediterranean.

But back to the *sentier*. A mile or so on, you come to the curve at the end; here you leave the protection of the mainland across the water, and the surf gets high and wild, particularly on a windy day. The path and the shore widen, now with 50 feet of rocks between the path and the water. It looks like the valley of the moon, with boulders strewn everywhere, the surf splashing, ocean spray wetting the rocks, sometimes even the path. The hillside flattens out, the trees have been replaced by low bushes and more rocks. The estates are still high above, but now they're farther away and invisible. (Renaud told us Chirac, or d'Estaing, I forget which, had an official summer home up there.)

As you walk on, the winds calm down and the water quiets; the path is protected now by another piece of land, the protruding thumb that forms a tiny harbor on the other side of Cap Ferrat. The walkway is now cement, easy to walk; you get closer to the beach of the small bay, little boats pulled up every which way. You can see the rest of the mainland now, with its background of mountains and little towns spread out: Beaulieu, that slides into Eze-sur-mer, and on up to the peninsula, with Rainier's palace perched atop, emerging from a bustling Monaco harbor. You're back into civilization at St. Jean, only blocks from where you started. The *sentier* of Cap Ferrat is one of the prettiest walks in France.

Palm Sunday in Cap Ferrat

One day in 1998, in early April near the end of our three-month stay in Villefranche, I was in the barber's chair on the main street in the village having my hair cut by Francis, in his *le Salon de Francis*. He was chattering away in French (I caught maybe one word in five) as he was cutting my hair really short, the French way. In this torrent of conversation, I heard the words *"Dimanche,"* and "*Paque*," and realized the subject was Easter Sunday, which was coming soon. Then he asked if I'd like to go to the Palm Sunday service at his church over in St. Jean Cap Ferrat, that it was "*charmante*." When I told him we had no car, "*Pas de voiture, Monsieur*," he said…in French, as Francis had not a word of English…"Madame, if you would be outside my shop here this Sunday morning at 8:30, I will drive you to church." Somehow, I understood and thanked him. "*Oui, oui, merci, Monsieur, merci*."

Sunday morning, a warm, sunny day, we walked down the hill toward the water and saw Francis waving to us from his apartment above the shop, across from the park. He, with his teen-age son, Albert, quickly backed out from the garage in a small, bright red Renault and picked us up; we drove around the *rade*, and in five minutes we were in the community parking lot of St. Jean under the town square.

Walking a few blocks, we came to the small *Église de Notre Dame de la Mer* (Church of our Lady of the Sea). Painted a baby-pink, with a tall bell tower to match, the church stood high above the harbor, where the small boats were bobbling in the forefront, the yachts quietly moored farther out. We walked up a short, steep flight of steps into the church. Here Francis left us, going toward the pulpit; we sat down.

I looked around. The interior was just as charming as the outside. A shell motif was repeated in light blue around the dome and on the cream-colored *faux-marbre* columns. The walls were bare and white; everything was sparklingly clean. Francis told us that the church was just recently newly refurbished. Quiet, understated, it had few decorations, the least exuberant Catholic church I'd ever seen; whether it was a reflection of Lent or just the restrained French, we didn't know.

After an introductory statement by Francis, evidently a lay pastor, we all were given programs of the service and small palm fronds; then Francis signaled the group to stand. Led out of the church by the acolytes and a group of teenagers carrying long,

10-foot freshly cut palm branches, we carefully navigated the steep steps to the street, then down more steps to the water's edge. The congregation assembled by the water on a concrete quay nestled into a curve of the street above. Next, the youngsters, all in blue jeans, filed, six to a boat, into several small rowboats waiting at the edge. After a blessing from the priest and a familiar hymn, with boys in each boat holding up two tall fronds, they silently moved out, the motors somehow muffled. Then, palms wavering in the breeze, they slowly disappeared among the other boats into a sea mist.

On shore in the morning sun, the priests resumed the service for the rest of us; we could follow it in the program. It was faithful to the familiar St. James version, and, to our ears, the Nicean Creed and the Lord's Prayer in French were poetry. The boats emerged through the maze of activity out in the water, and slowly motored in, palm fronds still high, and docked in front of us. The teenagers joined the group and were thanked by the priest. We sang the familiar tune of the Doxology, and the *bateau* service was over.

Following the priest, we climbed back into the church to finish the mass. The rest of the service was short, ending with Hosannas and much waving of the palm branches. Returning all the smiling "bon jours" offered us, we left the small pink church on the Mediterranean, grateful to Francis for a charming glimpse into a waterfront Easter on the blue coast of southern France.

– #49 –
Au Contraire
American Church

We had been in Paris only for several weeks when we went to church, which is something we do fitfully at home. Our guide books suggested the American Church on the quai d'Orsay on the Seine. Their 11:00 a.m. service is interdenominational Protestant. While travel writer Rick Steves says it serves some 30,000 Americans in Paris, the bulletin said Americans were in the minority. There were many Africans and Asians.

A twice-a-year seminar would soon be held, we discovered, to orient long-term visitors and expats. So we went to *Bloom Where You're Planted—How to Live in France,* a full day, weekday program at the church. A shopping bag full of information was free. It ranged from financial and medical information, communications technology, transportation, schools and food, to sports and culture—all to make living in France easier.

"There are two things you must understand about the French," said the minister's wife in her introduction. She had lived in France for many years.

"One, they are physically smaller than Americans. Two, in any discussion, their default position will be 'no.' Then slowly, they will often move to 'yes.' The Americans, contrarily, because we like to be liked, will often first agree, heartily nodding yes, then oftentimes, move slowly to 'no.'"

An art director from France who worked for our company epitomized this. Often, as I would begin describing a project, she would shake her head "no." Then usually, she would come around to "yes." Well, Americans didn't invent the phrase "au contraire."

My other favorite incident occurred on another Sunday during a service. After the sermon, we came to what many

Christians call "passing the peace," when you turn to your neighbor in the pew and say "God's grace." This time, the minister was a perky, black American woman with a theatrical bent and strong southern accent. She said, "now is the time to pass the peace. I want you to turn to the person next to you, look him in the eye and say, 'welcome. And God's grace. You're going to like me because I'm…lookin' guuud.'"

– #50 –
Chez Marcheroux

*Maxence corrects
Dana's French*

After we picked up a Peugeot in Tours, we aimed east. In 30 minutes, we found the château at Amboise, the oldest and most medieval of the Loire castles, riding high above the river.

We parked by the water's edge and walked through the town, past small houses cowering in the shadow of the ramparts' massive stone walls. Built into the side of a mountain, these walls formed the base of the fortress which dates from 503 A.D. The castle itself was added in Renaissance days and rose another 100 feet above those walls. Great defensive moats, one big enough for a powerboat, surrounded the château. It's hard to believe an enemy could storm this high citadel, extended by the wide moat and still-working drawbridge.

Once you're up there, you can see that it comprised a total world in those early centuries, with land for farming, stables and outbuildings...self-supporting for the hundreds of people living there. The kitchens opened a window into that life, with the large meat hooks, vast fireplaces, the cauldrons, the many storage rooms making it the center of activity for the castle.

In the French countryside this early spring, jonquils were pushing up, the huge surrounding forests greening; the royalty coveted this land in the 1500s for their hunting grounds. Chenonceaux, to us the most beautiful of the Loire châteaux, is on the river Cher, not the Loire, as we'd expected. The small original fortress from the 1200s had been connected to the land by a drawbridge, as now. But the structure we see today, completely spanning the river to the other side, is a marriage of a small part of the medieval keep with the bigger, more extravagant Renaissance building, finished in 1521.

This magnificence was decreed by the fashions of the times; the entire valley of the Loire was in demand by the nobility and their friends, each outdoing the other. Chenonceaux was soon confiscated by Francis I, and became a retreat for the king and his son Henry II, together with both wives and mistresses.

As the scene of the royal hunts, *fêtes*, suppers, the original decor must have been in the height of Renaissance opulence. Today the mansion is sparsely furnished with rudimentary wooden chests and simple chairs, decorated with tapestries and paintings. The indoor gardening is a vivid memory. On one of these old chests, in a grand hallway, stood a huge basket holding a live, blooming 10-foot tall rhododendron surrounded by small jonquils and little narcissi growing in moss. Live plants were abloom throughout the castle. We compared the dampness from the river with Fallingwater, the Frank Lloyd Wright house near Pittsburgh...built 500 years later over a waterfall.

The outside gardens showed the politics of the Renaissance: two beautiful formal gardens, on either side of the château, for two ladies who probably never wielded a trowel. One was for Catherine de Medici, the Italian wife of Henry II, the other for Diane de Poitiers who provided the king with more solace.

Back in the car and without a room, we saw a sign for Chez Marcheroux. Turning in a small wooded road, we found Caroline the owner, and Maxence, her two-and-a-half year old, in an *auberge* surrounded by forest. Caroline, who appeared to be in her mid-30s, said her husband was in Switzerland helping to build a house.

The inn wasn't large, a half-timbered house that appeared to have three or four bedrooms. Across the gravel courtyard, however, was a stable turned into a charming motel with four rooms, each with bath and a Dutch half-door entrance. We were the only guests. She said the inn was mostly for hunters in the fall. Behind it stood a French forest, different from American forests in its neatness. The forest floor looked as if it had just been picked clean by Earth Day volunteers. The next day I walked its roads, big enough for a Jeep, but saw neither a boar nor a stag.

"Do you want to have dinner here tonight?" asked Caroline. "*Absolument*," we said in our best French. So around 7:30 we walked across to the dining room. Caroline was cooking in the kitchen; Maxence was playing on the floor.

Before we left Paris on the train to Tours, I had bought the morning International Herald Tribune; it was Friday, March 21, 2003. The big headline: "U.S. AND BRITISH TROOPS OPEN GROUND WAR." A few days before, a New Yorker magazine had arrived quoting Condoleeza Rice from summer 2002: "Don't worry about Iraq, it's going to happen." So we were prepared, but worried. We agreed with those who wanted this to be a United Nations effort, and with those who said, "Yes, we can start a war but can we manage that country afterward?" The television was on, with CNN blaring the news.

After watching as much televised war as we could take, Caroline served *l'entrée*, a duck *pâte*, in front of the fireplace. Caroline likes *lardon* (French bacon) in her dishes; really good; fat fills the mouth. Then for the main course, tasty lamb chops. We were served Chinon, a popular Loire red wine that's chilled. We shared two bottles the two nights we were there, and they went down well. And with no driving, no guilt.

Dana was telling Caroline of seeing tourists in a hot-air balloon over a nearby castle, calling it "Montgolfiér," pronouncing the ending "ee-ay." From the floor, playing with little trucks, Maxence piped up, "Montgolfière," "ee-air." At two-and-a-half, he was correcting our French! And he was right. He knew the name well, as his parents were friends of the famous Montgolfière family, descendants of the original company that still runs balloon trips over the whole Loire château country.

Cheverny, we saw the next day. Smaller than Chenonceaux, yet with a grand and graveled entrance, it was all of a piece, symmetrical, not rambling like many of the castles. It still looked enormous to our eyes. The design was of a tall center building with two wings on either side attached to large square "pavilions" with unusual rounded roofs. The château, with its magnificent, intact furnishings dating back to Louis XIII of the early 1600s, has been in the same family for more than four centuries, the last owner being the Viscount de Sigalas.

As we walked in, a worker was polishing a lowered silver chandelier. We learned that the de Sigalas children were born there (pictures of a 1950s wedding were in one of the family rooms) and were in residence until just a few decades ago. The private rooms were decorated in a style similar to that of a wealthy American family of the time, comfortable and modern. The house was grand, complete with a ballroom, but it was livable.

Chambord, maybe an hour's drive north, is beautiful, but for a variety of reasons, we were disappointed. It's a lovely Renaissance château, enormous, tremendously imposing with turrets and chimneys everywhere, and a few really handsomely-decorated rooms. But it was just too big, with too many cold, bare, uninviting stone halls and rooms. Even the dramatic, double spiral stone staircase, designed by da Vinci, failed to enchant.

These grand palaces served as seasonal homes of the kings, getaways in summer or hunting trips in autumn, and were furnished only when royalty was in residence. The court apparently traveled with many bunk beds, trunks and chests, including the often necessary room-warming tapestries. Since the king had many choices of homes, for any purpose, the châteaux were often unoccupied and could thus easily fall into disrepair.

Although the child Maxence had been the star of this trip, he was upstaged by Leonardo da Vinci, or Leonard, as the French call him. Returning to Amboise on our way to Tours and the Paris train, we visited Clos Lucé, where Leonardo spent his last days. At the end of a small street, just under the big fortress, Clos Lucé had been yet another royal residence; made of pink brick and white stone, it was brought to elegance by Charles VIII in the late 1400s. After passing through many hands, the castle was restored 50 years ago to look as it did during Leonardo's time.

Persuaded by Francis I to leave Italy for France, Leonardo da Vinci made the journey by muleback. He traveled light, but his bag included, among several other paintings, the famous Mona Lisa. He also brought with him some of his innovative and prophetic engineering designs: one, a rapid-fire gun, another showing an attempt to fly with a parachute, then a printing-press invention, a catapult; so many creative ideas. IBM, just a few decades ago, turned da Vinci's futuristic drawings into reality, some full-size, some in miniature. These 20 or so models take up the ground floor of Clos Lucé and are fascinating to explore. Da Vinci's talent, ranging from superb paintings to engineering, using all sides of his brain, symbolized for us the revolutions that came to be known as the Renaissance.

In the Loire Valley, we went from the grandeur of the great estates to the reality of homelife at Chez Marcheroux with Maxence, whose French, at two-and-a-half, was far better than ours.

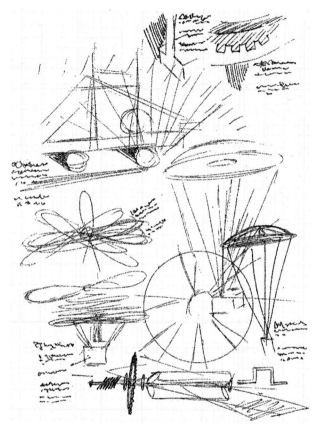

Da Vinci's drawings

– #51 –
Spearing the Brass Ring

I n the Luxembourg Gardens is the children's carousel. Old and creaky, it twirls the babies and the smaller kids in old-fashioned carriages in the calm center of the merry-go-round. Parents and nannies, grandparents like us, stand watching their charges. These little ones aren't in the game. They haven't a clue; they're looking at *Maman* or staring up the trees, totally unaware of the fierce competition ready to start. On the outside edge on the horses are the bigger children, maybe four and older. Poised for action, they're ready to ride, and ride hard.

The ringmaster hands each of these horsemen a baton, starts up the music, and the ride begins. Standing close to the carousel, he holds a clever wooden contraption that drops the shiny rings out, one by one; as the kids whirl by they try to spear...TA DA...the brass ring. Some are so adroit they collect a ring every time they pass; others are less clever and usually miss it. It's serious business; one little girl on a horse let her rings fall off the baton, she only had two...and sobbed and sobbed.

In the same Luxembourg near the entrance is a quiet area for all ages, with no competition or speed. At the wide, shallow basin, children are sailing boats, elders sitting in the sun around the water. The children use long sticks to guide the boats along. Some boats get stalled in the center, somehow they move free in the current. We sat in the metal chairs surrounding the pond, along with watchers, snoozers, tourists, parents, visitors like us, in the warm sun on a chilly March day, watching the boats gliding in front of the wind, and the children running after them. A good day in Paris.

– #52 –
A Weekend in the Country
Amiens and Beauvais

We had an invitation to visit the country house of the Desandres, relatives of friends in Pittsburgh. We knew this was something that doesn't happen to every tourist. It was near Amiens, about an hour's train ride north of Paris and famous for its cathedral, the largest in France.

When the train stopped, the loudspeaker announced "Amiens" and we jumped off with our bags, small this time, and began walking. But a sign said "Longueau," a suburb, so we hustled back onto the train, bags rolling, and <u>then</u> came to the *centre ville* where we were greeted by Claude and Jacqueline. We felt part of this warm French family, which needs saying only because of the negative stereotypes flying around at home in the summer of 2003. They bought us dinner at a *crêperie* close to the station: a fried egg on chopped steak with hard cider.

They had planned to show us the cathedral but, wisely low-key, didn't build up our expectations. We parked behind the church, then walked to the front where a small crowd had gathered. (Known as the Cathedral of Nôtre Dame, construction was begun in 1220.) We were going to see a *son et lumière* show, the first sound and light for Dana and me. Two platforms held laser projectors. Speakers soon played Bach. I didn't think this was going to work; too kitschy. I liked my cathedrals to look like stone. Then the large laser projectors began lighting the three grand doorways.

The portals were surrounded by full-size statues now <u>flooded</u> with oranges, golds, blues, reds and purples. We finally got it! Walking up close to the statues, I was amazed how closely the lights defined the folds of the robes, the scarves on the heads, the intricate cuts in the stone. The colors had been copied from a tapestry; we were standing <u>in</u> the Middle Ages. *Merveilleux!*

In the morning I could see the house was big and comfortable, part of a hamlet of just three houses in the middle of farms with rabbits darting in the yard and sheep grazing in the field. Breakfast was served in the big kitchen. It was an old-shoe kind of house, perfect for us.

Then we drove off to Beauvais, home of another cathedral designed in 1227 to be the highest in Christendom. Never totally completed, it also suffered from a weak foundation. Now, great wooden braces supported columns perhaps too graceful, too thin; steel reinforcing beams strengthened the flooring.

Once home, Jacqueline presented a dinner on the terrace: lamb chops and fresh greens with a Medoc. Without the rush of Paris, it was very quiet, *très calme.*

– #53 –
Gardez Votre Sac, Madame

We've realized we look pretty American, or at least not French. It's part attitude, part clothing; shoes are often a giveaway. Sometimes people speak to us in English before we've said a word. And, discouragingly, they'll do the same thing even as I get out the "Bonjour, M'sieur." We just don't have the accent down yet…one syllable, and they know, which makes us fairly obvious sitting-ducks on the Metro.

The Metros are safe, really at any time, in most areas of the city; it's just your wallet that's in danger. Pickpockets are prevalent, particularly at the rush hours at heavily-traveled *correspondance* stops. However, I wear little jewelry, don't carry much money, and can clutch a purse with the best of them. Don's back-pocket wallet is a little more vulnerable, and he was robbed in the Metro. Never felt a thing.

My moment came one evening at Chatelet, one of the biggest exchange points. I was behind Don, getting into a rush-hour 6:00 train, when I realized the crowd was pushing me into a corner, two young girls in the forefront. As I was pushing back, out of nowhere came a man in blue jeans brandishing handcuffs, which he snapped on one of the girls. He spoke to me, which, of course, I didn't understand, but the man next to me explained that the jeans-clad guy was a French policeman, telling me to get back off the train to testify against the girls.

Don saw me being taken off the train, yelled, "That's my wife!" and followed us out. It was all fairly anti-climactic; they asked if anything had been taken out of my purse. I looked down and saw the zipper undone (which I never felt), but no, nothing was gone. We answered some questions, looked at the five plain-clothes cops holding the two young gypsy girls, and got on another train and came home. End of story. But still exciting.

– #54 –
The Beaches of Normandy

The first thing we did after arriving in Caen, the small city near the Normandy beaches, was to find the museum where I discovered a stunning timeline. Printed around a large column, it started with Moses, who left Egypt in the 13th century B.C., and ended with Kafka, the influential German writer who died in 1924. This placed World War II in the context of thousands of years and, ironically, after the end of time, in the Caen museum.

Posters, films and audio tracks present important speeches of Roosevelt, Churchill, DeGaulle and Hitler. There's footage of the inelegant 1918 peace treaty leading to unemployment and wild inflation, resulting in the rantings of Hitler, the invasion of Czechoslovakia and the Nazi movement, the bombings in France and Great Britain, the capitulation of France, the planning and execution of the Normandy invasion, the death camps and the eventual end of the war in 1945, known to the French as *"La Guerre de 1939-1940."* The message is from France and gives fairly short shrift to the Allies' roles in both the amazing invasion and the successful end of the Second World War.

We spent the whole afternoon in the Caen Museum; then the next day, on May 8, the celebration of the war's end, we toured the beaches. The incredible building of Port Winston at Arromanches became vivid to us; it's an artificial port made to transport Allied men and materiel. Seventeen British destroyers were brought over and sunk along the beaches to make a barrier reef. Enormous concrete caissons called "mulberries" were towed from Britain and sunk. A floating highway was built on these foundations to move in Jeeps, tanks and trucks full of soldiers, ammunition and all the supplies of war, done without detection by the Germans! You can still see the remains: mournful pieces of ships, German defenses and parts of the foundations of Port Winston.

With our French tour guide we entered German pillboxes, some with telephone poles serving as decoy guns that overlooked the cliffs scaled by U.S. Rangers in the face of German machine guns. We walked silently among the thousands of white marble crosses facing the sea. In the separate Canadian cemetery, crosses carry a poignant phrase from the family of a fallen hero. The French government has wisely made the whole memorial uncommercial: no tourist signs, no advertising of any kind. Dana and I, young teenagers at the time, remembered some of these sights from Life magazine and the mental pictures painted by Lowell Thomas on the radio.

On June 6, 2004, in a hotel in Yerevan, Armenia, I watched the moving 60th anniversary of the Normandy landings on CNN. (I had volunteered there to consult with non-governmental organizations in fund raising.) The pictures of the soldiers who fought there, now in their late 70s or 80s, the coming together of U.S., British and German soldiers meeting on the beaches and the bear hugs between Presidents Chirac and Schroeder were vivid reminders that wars don't always have to keep repeating and repeating.

55

Mont-St-Michel

When you drive from Caen in Normandy to Mont-St-Michel, it takes only an hour, but you lose eight centuries. That's going from the D-Day invasion in June, 1944 to the erection in the 11th century of the cathedral on the sometimes island of Mont-St-Michel; "sometimes" because much of the time it has a sandy land bridge that can be navigated on foot.

But we're ahead of our story. Dana and I had long believed that when you walked on the land bridge you were in danger of being swamped by the racing in of the sea. Further, when David was in the seventh grade, his teacher asked, "Who knows how fast the water comes into Mont-St-Michel?" Remembering a family dinner table conversation, David said "Faster than a galloping horse."

We had checked into a cute hotel half way up the Mont. Before we went to bed, we looked to see if the sea was roaring in. Nothing. The next morning the sand was still dry.

"Ou est la mer?" I asked the hotel manager standing at her desk. Where is the sea? Feeling sprightly and prepared with a pun, she responded *"Je suis la mere."* I am the mother. Good for this lover of French puns, which I got, but it shed little light until she explained that the water came in only twice a month with the lunar pull.

We learned the causeway was built in the late 1800s, but there is talk now of removing it and returning Mont-St-Michel to its sandy origins.

At the top of the Mont is an ancient cathedral which was closed the hours we were there. But I found on our bookshelves a book from Dana's mother, "Mont-St-Michel and Chartres," the classic written in 1905 by Henry Adams, which takes up Middle-Ages architecture and this very cathedral in his personal style:

(Mont-St-Michel) is your first eleventh-century church! How does it affect you? Serious and simple to excess! Is it not? Young people rarely enjoy it. They prefer the Gothic, even as you see it here, looking at us from the choir, through the great Norman arch. No doubt they are right, since they are young: but men and women who have lived long and are tired—who want rest—who have done with aspirations and ambition—whose life has been a broken arch—feel this repose and self-restraint as they feel nothing else. The quiet strength of these curved lines, the solid support of these heavy columns, the moderate proportions, even the modified lights, the absence of display, of effort, of self-consciousness, satisfy them as no other art does.

As a fan of Chartres since college, I had learned to appreciate Notre Dame, Amiens and Beauvais and others on this trip, and other cathedrals on other trips. But Adams' musings really speak to me except for "the broken arch" and end of "aspirations and ambition." Without aspirations and ambition we wouldn't be climbing these old stone steps with awe and sometimes a little angina.

56

Serendipity in a
French Underground

Cavemen were drawing on their walls in southwestern France as long as 14,000 years ago, in the Iron Age, pre-dating any known history. Only discovered in the mid-1800s, these engravings have fascinated modern man ever since with their artistry and creativity, talents not usually associated with an ancient, presumably uncivilized world. The paintings depict the animals they knew best: bisons and mammoths and horses, wolves, deer and squirrels. Some are line drawings, others are fully painted in, and the most interesting use the contours of the cave walls to form the bulk and bodies of the animals.

We had planned to see some of these drawings while visiting the Dordogne in central France. Lescaux, the most famous of the French caves, second only to Altamira in Spain, is now unfortunately closed to the public, whose very breath was contaminating and destroying the fragile drawings. Another cave, however, serves as a replica, totally faithful to the original Lescaux, complete with expert artist's copies of the animals. But we decided we wanted the real thing and settled for Font-de-Gaume, a smaller but authentic cave not far from our hotel in Sarlat.

Don had asked the desk man at our hotel to make reservations for us at Font-de-Gaume. As the cave didn't answer the phone that morning, the hotel told us to just drive over, and we probably could get in. We knew they only took small groups through the cave, for perhaps an hour tour.

You can guess the answer to our gamble after making the 40-minute trip: "*Non*, M'sieur, no place. *Non*, *non*, for any tour this afternoon." We tried to tell her if they had answered their phone, etc. It didn't work, and we left the small entrance fuming and talking to ourselves…one of the few times we ever were angry at the French stubborn reluctance to bend a rule. We went outside, venting to a small group of Americans waiting in the parking lot. One of them, a quiet man, said, "If you sweet-talk that woman over there," he pointed to a group member, "I bet she'd let you go with us." We did, and within a few minutes we were in their group, passing the dragon lady at the entrance, and on the path to the cave.

This turned into a major hike, a 15-minute climb; it wasn't an enormous challenge, but it was definitely a hill to remember. On the way up, while also trying to keep breathing, we chatted with the man who had kindly paved the way for us. Don thanked him, and we introduced ourselves, mentioning Pittsburgh. He said his name was Jack and, "Oh, I'm from Buffalo, but I grew up in Pittsburgh, on South Dallas Avenue." Don threw out a few friends' names, this man knew them all. When he mentioned something about New York, and a play he was producing, all the pieces fell into place. And Don yelled, "You're Jack Cullen, the McCallum's cousin!…the play producer! We know you!"

And we did, or least we'd heard about him, and just recently. We'd known a lot of the Cullens in Pittsburgh for years; they were Jeanne McCallum's family, a large, closely-knit Irish clan, all doing well in various cities around the east. And the McCallums, after seeing us in Paris a month ago, had just spent a weekend with Jack Cullen, seeing his play on Broadway.

Jack was hosting a six-week trip for his son's family. It sounded perfect. They'd sailed around the Greek Islands, toured through Europe to the Dordogne, to end up in Paris, heading for the States and home. Here, they were having a guided tour by a local anthropologist, a cave expert, and we had lucked into it. We all marveled at the "six degrees of separation," finding "friends of friends" in such an unlikely place in the middle of France.

The group was perhaps 13 people, including two of Jack's small grandchildren. Finally at the cave entrance, depositing bags and purses in an adjacent opening in the mountain, we were led in, single file, by the young guide who told us not to touch the walls with hands or clothing. The passageway was narrow and low-ceilinged as we made our way through the dimly-lighted cave. When we reached a certain point called the "Rubicon," the few overhead lamps went out, leaving strips of red lights on the bottom sides of the cave floor. Little murmurs came from the children, who were reassured by their parents and quieted.

We were in a high-ceilinged, small area, the walls narrowing slightly just above our heads. The floor was smooth and dry, no water anywhere. There was just enough room for our group to stand without touching anything. The guide shone a red laser light on the cave wall; I saw only the sand-colors with markings at eye-level. As she traced the faint lines with the light, the drawings took shape for me. I could see the outlines of an animal's hump, a bison, and its body. Then more details of the drawing emerged: the bison's eye, sunk into a small cavity in the wall, the bulk of the body, the tail. The guide pointed out the artist's clever use of contours, both convex and concave, of the cave wall to form the details of the bison. Several animals were drawn on this wall. Some were static, one had more motion; it was a horse running, the head raised, two feet off the ground.

As we went farther into the darkness, guided by the faint red lights on the floor, we saw a dozen more drawings, each different, some painted, some just in outline. The guide also showed us a bison full-face and profile super-imposed on each other, remarking that Picasso wasn't the first to use this technique. She made us see that at Font-de-Gaume the animal outlines are carved, then painted inside the carved lines, a more advanced technique than simple drawings.

The tour was over; we made our good-byes to the group, reimbursing Jack for the fees, and walked down the mountain. We were happy with Font-de-Gaume, despite the fact that the Lescaux drawings were said to be superior in techniques and coloring. This was real; the drawings were authentically 14,000 years old. That was the best part, knowing that a man of the Iron Age had been here, carving out his drawings by torchlight, in this very cave, standing in this spot.

– #57 –
Put Your Feet Up
and Read a Book

On any given day, Dana and I will be reading: over the kitchen table, in the tub, on the bed. Since you can't walk all day, we read all over Europe. We often read about what we were seeing (see the *Louvre*, come home and study it more) but we didn't make that an imperative. We bought books in English-speaking stores, browsing until we could stand no longer. Rome has an excellent Anglo-American Book Store near the Via Condotti, the fashionable street just down from the Spanish Steps. Vienna has a British book store between Kaerntnerstrasse and the Ring. Paris has the made-for-browsing Shakespeare & Company, near Notre Dame, the Hemingway hangout in the 1920s that helped James Joyce publish "Ulysses." WH Smith, on the rue de Rivoli, is abuzz with college students and retired business people looking for maps and books on travel and language. Brentano's on the avenue de l'Opera, has been in Paris since 1895.

Although the average rushed tourist must read maps and tour guides, we had time to go beyond. In Vienna I liked some new fiction by Nick Hornby, an English writer I'd never read. I read a long treatise about the Habsburgs, really setting us up for Vienna and for Prague and Budapest when we got there. From the 1300s, they were the European power family until Emperor Franz Joseph fell in 1918. They married into the royal families in both Spain and France, where Marie Antoinette best represents the Habsburgs.

Over our 18 months in Europe I made several vivid book discoveries. In February 2003, when we started our six months in Paris, we visited the American Church just to meet some people. Located on quai d'Orsay, they were having their semi-annual orientation seminar for Americans.

The "textbook" of the orientation is a must if you stay in Paris for a while: "Bloom Where You're Planted—How to Live in France." It covers everything from health insurance to the word for starch at the laundry *(amidon)* to a list of websites for practical information. For a copy, contact *www.americanchurchparis.org.*

The briefing included recommended reading which encouraged me to, so to speak, enjoy "Madame Bovary" after all these years, and she wowed me. Dana helped by bringing home "Lectures on Literature" by Vladimir Nabokov, who dissected a famous passage of an assignation during a long carriage ride.

More rational but no less exciting than "Madame Bovary" was "Guns, Germs and Steel," which our son David had discovered. It's an anthropological examination of the question "why have Africa, Latin America and the South Pacific developed much later than Europe?" Or, conversely, "why did Europe and Asia develop so much earlier?" Is it inherent in the people who lived there? *Au contraire* argues the author, with a plausible hypothesis.

I tackled the book "Genome" about the human body's 23 pairs of chromosomes—at least when the book was published in 2000. I read it in Rome. Author Matt Ridley makes an extremely complicated issue very clear. While I was totally engrossed, Dana was reading, of course, and listening to books on tape. Some of the books she heard included "John Adams" by David McCullough, "A Man in Full" by Tom Wolfe, the Robert Caro biography of Lyndon Johnson and a biography by Scott Berg of Charles Lindbergh, whom Dana came to remember as "selfish, unpleasant and dull." But that was before we knew he had two sub-rosa families in Austria.

Why am I telling you this? Simply to underline the time we had to pursue more than train timetables, to add dimension to almost two years of renting apartments. When friends would say to us, "but what did you <u>do</u> for 18 months?" Dana responded, smiling, "we did everything you did only we did it in Europe."

– #58 –
The Day the Computer Crashed in Paris

Traveling with a laptop is a lot like dealing with a four-year-old; you never know when it's going to blow up in your face. And mine did.

We had started out with this little baby computer a year ago in Rome; I was the official courier of the laptop…Don had even more poundage…and had lugged it from the States in my shoulder bag. It's a small turquoise Mac iBook, one of those pretty colored ones popular a few years ago, weighing maybe five pounds. I know that's nothing; we've all had roast chickens that weighed more. However, when I'm slogging through the airports with this five pounds of nothing on my back, it became a definite something. But, as I wanted it with us, I lived with it.

In Rome, we used it just as a diary, no e-mail connections; it was too hard. But we had Maria's computer for that; she was our trusting landlady who let us use her computer, and her empty apartment when they went on vacation. In Vienna, our landlord Alfred was a computer whiz, who not only switched the laptop to a local server (as part of the contract for our **** apartment), but also lent me his expensive Sony laptop. London, I didn't even take it with us. Our three-month projected visit had been sliced in half by Don's foot surgeon, and there we existed on cybercafe messages.

The laptop and I started our Paris life together easily enough. I got it over the first stage, using the same converter I had in Rome, the one that reduces European house current from 220 down to our 110, then the adapter to marry American plugs to French ones. That gave me electricity; we could word-process. But that wasn't the goal. We wanted it all, e-mail, right here in the dining room. We were tired of trekking to our local cybercafe, where we'd be closeted, at 3.5 euros per hour, with Parisian Arab teenagers playing shoot-em-up video games all around us, literally as the U.S. was marching into Iraq.

Like many things, hooking it up didn't seem too hard to do. Once I realized that the funny little plug in the wall was the telephone jack, all I had to do was to cross the street to France Telecom, buy the attachment that my U.S. telephone line would plug into, and sign up for Wanadoo, the French server...get the free Wanadoo installation CD, and *voilà*, we'd be connected.

<u>Wrong</u>. All sorts of warning signs came bubbling up on the screen. As it was in French, I never knew exactly the problem, but I did know it was talking about memory. I asked France Telecom what to do; they very politely threw up their hands and suggested the FNAC over in St. Germain. This is the big technical discount house across town selling TV's, computers, copiers. So I lugged the laptop through the Metro to the left bank, and bought 64 things of memory. I probably should have bought a lot more, we all could have used some.

But the screen kept displaying bad news. By now it was way over my head, and I realized I needed a French techie. Back across the street at France Telecom, I asked the young English-speaking clerk there who told me of a young Bulgarian at the Sorbonne, studying Kirkegaard, who also moonlighted in computers. Of course.

Lachizar arrived as planned at 8:30 one spring evening, early April. Tall and bearded and studious-looking, he spoke English and seemed computer-friendly. (If I were 50 years younger, yes, and single, it could have been the plot to a new movie, or a sitcom.) I took him upstairs. He sat down, turned on the computer; nothing. Then a small, trembling question mark appeared on the screen, and that was it. Crash! It had been working beautifully all day; I'd just been playing solitaire on it before he came, and now death...and disappointment.

I paid him 15 euros, and he left. He offered to work on it at home, to see if he could fix it, but I didn't have the confidence to entrust the little blue laptop to a total stranger, even a Philosophy major at the Sorbonne. We decided I should take it back to FNAC, my house of memory.

Thus began my longest day. When the technicians looked at it, all shaking their heads, they did the "wha wha wha" mouth-blowings that the French do in moments of stress, or confusion, and then "*non, Madame.*" The most verbal of them got it across that I would have to send it to Finland. "What?" I said. The other one quickly said, "*non, Madame,* only Ireland." That was supposed to make me feel better. I gathered my wits and asked if there were an English-speaking clerk near…"*Pardon, M'sieur, est-ce qu'il y a quelq'un qui parle Anglais*?" One appeared and said, "no, Madame, you have only to go to the first floor, to the *rez de chaussée.*" Here my head started to hurt.

The downstairs seemed to be a combination "will-call" and coat room, people milling about, but my English clerk introduced me to a youngish man, who, after some questions, said, "it will be easy, Madame. You have only to go to the Apple Shoop, very close, and they will fix you." He wrote the name again, Apple Shoop, wrote the words "*disc d'installation,*" and gave me the directions, the final all-important Metro stop. We took off, the blue baby laptop and I. (I was losing a little confidence here, but I was determined.)

This is where it got surreal. I asked the woman in the cage down inside the Metro for the location of Place du Thermes, adding that I'd been told it was nearby. She instantly was furious at me. "*non, non, pas du Thermes,*" she sputtered. "*C'est de Terne!* Do not speak!" She seemed to be angry at my confusing the names; maybe too many lost Americans had been cluttering up her space. I meekly asked where it was; she gave me the three Metro changes I would have to make, and the moment was over. I'll never know what was wrong.

By now it's the rush hour in Paris. Trains were full, the platforms crowded, and everything had gone out of my head. (If I could only buy 64 things of memory, that would fix it.) I remembered she'd said Chatelet; I found that platform, and was hopping on the next train, when it came to me that was the big exchange point where my purse had almost been stolen. I clutched everything to my chest. Then a switch there to Charles de Gaulle Metro stop. Looking at the map on the train, I saw it, right there on line 2, just up two stops, Place de Terne. I had done it; I couldn't believe it.

We three, the blue laptop, my purse and I surfaced and looked around a busy, enormous traffic circle, the elusive Place de Terne. I saw no Apple Shoop, nothing resembling it. I did see a Pharmacie, where someone usually speaks English. This one had only French. But she was very nice, and finally suggested that it might be in the FNAC right down the street, which was really so logical.

Two long blocks later, down in the bowels of the FNAC, I waited in line, only to be told, "*Je suis désolé, Madame, pas ici.*" "Sorry, lady, not here," only a little more politely. I asked again for the Shoop and somebody remembered it, which by now they called by its right name, and yes, it wasn't far. "*Voilà, Madame, l'adresse.*" True, it <u>was</u> close, but by now, I was all turned around. I was leaving the store by a different entrance, to the wrong street, and couldn't find the original street. Nobody I asked knew where the Shoop was, and it was an eternity of well-meaning but feckless directions before I staggered into a charming little cul-de-sac of a street, with a big sign on the building at the end, The Apple Care Shop.

Here another frazzled lady heard my plaint, and quickly said, "Oh, we're closing now—they're always sending me people like you." This is where I started to cry. But she helped, gave me a number to call. I had my cell phone and dialed it right there. A voice, thank God it was in English, said they were closing, but I could call yet another number tomorrow morning, and yes, those people will speak English, something I knew was a necessity.

The next morning, *dans l'appartement*, I took my *café* to the telephone; I took a deep breath, dialed the number, and found the Holy Grail. They spoke English, they found my registration number (all computers are registered by name), and with the credit card, for 72 euros they would send me an installation disc that solved all problems. I noticed an accent and asked him where he was located. He answered, "Dublin, Ma'am." I was in Ireland, just as the man had said.

Two weeks later my disc arrived; I called Lachizar, he Metro'ed over and connected us up. We were on Wanadoo.fr and the Internet was ours. And all it cost was 72 euros and my entire nervous system.

– #59 –
Restoring a Medieval Castle

*K*atie McCallum is the daughter of our old friends, Tom and Jeanne McCallum. She's an enterprising young woman...and this is her story of a recent work-play vacation in France.

Subj: Working in France
Date: June 2, 2003
From: Katie.McCallum
To: Manges.Dana@Wanadoo.Fr

So, you wanted to know about my working week in France, right? Well, I first heard about it on the Today Show when they were doing a segment on Volunteer Vacations. I followed up online and got the particulars. La Sabraneque in Provence, France, intrigued me, so I chose that. But I didn't want to do it by myself, so I found a buddy in Amanda O'Dea, a malpractice lawyer friend here in Philadelphia. We flew to Paris, where we had dinner with you and Don...I guess you weren't listening when we told you about it...then a train to Avignon, where we were met.

First of all, this Sabraneque is a non-profit organization based in St. Victor la Coste, a beautiful little village about 45 minutes east of Avignon. Their mission is to preserve 'rural Mediterranean habitats.' They import people like Amanda and me to help, giving us housing and food and tours of the area; I think we each paid $450 for the week.

The rooms were rustic, with communal bathrooms and showers. We worked every morning on Castle Gicon, their latest project. There were seven people in our group, three of us from the States, of all ages, backgrounds and abilities. Our group was taken to the work site after breakfast, arriving by 9:00 a.m., to work on the consolidation and restoration of the medieval castle ruins, and of the path leading from the village to the castle. In our week, we built a dry stone wall, laid a tile floor, and pointed a stone wall. It was hard, really grubby work, but the views were fantastic. Did I mention we were in the Luberon, the chic area of Peter Mayle country?

The meals were simple and delicious and served family style; all local cuisine and prepared by a cook, lunch was the biggest. Wonderful platters of cheeses were served at every meal; we had wine with dinner only. They fed about 30 of us; volunteers, some paid workers and some locals. We all pitched in to clean up, maybe 15 minutes total.

Then, after lunch, we'd be taken on tours to Avignon, and Uzes, and other quaint villages around there. My favorite sight was the enormous Pont du Gard, the Roman aqueduct, which brought water into Nimes up until maybe 100 years ago. At any given time I could hear 3-4 languages spoken: French, English, Italian, Spanish. Nights were usually fairly quiet, as everyone was tired.

It was a short week; arriving on Monday, we left Saturday morning. Would I do it again? Probably not, but it was a great experience.

– #60 –
Haute Cuisine

O r High Kitchen, as Don calls it. We made a foray into that world to the new, highly-touted Joel Robuchon restaurant on rue du Bac. I hadn't heard of him, but Patricia Wells, the food editor of the Herald Tribune, and Pariscope, the little weekly magazine of "what's happening now," they all know him, and they think he's swell. He's a chef in a second career, who's opened a restaurant to his own liking: *L'Atelier de Joel Robuchon.*

It's very different. No reservations; you just wait in a line outside, in the heat, on the sidewalk, take your turn. No tables, just comfortable, high-backed bar stools around an open, chrome and glass kitchen. And all a la carte. Most restaurants, good or bad, have a rigid formula of *entrée, plat* and *dessert*, so for one of the classy places in Paris, it's really a change…with cloth napkins, but just high quality paper place mats, and stunning, non-silver utensils. And great presentation. It was an expensive night for us, $150, but so delicious.

I didn't order as well as Don. There were too many caviar/oestra/legume touches that I'm too much a peasant to appreciate; I settled for a spicy gazpacho, then three little lamb chops that came with a small pot of something white. The man on the neighboring stool was eating the same thing…I asked him, pointing, what it was: "*Pardon, Monsieur, qu-est-ce que c'est?*" And as usual, I couldn't hear <u>or</u> understand the answer. It looked like a sauce of some kind, thickish…it took me several bites to find out it was simply mashed, or puréed, potatoes, very different, and good. Definitely not your mother's mashed potatoes.

Don had exquisite little deep-fried vegetables, delicate, then a fish thing with all kinds of herbs and twitters and spangles. And a soufflé, chartreuse, with pistachio ice cream. He liked it. I'm not adventurous; I had a chocolate mousse.

One of the best parts of the night was seeing how the restaurant worked. It really was like a stage play, with the diners as audience. The room is designed, I've read, as Robuchon's version of a New York diner. Two big semi-circular counters face a totally exposed kitchen area, with the work and food assembly stations also in clear view. The barstools are chrome and comfortable; the food is served, slightly awkwardly, over a low divider of condiments and flowers. All was total calm and quiet, only the normal buzz of the diners' conversations. As this was Paris, the talk was low in pitch, civilized and, I assume, discreet.

The kitchen was also the epitome of calm. Nobody ran, or screamed, no classic outbursts of temper or despair, just a lot of men in black costumes, *sous-chefs* and servers, moving quietly about. Knives flashed, large sections of meat were dismembered, salads mixed, plates assembled, and all was eerily silent. It looked like the set of Star Trek, only with much better food.

– #61 –
Renaud and Luc

As we were reaching our late 50s, we met two students from France whom we got to know better in the next 20 years. Renaud Calaque and Luc Robert have never met each other—one lives in Paris and one in the Côte d'Azur—but both of them helped us understand and enjoy France. But first, you have to understand PCIV. For 30 years, Dana and I belonged to the Pittsburgh Council for International Visitors, started in the early 1960s to connect students and visitors with Americans for a long visit or, in our case, for a dinner. We have entertained: five sailors from a, yes, landlocked country in South America; three engineers from Communist Yugoslavia who wanted to know my salary; the mayor of Ankara and his interpreter; a tiny lumber buyer from Chad whose watch wouldn't stop playing "Stars and Stripes Forever," and scores more. And then we met Renaud.

We had a phone call in January from the PCIV asking if we would like to meet Renaud, studying artificial intelligence at the University of Pittsburgh. We said *"oui."* He was 21, tall and skinny, liked to laugh and—we were in our late 50s—was easy about the differences in our ages. We met him on a Tuesday night in January and decided he should come every Tuesday night, have dinner and teach us French. Well, you know how that works! Speaking French quickly devolved into speaking English about France and the U.S. (politics, manners, economics, cooking) laughing at both the differences and the similarities. He would occasionally join in the yard work until summer 1988 when he returned to France.

A few years later, when Renaud married Isabel, a young, Francophile German, they invited us to their wedding in Germany. We said *"non"* to that, something we've always regretted. So, instead, they spent two days of their honeymoon with us in Pittsburgh. Although they puzzled through their first baseball game, they saw the Pirates win.

In the mid 1990s, Renaud asked us to help his sister Aurelie find an internship with an advertising agency for her master's degree. She preferred San Francisco. I said, well, I could arrange one in Pittsburgh, and as much as that sounds like an old joke, she came, stayed with us for a while, then moved to a more communal student house in the university area. She was good looking, bright and practical enough to pull up the kitchen floor, moving appliances and cleaning under them, giving new meaning to the stereotypes of a young, usually-in-black Parisian woman.

We hosted Aurelie's parents at dinner when they came to see her, and months later they returned the favor in Paris, where I upset my share of international relations by ordering red wine with fish. In 2003, when we were in Paris for our six months' Odyssey, we saw Renaud and Isabel often, in their apartment, in our apartment, in a café, wherever it would work. Renaud consults on computer techniques for marketing. Isabel handles customer relations for a helicopter company. And we visited Aurelie, now with a baby Cedric and deep into worldwide advertising for L'Oreal. All of them, productive and successful.

Luc Robert, a post-doctoral student at Carnegie Mellon University, and I met at a seminar on jazz piano. I invited him to our house to play two-piano blues and we've been good friends ever since. He had a degree in computer science from the École Polytechnique, which some have compared to a combination of Harvard and MIT; was an unusual mix of smart, practical and nice, and engaged to a Brazilian girl named Monica, with her own computer Ph.D. (Doctor and Doctor Computer.) Before he left for Paris, he said, "uh, would you like to come to our wedding? It's in Brasilia." I thought for two minutes, called Dana who was up for it, remembering missing Renaud's wedding in Germany, and answered with an exuberant "*si!*"

Luc is now a partner in a software company in Sophia Antipolis, a park of young, brainy techies in the south of France in a quasi-government partnership. He and Monica have two babies: Lisa, who came with them to Rome to see us, and Ivan, named for the Brazilian singer, Ivan Lins. We spent several days with them in the summer of 2003, playing as much piano as you can with two babies, and watching Luc grill in the backyard, *bossa novas* in the background.

Luc arranged one incredible night in Paris in the late 90s. We were staying with Renaud and Isabel when Luc had business in the city. He called Philippe Souplet, a teacher of mathematics at the École Polytechnique and master stride pianist, and Aaron Bridgers, the American, former good friend of Billy Strayhorn who was a close partner of Duke Ellington. The four of us, in turn, played Philippe's shiny grand Yamaha. Aaron, for years the pianist at the Hotel Crillon, had lost a lot of technique by his late 70s, but Souplet was strong, commanding the energetic strides of songs like "Honeysuckle Rose." He plays regularly in Paris. Compared to them, I was a novice, but appreciative.

Maybe someday, after Renaud and Luc read this, they will meet.

– #62 –
Paris on Rollerblades

The Friday night rollerbladers wheeled by our apartment one evening about 10:30 p.m. I had been hearing a constant whirring, a sound like enraged locusts, coming from the street...and when we finally opened the windows, there they were: roller skaters, thousands of them, young and old, racing down our rue de la Convention toward the Seine. The cars had disappeared, the street was a blur of people, of color and sound and motion. Skaters filled the entire four lanes: graybeards, family groups with little kids perched on shoulders, teenagers holding hands, even white-haired ladies in spandex tights. The right side was for the slower ones, the left lane belonged to the really fast, the serious skaters barreling along, weaving in and out, bent over, heads down.

We learned it's an organized three-hour spin, with a route that changes weekly. The group gathers at Gare Montparnasse at

10:00 p.m. Fridays and has an impressive police guard. Fronted by six policemen on motorcycles, two official cars plus six "roller cops," the skaters have a clear road; with French practicality an ambulance brings up the rear.

The Friday night run is the biggest; up to 20,000 bladers join the race. There are also smaller runs. Sitting casually one Sunday afternoon at a café near the Place de l'Opera across town, we saw a group of perhaps 300 skaters rounding the corner onto rue de la Paix. They were a little more relaxed than the Friday nighters; going slower, most were chatting away. It was more a casual afternoon run than a real race. It must have been official, however, as the police were in front clearing the path.

The big Friday night skate was great fun to watch...the only thing better would be to be out there with them. Hardly a helmet, and forget the knee pads. They're out to <u>run</u>.

− #63 −
Le Jour de Desrue

Sophie Desrue, our cute Paris landlady, lived in Rome, leaving her parents in charge of the actual paying of the rent. M. and Mme. Desrue came the first of every month to pick up the money. It was all done in cash; opening a checking account in a local bank was too hard, if not impossible. Americans like us, on our own, lacking contacts, the language, or the umbrella of a corporation, had a hard time with official France. And banks were the worst. However, the ATM machines and the VISA card did the job. As the income generated by our pot of gold was automatically deposited monthly into our bank at home, we could access it by the same cash card we used in Pittsburgh.

Once a month, Don or I would hit the ATM machines to withdraw 1500 euros from our account to pay the rent. It took five days to accumulate it all, as 300 euros was the daily limit for withdrawals. I'd pile it up in Don's sock drawer, figuring that the burglar, if he ever got past all the French key pads and locked doors of our apartment house, would never find it there. We learned we had to find the machines that dealt in the bigger denominations…1500 euros in 20 euro bills was a big wad for Madame to carry to the bank.

On the day of reckoning, the doorbell would ring at 11:00 a.m., and M'sieur and Mme. Desrue were standing there in the hall. They were our age, early 70s, lived in the 11th *arrondissement* across town. A retired salesman, M'sieur was a voluble, excitable man, dapper, smiling, very friendly, with a little bit of English. As a young man he had played the drums one memorable night with Dizzy Gillespie, and loved to talk about it. Madame was a large round lady but not unattractive, spoke only French, and was the money manager. I'd retrieve the cash from the sock drawer, and we three would sit at the dining room table and talk as she counted it.

And slowly, we became friends. Probably humor was the common denominator; they both laughed easily, and particularly so over our mutual gaffes in language. Often they'd stay for several hours as we discussed, in our pidgin Franglais, politics, World War II, French customs. We all learned a lot. (M'sieur had tears in his eyes one time as we talked about the Normandy landings and how, in his words, America had saved France.) Once, Madame took me to our local *supermarché* to make sure we had the best *foie gras*; another day, shortly before we left, M'sieur insisted on driving us around Paris to some of his favorite spots.

Now that was a day. Bernard (we were finally on a first name basis) called on the appointed morning and said "11:00 today, OK, yes?" And we said, "yes, today." He appeared without Madame, and we went off in his big Saab. Bernard was a nervous man, and he drove just as you'd expect, but we never actually hit anything. He was always frustrated by his lack of English, although he was really pretty good, and would say "excuse me..." practically after every phrase. He looked every way except at the car in front, gestured, pointed, talked..."excuse me"...laughed...a funny, and very nice guy.

We dived into the traffic on our street, rue de la Convention, crossed the river to the right bank and barreled along the Seine, raced past the Tour Eiffel, past Place Alma where Diana died (it's amazingly short, that underpass), then into a long underpass under Place Concorde and the Tuileries and the Louvre. We came up into the light. He pointed out the oldest house in Paris, "*le plus ancien maison à Paris*"..."excuse me"...just missing a truck in front of us. Then a fast right turn over the Pont Neuf, whirling over to the left bank, ducking underground into a big parking lot at Place Dauphine, right by the river. And stopped.

This was new territory for us, although we knew other parts of this side of the Seine. There was a pretty park in the *place* shaded by the sycamores that the French call *plane* trees. He pointed out some expensive river-front real estate, including an apartment, costing many millions, where Yves Montand and Simone Signoret lived. And here was his favorite bistro, Henry IV, smallish, dark, crowded, a friendly place. He and Don had *escargots en croûte,* I had *salade chèvre chaud,* the hot goat cheese, and he insisted on buying champagne. A long lunch hour, talking, talking…"excuse me"…much conversation…the more we talked, the better we all became in both hearing and speaking. He spoke of grandparents he sailed with on the ill-fated Normandie to New York in the early 30s. He had some memories of the city, more of the ship.

Bernard wanted to show us Le Train Bleu, a famous restaurant at the Gare de Lyon. So we piled back in the car, crossed the river again, then here I was lost. I saw the Place de la Bastille with the famous obelisk, and the new Opera House, then suddenly we were in a large parking lot at the train station. We took an elevator up to the second floor, and there it was, just as he and Madame had said, "a classic restaurant *à la belle époque.*"

An enormous room, the restaurant stretched horizontally across and above the tracks, all 25 of them, with a stunning view through a glass side wall down to the trains and passenger hurly-burly. It was out of a movie set: tables with starched linens, shining silver, crystal stemware, the black-tie waiters moving about, mirrored walls with paintings, comfortable couches and chairs, well-dressed people, not your ordinary train-station restaurant. We had tea and ice cream, talked, paid a big bill, and left for home.

By now we're in the 5:00 Paris traffic, lurching, stopping, illegally moving in and out of the bus/taxi lane (as far as I could see, it was not for us), talking…"excuse me"…but he never hit a thing. I couldn't believe it. We sped along the rue de Rivoli, behind the Louvre, passing Le Cabaret, a jazz club we'd been to, then a fast left through a Louvre wall that took us roaring past the I.M.Pei glass triangle entrance, past the buses and tourists and pedestrians there in the middle of that vast Place du Carrousel. We crossed the river right there, took another right along the Seine past Musee d'Orsay, the Pont Alexandre III with the shining gold columns and eagles. Then I saw more familiar sights where we'd walked before, as the American Church, then Pont Grenelle and the big appliance store, Darty, left at Convention, our street. Here he slowed down, and, finally, our apartment.

I was breathless...he was still talking, laughing, saying, "excuse me..." We thanked him for a wonderful day..."*merci, merci...le jour, c'etait merveilleux, merci.*" I gave him a big kiss, the men shook hands, and we staggered up into the apartment. And that was the day of M. Desrue.

– #64 –
Day Trips from Paris, Giverney and Vaux-le-Vicomte

After we came home to Pittsburgh, several friends asked if we didn't get a little claustrophobic living in Paris for six months. Although that never occurred to us, it's a reasonable question if you define travel solely as movement, or if you live among the green of the suburbs and don't enjoy being surrounded by bricks and concrete. Another reason, however, for rarely feeling penned in was that we took frequent, same-day trips from the capital. Two good short ones were to Giverney to see Monet's gardens and to Vaux-le-Vicomte, the fantasy palace-in-the-country built in the early 1600s.

To get to Giverney you take the train from Gare St. Lazare northwest to Vernon, which is only two-and-a-half miles from Monet's house, easy by taxi or even bicycle. In our case, we chose a holiday Friday late in May when the kids were out of school and the temperature soared to 81 degrees Fahrenheit. Monet is the Nascar of art tourism; Monet is huge. Better to arrive before 10 o'clock in the morning.

Behind the Monet house you see a large, two-story iron arbor covered with big pink tea roses. In the back garden are rows of irises and small lavender pansies punctuated with orange and yellow poppies; the beds are separated with gravel walkways. The overall effect was of a slightly run-down suburban garden center with a 21st century sense of color. Keep walking and you come to the lake edged by weeping willows, covered with those water lilies you know from paintings. The scene of green is dominated by the famous red Japanese bridge. Here, it is shady, cooler, the light absorbed, more contemplative.

So much of the enjoyment of travel depends on expectations. We like surprises. Giverney suffered from overexposure. We had seen too many pictures of the gardens, paintings of the water lilies, read too much of the 43 years Monet spent here.

After a nap in the Hotel Normandy, we asked about restaurants and strolled along the Seine (on its way to the English Channel) to the restaurant Côte Marine. Here was a quiet meal worth reporting: an *amuse gueule*, a bite of fish in creamy, salty sauce; then filet of sole stuffed with spinach and camembert; profiteroles and a kabob of fruit.

At dinner we remembered the story told by Jean Kerr, author of "Please Don't Eat the Daisies," on the Johnny Carson show. She and her husband, Walter Kerr, drama critic of The New York Times, lived in Westchester with four or five kids. A hassle getting them ready when going out to dinner, they were exhausted by the time they sat down in a restaurant, with little to say, but people would gossip about their marriage. So they learned to recite nursery rhymes to each other in a highly animated manner. We're not celebrities but we do relish that restaurant story.

Vaux-le-Vicomte lies southeast of Paris and should take a 35-minute train ride and 15 minutes in a taxi. A good same-day but all-day trip. With its palace and charming gardens smaller than Versailles, Vaux-le-Vicomte wags a finger at us: if you're going to build a house bigger than your boss's, don't invite him to the house-warming. Nicholas Fouquet, finance minister to Louis XIV, built Vaux-le-Vicomte in the early 1600s. With family money and we-don't-know-what-from-collecting taxes, he hired 18,000 workers to "clear a few villages" and convert 80 acres into a magnificent palace with model gardens that came to be known throughout Europe as "French." Fouquet hired the best artisans of the early 17th century: Le Notre the landscape designer; Le Vau the architect; Le Brun the artist. To celebrate the opening of the château, Fouquet threw a party—with a massive banquet, dancing to an orchestra, an original play under torch lights, walking the gardens with fountains and lakes—and invited the king whose hunting lodge, Versailles, was just down the road.

During the house tour, just like today, Louis, the Sun King, discovered on the ceiling over Fouquet's bed a painting of the flaming...sun. He was enraged.

"Shall we arrest him now or wait until tomorrow?" whispered the king to his mother. "Not when he has created this evening for you," she suggested.

Louis, determined to make Versailles even grander than Vaux-le-Vicomte, hired Fouquet's architect, builder, weavers, painters and craftsmen. He also simply commandeered the paintings, the furniture, the rugs and tapestries for Versailles and arrested Fouquet on trumped-up charges, throwing him into jail, where he stayed the rest of his life. Versailles then became the immense palace it is today, but not necessarily (finger wagging) the most tasteful.

Just a-Sittin'
and a-Sippin'

Four blocks from the apartment is our park. Built in 1980, it's named after a popular French singer, Georges Brassens, and sits on the site of a former *abattoir*, appropriately commemorated with two bronze bulls high above the entrance. It's a neighborhood park, with everything a Paris park provides…and everything a hot apartment house lacks. You're greeted by a big, formal, shallow pond at the entrance to cool off a hot summer night; then paths appear that wind around magnificently-tended flower beds and shade trees. On to an amphitheatre of climbing rocks for children…some of the original *abattoir* stones; a covered theatre doing everything from Shakespeare to kid's puppet shows; special lanes for the joggers; a vineyard and an apiary with bees a-humming; a small stream that winds downhill and disappears under a foot bridge.

Two of our favorite cafés face the park. We like the corner one for people-watching with a glass of wine; the other has better food "*a la terroir.*" No, it's not for terrorists, it means "from the land." Sitting outside on a hot summer night, we see the young gathering in the park, some flirting, some with babies, some walking dogs. All ages are beside us, some eating or drinking or reading the paper, others just arriving from work in suits and ties. We watch cars, always driving too fast, somehow avoid total catastrophe at the foliage-blind curve right in front. Dark doesn't come until 10:15, later still as we approach the summer solstice, and it's cool. One glass of wine or beer gives you the table and the fresh air for the night.

At the edge of the park is the old covered cattle shed, now filled every weekend with antique/used book sellers from France, northern Germany and a few from Scandinavia. One rainy Saturday Don found a bound book of the April 1953 issue of Holiday magazine, with the cover of Paris! Paris!...the very one that came on the stands 50 years ago, the day he arrived in Paris on leave from Germany...the same one he's been talking about forever, and the probable inspiration for our spending six months in Paris.

– #66 –
Small Favorites
of Paris

    –   The *sucre beurre* crepe I can get at the outside, open-counter of the corner restaurant on the way home from the Metro: it's a simple sugar and butter pancake.

    –   The cleaning crew for our three-times-a-week open market: at 2:00 p.m. the market is finished, and an army of men and machines appear in matching green and chartreuse suits, with a truck to match. There's a smaller motorized sidewalk cleaner, like a Zamboni, and with hoses, brooms, and vacuums, they finish by flushing the detritus down the street, washing, grooming, and by 4:00, it's all tidy and clean again. Amazing.

    –   Place Furstenberg, the tiny but exquisite little square just off rue Jacob in the 6th: Tony O'Reilly, the charismatic and cosmopolitan ex-CEO of the Heinz Company, chose this spot as the background for a photo shoot.

– The high-backed plush seats in the movies…that recline, just enough.

– Our Metro line 12 that comes up into the daylight as we cross the Seine right beside the Tour Eiffel…going into the 16th *arrondissement,* it stops at Passy, where Ben Franklin lived, then dives down to Trocadero with the stylish apartment houses.

– The musicians on the Metro: accordions, sax players, a violin or two, some great, some terrible, always colorful; sometimes it's 'Lady of Spain,' sometimes 'Hello, Dolly.'

– The second floor of Musee d'Orsay, with Renoirs and Monets and Manets: a feast of Impressionism.

– Ile St. Louis, floating in the Seine, serenely residential right in the heart of Paris, lies just east of its sister island, Cite. A sunny day brings tourists and explorers looking for the famous ice cream shops; nighttime is quieter, with small hotels, great apartment living, and its restaurants for locals and tourists alike.

– That totally French "ooh la la" (they really say it)…and the waggling finger that says no.

– The ingenious glass pyramids by I.M.Pei at the Place du Carrousel entrance to the Louvre: the biggest serves as the main entrance to the museum, leading to an elevator, an escalator or a circular staircase down to the new reception area of the museum. The several other smaller pyramids help to bring in light to this enormous underground lobby.

– Parc Monceau, on the right bank in the 17th: a wonderland of flowers, water, with a replica of a Greek temple, walking paths, and a neighborhood of elegant townhouses, nannies and yuppies.

—   The five famous Unicorn tapestries at the Cluny Museum, showplace of the Middle Ages in St. Germain: the lady with her smile and her unicorn hold court on the top floor, complete with benches for us to sit and admire.

—   The view of the Eiffel Tower from the 16th, right across the river at the Palais de Chaillot, high and open and crowded with people: you walk through them and the river appears with the enormous iron Tour Eiffel and its long, long field of grass full of picnics and tourists.

—   The ingenious and beautiful facade of l'Institut du Monde Arab: facing southwest into a hot summer sun, it consists of multiple squares of movable sun-controlled panels, really irises; each large iris is surrounded by numerous smaller ones. When the temperature reaches a certain height, the thermostat-controlled lenses shutter down, shading and cooling the building. The effect from the street is somehow reminiscent of the fine lacy-filigree cement-work used in Spanish and Moorish architecture.

—   And my favorite street sign of all time depicts a puppy lavatory. It shows a small dog…circling an area labelled *"ici"*…meaning "Here."

– #67 –
"We'd Kill Each Other"

When we talked to friends about our plans in the fall of 2001, some would give us the sheep's eye.

"Oh, we could never do that," said one friend. "We'd kill each other. We'd be with each other, and I mean <u>with</u>, 24/7. Few friends to see and, in a small apartment, no place to hide. No volunteer work, board meetings, having lunch with the boys, no coffees, no friends, no grandchildren. No phone calls with buddies." He had painted a picture different from what I had in mind, but he did have a point.

I said, "Dana, if we stay alone together, our conversation over a drink in the evening will be "which did you like better—the 11 o'clock this morning at the *supermarché* or the 3 o'clock in the museum?"

How did we handle this "alone together" issue? We read a lot, we can be quiet a lot. We also stayed stimulated with current events, reading the International Herald Tribune, the New Yorker and The Atlantic that came by mail, paying bills, wondering if we can afford all this, and we laughed a good deal, much of the time at ourselves. We started doing more things by ourselves, so we had two places to talk about over drinks. We've kept notes for this book and most days we sent e-mails, either from a cybercafe or the apartment when we had a computer hookup. And we had phone calls from Hardy, our youngest, the most palpably concerned about us. We also learned to vary the schedules, go to a café before dinner for a drink, or the movies.

When we got to Paris, however, we decided to put some time and money into a little more separation. Dana took the train to Nice, stayed in the Welcome Hotel in Villefranche-sur-mer for a week, where we had stayed the winters of 1998 and 1999, and she would see her Scottish friend Andie, her friend from Edinburgh.

So I had this idealized time in Paris, going to jazz bars, responsible to no one. I looked up one on a barge in the Seine on a chilly night and—it was closed. So expectations in my 70s were beyond my ability to realize the bachelor dream.

Once, we even considered Dana's going to Kiawah Island to rest while I would go to Sicily—both good ideas for the winter but outside our budget.

Being alone together in small spaces in foreign countries just has to be acknowledged. It's not inherently wonderful all the time.

– #68 –
Of Joys and Heartbreak:
Subways and Buses in Europe

Europe's city transportation systems were, to us, fascinating, very big, and sometimes very complicated. Rome, the first city on our itinerary, at first was almost a total mystery to us. We set off our second day to find the Michelangelo steps down by the big Vittorio Emanuele monument; we got there and back by tram, that was easy. Ticket sellers are everywhere, at a Tabacci or the magazine kiosks on the street. The trouble with day tickets is that they're timed; you have to return in either 75 minutes or in six hours, all bad choices. Second, there wasn't anybody to collect them. The conductor didn't want money or tickets; he was there to drive. He didn't care what we did. Some people punched a ticket in a gizmo on a pole inside the bus, most didn't. It seemed very devil-may-care, very Italian. We decided we didn't care either.

Down in the subway we just walked through an open gate into the train area, and went on our way. No problem. So for some time we used the system as we pleased, just got on and off wherever we wanted. Finally, when one of our sons, in a phone call, said that he didn't want to read about our being hauled off to a Roman jail, we acknowledged reality and asked Maria. She led us underground and showed us a (hidden, to us) window where we could buy monthly passes. We obviously hadn't tried too hard.

Now that we were legal, it reinforced how easy it had been to cheat. Underground, the pass holders merely walked through an open gate (which was what we had used in our illegal phase); surface, you just hopped on a bus. Then we learned of the police; we were stopped maybe twice, in our three months in Rome, both under, and above ground, and had to show our passes. Somehow we had avoided bus jail, and/or a hefty fine, during those first puzzling weeks in Rome. From then on we were with the system, definitely international travelers.

Rome didn't seem to have enough trains, at least for the busy routes, so they were always crushingly jammed at rush hour. One time, getting out at Barbarini, our computer stop, Don had to literally pull me through the mass of people crowding the door. And the cars were messy, inside and out. Some had so much graffiti that you couldn't see out of the windows; you only knew where you were when the doors opened. No, Rome wasn't pretty underground.

Vienna subways, after Rome, were like trading your teenage son's Honda for the minister's Buick. The subway cars here were new, totally free of graffiti, shining clean...no dirt in Austria! Probably not all of them looked like this, but a lot did. The crowds also seemed better controlled, maybe fewer people, or all those Germanic genes. Right away, we bought our passes at a big tourist window on the *quai* at Schwedenplatz, the center of town and a ten-minute tram ride away from the apartment. So we were always legal. The passes are never cheap, but they're a bargain compared to the daily rates. We tried for senior prices (in Italy we were the *anziani*) but we were out of the EU and not eligible.

The surface trams were just as convenient as the underground; we basically used them to get into the city, out to the Prater, and also to get to the Ringstrasse, to the big museums. From Schwedenplatz, one tram went clockwise around the Ring, the other counter-clockwise...a clever touch; they made for wonderful sight-seeing.

Now, the London tube. It usually worked, trains came often, but it wasn't pretty. Compared to Vienna, it was a rat's nest (probably true!), grungy, crowded, and often quite deep underground. The exchange points were usually <u>really</u> deep, like several escalators down, down, down, always slightly unnerving when you thought about where you were...something I tried not to do. From what I read now, the London underground, for several years before we arrived, had been threatened by various terrorist Irish groups. We fortunately knew none of this.

One day, Don, doing a dark load of washing, found he had also turned his bus pass, worth 37.5 pounds, about $60, into a sodden, unreadable mess. So, now to replace it turned into a big megilla. All the tube stations we approached disclaimed any knowledge of us: "Sorry, guv, you're not in the computer. You must've bought it in a sweet shop." We didn't know what he was talking about...as in, "What's a sweet shop?" All we could gather was that we had apparently bought it in some strange place, and we had to go back there to get a new one. But of course we couldn't remember. Then, a miracle! I read my notes, and there it was: "Bought two monthly passes on our way to Carnaby Street." And it was at Oxford Circus, an ordinary tube station, where we had fallen into some kind of a travel agent down there...what did we know? We thought it was just a regular window...<u>wrong</u>. So here the computer knew us, and another $16 later, Don was legal again.

The double-decker buses in London were fun, and went everywhere, early and often. The top front of the bus was a prized seat; you were the leader of the parade up there, with a marvelous view. And the running leaps I saw of people getting on or off at the back door...once by a stylish woman in high heels. Now that's a good trick.

Paris was definitely organized, Metro-wise. Not as clean and sparkling as Vienna could be, not quite as crowded as Rome, and not as many deep spooky stations as London, the system was wonderful. It was business-like, it ran from 6:00 a.m. to 12:30 a.m., and was our link to all Paris. Our monthly pass had our pictures, our address, and the magic ticket for the turnstile. Everyone had to put some sort of purchased ticket, bought by the ride, the week/month/year, into the meter. Then all Paris is yours, you just have to study the underground maps, which are easy. And it was all made easier by every business, café, restaurant, movie etc. listing its Metro stop on the address. A good system.

In true French fashion, the Metro stations can be works of art, as shown by the original, wonderfully ornate, turn-of-the-century entrances designed by Hector Guimard. Constructed of green cast iron and glass in the leafy Art Nouveau style, only a few are left standing. Some have lamp posts resembling long-stemmed flowers, some have a canopy of glass and metal in a sunburst pattern over the stairways. Others are plainer, but still distinctively Art Nouveau, with an ornately designed word "Metropolitain" on the arch support.

Many Paris stations are also decorated underground in some way. The Louvre Palais Royale station has copies of some famous statues and exhibits from the Museum...totally neat and clean with no graffiti. The Louvre stop is on the right bank's Line One that goes horizontally across the city through fairly fashionable areas, like George V, or Franklin D. Roosevelt, done in an Art Deco style, with its hallmark of more rigid lines and circles. Line One also had better-dressed passengers. A lot of the men were in suits and ties, or at least in the fashionable black turtle neck; the women were definitely more chic than on our more middle-class Line 12. The prettiest stop on the left bank is at St. Germain, in the heart of the student section, with moving lights playing over the names of authors and painters written in gold letters on the big vaulted ceiling.

The moving sidewalk is in only a few Metro stations, usually at the big *correspondance* points. And at Montparnasse, one of the largest on our line, they've improved it, at least I hope it's an improvement, by speeding it up. They've added another sidewalk, three times as fast. A sign said it was 9 km/hour vs. 3/hr for the regular one, and you can definitely feel the difference. To me, they made it harder by a warning system of round, rolling, bumpy things...they looked like roller bearings...under your feet at the start, which served to put me out of balance right away. Then that disappeared, and it was just plain fast. It took several months, that winter we were there, for the workmen to get it up and running, and when finally in use, many warnings were posted, along with a guard who presumably would pick up us *anziani* who had flown off. The businessmen loved it; the little old ladies usually kept to the slower one.

Music in the Europe's underground was a common denominator. Most of the city stations, and a lot of the trains, had various entertainment, with Paris leading the hit parade. London had a few sad accordion players wandering the cars; Vienna, maybe only sporadic violins in the stations, really very few. Rome, I remember no music, only gypsies huddled in the long passageways: a mother, head bent, mutely holding out a hand, always with two to three small children and a baby at breast.

But Paris had it all, everywhere underground. There were jazz combos in the passageways, or a string quartet echoing through the halls, sometimes a solo trumpet or saxophone player with a wheeled recorded accompaniment in the cars. You saw, and heard, everything in the Paris Metro, some was good, most not, but all was colorful and picturesque. A lot of the music were old war-horses of tunes, many from old movies trying to capture French atmosphere: recognizable but nameless. The more agile and/or portable musicians went from car to car at each stop; you had the feeling they lived underground, never saw the light of day. There were so many musicians that I kept a special, easily accessible change purse, to put my contribution into the passing cup.

We thought these big-city transportation systems were marvelous. Efficient, far-reaching, fairly cheap and totally convenient, they were our lifelines into these fabulous cities. We couldn't have done it without them.

– #69 –
Sun and Sand
on the Seine

Hey, want to lie in the sun on a beach in Paris? Now you can, only don't go near the water, it's forbidden, *interdit!* A summer treat for all, they call it "*le Paris Plage*," the Paris Beach. Countless tons of sand are brought in, making a respectable, 10-foot wide beach all along the stone flood wall. For a month in July and August it's beach chairs, suntan lotion, pretty girls, men in tight little French bathing suits, young and old, soft drinks (perhaps wine, it's Paree!), open showers to get the sand off. Even on a gray day, Paris flocks there.

Le Plage is on the right bank, the lowest road by the river, several levels down from the buses and traffic passing the Louvre...probably where Gene Kelly and Leslie Caron danced in the old movie "American in Paris." The city has turned a two-mile stretch along the riverside into a sandy beach for a month, extending from the tunnel at the west end of the Tuileries to the farthest end of the pretty little Île St. Louis. From down here, you have a fish-eye's view of the river, all the famous bridges, and a largely naked Paris. It's a great success, crowded and free...come on down, you'll love it!

– #70 –
The Jaoul Houses

I was having lunch one day in Pittsburgh with Michel Jaoul, a client who is French, and president of an international consortium of aluminum companies. Michel, a fit man in his 60s, asked us to produce a brochure and film about the company's bauxite mining operations in West Africa. That day, after Michel narrated the French version of the film, we dropped into a Chinese restaurant where our conversation somehow got around to architecture.

"Don, did you know I have a house by Le Corbusier?" he said. "I had no idea," I answered, and asked him all about it. "Well, actually, I have two houses. My father was a friend of Le Corbusier, so he designed one for my parents and one for Nadine (his wife) and me side by side in Neuilly. Corbusier carved into a floor tile the instructions for cleaning it," he said. When the Jaoul houses were sold to Lord Palumbo of Great Britain in the early 90s, they made headlines in The New York Times.

A tennis player, Michel asked me if I could recommend him for our tennis club. We helped propose him and had a little party to introduce him. He played tennis until he returned to Paris in the 1990s. To thank us, he gave us a case of *Sancerre*, the Loire white wine, and a handsome book of Bruegel's paintings.

Early in our Paris stay, we visited the Corbusier museum, formerly the family villa, called Villa La Roche, a three-story, white rectilinear house built in 1923, located in Auteuil, the vaunted 16th *arrondissement* famous for its racing track. "Le Corbusier," said our guide, "means something like crow. His real name is Charles Edouard Jeanneret-Gris." Photographs of the Jaoul houses are hung in the museum.

In spring 2003, in Paris, when we had dinner with mutual French friends, Michel said something unforgettable. We were talking about the Iraq war. It was no surprise that he was against it, as were most French people, Chirac and the media, and we were against going alone and without a plan for managing the peace.

"However," I said, "I can well understand how an American who fought for France in World War II would hate the French for not going along with Bush." "Well, so can I, Don," he said. "But there's one big question: In World War II, what took you so long to get here?"

That was ungrateful and hitting below the belt. I include it here only because it demonstrates both the graciousness of many French people, counterposed to an unfortunate attitude, and one that would rarely get expressed to an American.

– #71 –
Le Spectacle

In June, bachelor son Ted brought over his niece, our 12-year-old granddaughter, Alexandra, for a planned week in Paris. They arrived into the hurly-burly of our Sunday market, right in front of the apartment. After breakfasting on the local *crèpes*, Ted left us three to "bond away," and he drove up to see the Normandy beaches.

Alex is David's oldest, a cute kid, really bright, a reader, and she speaks French; well, just a little, but she has a great accent. Margaret, her mother, had been an *au pair* in Lyon after college, and still has a good guttural French 'r.' One time that week, over on the right bank, Alex and I were asking directions. I told her to start with "*Pardon, Madame, ou se trouve...?*" Alex rolled those r's; the woman not only understood her, but replied in French, which I've never gotten. (They take one look at me, or a listen, and instantly come back in English.)

The whole week was a lot of fun. We did the bus tour, went up to the top of the Eiffel Tower; we ate at the café by the park and wandered the Louvre. We even got Alex and Servane, the grand-daughter of Paris friends, to the fair in the Tuileries. Starting out early, we'd be back on the couches by 3:00, where Alex had the new Harry Potter book to keep her happy.

When Ted returned on Thursday, we all had dinner near his hotel on the rue de Lille, right behind Musée d'Orsay. Afterwards, we walked to the Seine, and on a pedestrian bridge we turned tourist, taking pictures of each other, facing west into the setting sun, with le Tour Eiffel in the distance. Alex was enchanted. Here Ted told us of his surprise for Alex's last night in Paris: he had four seats for the 11:00 show at the Moulin Rouge. Anticipating a few negatives from us, he had talked to the manager of the theatre, checking on the minimum age for the audience. He was told that "of course, M'sieur, no one under six years of age is allowed to see *notre spectacle*."

With that Gallic reassurance, we arranged to meet Ted at the Metro stop closest to the theatre. The Moulin Rouge, as far north of the city as we were south, was an easy ride on the Metro. The part we forgot was that on this particular night the end of the line was to be closed, two stops from our destination. We emerged into the hubbub of Montmartre, still daylight at 10:30. Don hailed a cab and in his best French accent, said "*Le Moulin Rouge, M'sieur, s'il vous plait.*" The cabbie took a look at us, two 70-some-things and a teen-ager, all dressed up for a night at the Moulin Rouge, and he broke out in laughter. He laughed for four blocks.

Don had seen the Folies Bergeres in the 50s, Ted had been to Las Vegas; only Alex and I didn't know what to expect. The house was crowded with all ages, including some little ones as adver-tised. We were seated at a table, the champagne was ordered (when in Paris etc.), the lights went down, and the show began.

From the very first moment, it was a true spectacle: beautiful girls, statuesque, bare-breasted, of course, in elaborate costumes of satin and lamé, with feathers, spangles, sequins. No longer the Red Mill of the 1890s, of can-can dancers and absinthe drinkers, today's show is totally modern with computerized lighting and tomorrow's music. Alex was cute; she watched the first five minutes between her fingers. Then she forgot any embarrassment, and she giggled and applauded with the rest of us.

The show was vaudeville and burlesque, a combination of beautiful girls, dancing, music, jugglers and acrobats. To me, the worried grandmother, the best part was that it wasn't the least bit lewd. The girls danced, kicked those gorgeous legs high, pranced all over the stage, but there wasn't a jiggle or a bounce, not a wink or a leer. Aside from their being topless, the whole show was out of Ed Sullivan.

The cabbie had promised to return at 1:00 a.m., but we either missed him or he never showed. We walked a few blocks, trying to find a cab home, talking, talking, hoping Alex wasn't seeing all the sex shops and the girls waiting in doorways. Finally we got a cab, and left a slightly seedy Montmartre and its ghosts of Toulouse-Lautrec and sped through the Paris night back to our ordinary, dull, but sane world of the 15th *arrondissement*.

– #72 –
How to Entertain
a Teenager in Paris

When I realized that our new friend's daughter, Servane, could be a buddy for our granddaughter who was to visit us in Paris in late June, I had asked her mother if Servane would like to spend an afternoon with Alexandra. The girls were just the same age, and she spoke fairly good English, a sweet and friendly girl. So we arranged for the two teenagers to meet.

Unfortunately, neither Don nor I had any ideas for entertaining the girls. It was summer, the kids would be out of school, but we couldn't come up with a thing. We read the papers, and *Pariscope,* and the guide books on Paris; nothing seemed right for two 13-year-olds. It wasn't until Alex was here, and we were on a bus passing the summer fair in the Tuileries with the big Ferris wheel, she had said, very determinedly, "That's where I want to go with Servane." Problem solved!

On a beautiful, blue-sky day, we all met at W.H. Smith, the bookseller right across the Rivoli from the park...Servane and her parents, Alex, and Don and I. The two girls were clones of each other: budding teen-agers, they each had on jeans and the tight shirts the young teens love, hair pulled back in pony-tails, same height, same cute tight bodies, they could have been twins.

The parents left; we, with the girls, walked over to the park. We gave each some euros, and they instantly raced off to the big roller coaster. Alex has maybe 20 words of French, but Servane studies English in school, as do most French kids, so language wasn't a problem. Don and I had books and sat under the big plane trees, reading in the shade. I could see the girls up on the big ride, laughing and talking; ten minutes later they raced by us on their way down to the next ride. They surfaced every 30 minutes or so, came over and chatted...then ran off. Coming back for more cash, they ate at the little café in the park, found cotton candy somewhere…and went on every ride, through the Tuileries all the way down to the Louvre.

Finishing up with Cokes someplace on the Rivoli, we started to hail a cab for Servane's house, when she said she often came to this part of town, and would take a bus home. We saw her onto the next bus, saying *"Au revoir,"* to a very self-possessed, cute young girl, very adult for 13. We were all impressed.

– #73 –
A Birthday in Burgundy

We left Paris for Dijon on July 7, not because we were inordinately fond of mustard but because we had never seen Burgundy and because it was my birthday. We went to the Gare de Lyon early for breakfast in the station. I asked a server for a *croissant*, not a wild request. "No *croissants* here," he said, pointing to his counter. "They're over there." Which reminded me how much we didn't like the French love of rules. Weeks earlier, we had expanded this notion with our young friend, Luc, a principal with a startup company.

"No, Don," he said, "you may be right. The French like rules and worse, are slow to take risks. For example," continued Luc, "there are 1,000 times more startups per capita in Israel than in France." All this deep thinking happened in the Gare de Lyon over a croissant. In Pittsburgh I had clients from both Britain and France. Both said it was a dream, relatively speaking, to start up and conduct business in the U.S. compared to working in Europe.

Dijon is a short train ride south. A taxi drove us to the Hotel *Phillippe le Bon* and we celebrated with dinner on the lawn of the hotel's restaurant, *Les Oenophiles.* (Gone are the days when you race from the hotel to eat. Some of the best restaurants are now <u>in</u> the hotels.) We started with a glass of champagne, a sometimes-love, competing with that famous aperitif, Jack Daniels on the rocks with a splash of soda.

Dana had a terrine of *foie gras* and *aubergine.* I had sea bass with tapenade. The food grew tastier as the champagne flowed and the light fell. I was turning 74 and wrote that my speech was slower and remembering names was becoming harder. Dana gave me a fine wallet and Margaret sent a red linen shirt. So I put the wallet <u>into</u> the pocket of the linen shirt and we had another night cap. If you have to turn 74, why not in Dijon dining on the grass on a warm July night?

In the morning we rented a car and took off for Beaune. Our plan was to drive north on la Route des Grande Vins and to try some of those great wines that *les oenophiles* talk about. We have to be honest here. We have been drinking wine for 40 years. But the only opinions I have on wine are: 1998 was good for Côte du Rhone and Pontet Canet is a wonderful Bordeaux. At least it was in 1975. That's it. At least, *généralement,* we don't buy wine by the half-gallon anymore. This trip, then, had an objective as specific as anything Donald Rumsfeld could espouse: learn four new Burgundies.

The area that we traversed is the *Côte-D'or* of Burgundy. We stopped, tasted and bought bottles of *Puligny Montrachet* 2001, *Pommard Les Jarollieres* 1997, *Bourgogne Aligote* 2001, and *Bourgogne Hautes Côtes du Nuits* and *Aloxe Corton* 2000. The best was the *Puligny Montrachet* for 48 euros, for which Dana grilled a fish from our market. It was simply the best wine we had ever tasted. But we soon returned to the ones we can afford, one-fifth that of *Puligny*. We did learn the difference between *Grande Cru* and *Premier Cru* but also enjoyed seeing the vineyards and the crisp towns, lovingly cared for and even prettier than the Sonoma Valley.

– #74 –
Champagne Lights
in Paris

One night in July we took a picnic supper to the Champs du
Mars, the large greensward in front of the Eiffel Tower.
The grounds were crowded with *boules* players, eaters,
drinkers, sleepers, a motley crew. We went late, about 8:30, still
full daylight, because we wanted to see the special light show on
the Tower at 10:00. *Pariscope*, the weekly 'What's Happening in

Paris,' had said the flash bulb effect from the Millennium display would repeat every hour, for ten minutes, up until 1:00 a.m.

We ate, we drank some wine, it slowly darkened, and right on schedule the Tower exploded in light, like Champagne bubbling and fizzing, sending gold flashes into the night. The big, dark industrial tower was transformed into a blazing beacon of blinking gold and white lights. Bulbs, strung on every strut and support, twinkled and sparkled exuberantly over the entire massive structure for ten minutes. The audience, standing silhouetted against the light, cheered and applauded.

Then it was over, the gold lights were gone. We gathered up the blankets, the empty bottle, the basket, the cushions, and made our way to the Metro and back to the 15th.

– #75 –
44 Vendors
Our Paris Street Market

On April 3, 2003, I wrote down what each merchant was selling on both sides of one block of *rue de la Convention* in Paris, "our" street. The market went up and was taken down on Sundays, Tuesdays and Thursdays from early morning until early afternoon.

First Side:

Specialties—Italian and Portuguese olives, sausage, *bacalao*, port, vinegar
Chinese take away, cooked on street
Sunglasses
Sweaters and shirts
Women's shoes and boots
Luggage and purses
Wooden flowers
Women's and men's underwear*
Beds and mattresses
Slippers, men's, women's
Women's pants, blouses
Purses from India
Combs, barrettes
Scarves, jewelry
Crêpes, savory and sweet, made on street
Greenbeans, 4.50/kilo
Tomatoes, asparagus, endive, strawberries
Apples and oranges
Linens
Baby clothes
Women's coats and jackets
Potatoes and greens

Seafood: *daurade, raie, coquelles St Jacques, truite, pave de saumon,* shrimp, haddock, *maquereau, filets de harang*
Artichokes, red beets
Pig's feet, pork and veal organs
Cheese, milk, butter, yogurt

Second Side:

Pottted azaleas, rhododendrons
Lard, ribs, ham, sausage
Purses and wallets
Poissonerie de Evelyn & Charles: *coques de Brittany, oursin,* big *saumon*
Chickens being grilled over potatoes
"Mister Paella," made on street
Jackets, jeans, tee shirts
Dried nuts, seeds, beans, raisins
Olives, dates, herbs
Women's sweaters
Watches, blouses
Sunglasses
Women's pants, shirts
Men's socks
Cut flowers, plants
Seafood
African art, jewelry

*Men's jockey shorts are called "slips."

– #76 –
Still Cooking at 72

One of life's little ironies is that I am writing about cooking in Europe. I'd put myself as a beginner, except that I fed a family for 30 years. The truth is that food never really interested me until I was 40, on our first big trip abroad. I still remember that first meal; it was in Rome, we'd just arrived about lunchtime, and decided to eat in the hotel only because it was included. It was just a simple baked macaroni dish…we've all had it a million times…but it was crusty and creamy…and somehow the veil was lifted and I started to realize what I'd been missing.

I'd spent a lifetime ignoring meals; always thin, I was the original fussy eater. Not much tasted good to me, so eating wasn't that important. But somewhere in my 40s, after that epochal macaroni and cheese dish, after I quit smoking and found myself pudging up, I started getting interested in food. I bought The New York Times Cookbook, made a *béchamel* sauce, bought a whisk. I was ready! Now, I'm not implying that this change transformed me into WonderCook. Not at all. I know what's out there, and can order a good rare tuna filet with *coulis de tomate*, or a Grand Marnier soufflé with the best of them…it's just that I can't prepare these jewels.

What I fed to our three children is embarrassing to remember. I knew nutrition…after all, I <u>was</u> a Wells College graduate…and vegetables and milk and fruit and iodized salt; I just didn't make anything terribly good. I remember opening a lot of cans in those years, Chef Boyardee, packages of Manwiches, Hamburger Helper. (Our son Hardy, when asked what he wanted for his seventh birthday dinner, answered "Hamburger Helper.") So, everyone was fed, no one complained, I don't think, but food-wise, those years were very ordinary. The dinners were palatable, probably, because we played word-games and laughed a lot.

So, while many others could tell you much more about cooking in Europe, this is my story of how I handled meals in strange city kitchens. First, it's not hard, it's just different. Most kitchens, of course, in our apartment rentals were smaller than at home. However, they all worked, they had most of the necessaries, few of the frills. And we managed to follow our budget plan of eating in-house most of the time.

Right there, that disappoints many people. Of course we had meals out, but rarely of the wonderful, expensive ilk that most associate with European visits. Remember, this was real life, we were there for months, trying to stay on a budget. One thing our cities share is that dining out is expensive. There are exceptions, as when we've visited in the eastern parts, such as Lithuania, Prague, or Budapest. There you can get fantastic meals quite cheaply. If we'd known the language in Rome, or Vienna, or Paris…I have no excuse for London…or really searched out some good local places, it would have been different. But in western Europe, in a nice restaurant, a "tablecloth" one, an ordinary meal for two can easily be $100. And I repeat ordinary. We learned that a bad meal will break the budget just as easily as a good one. So we didn't eat out too often.

As far as buying food is concerned, almost everything in our American markets is duplicated in even the small stores abroad. All the American cereals, for example, Kellogg, Post, etc. are in the stores; big brands like Kraft, Nabisco, Coca-Cola fill the shelves. One small difference I noticed was in the packaged cookies. They're sweeter and use different flavors, as in the wonderful hazelnut wafers I found in both Rome and Vienna stores. Of course the gourmet places, like Fauchon in Paris, have exotica far beyond the ordinary. But buying and/or thinking up interesting meals was still hard. The little things…let's say capers…that we take for granted in America, the extra touches that make a meal good, that we know where to find in a favorite market…I either couldn't remember, or devise, or find. And as much time as we had, the days we spent wandering the museums, parks, shops and funny little streets trumped any time in the kitchen.

Maria, our landlady of Rome, had equipped our small kitchen with the basics: a gas stove, a working rehabbed dishwasher, plates and silverware, glasses, placemats for two, a few pots and pans, some tools. Arnoldo had to explain the gas oven (it seemed from the 30s), and the vagaries of the dishwasher, but nothing was a big deal.

Before our Pittsburgh friends, the Bechtols, arrived for Easter in Rome, we researched good restaurants, tried a few out, didn't like them. Finally, from one of our better guidebooks, "City Secrets of Rome," compiled by Robert Kahn, we chose Vecchia Roma, over in Piazza Campitelli, that was touted as a "not-to-miss" restaurant. It was true; everything tasted Italian, good and very special. Don had *baccala,* codfish in a sauce he's still talking about, and I had a delicate calves liver with a sweet/sour marsala sauce, then an exquisite many-layered dessert, *millefoglie* with *zabaglione. Mamma mia!* Our guests didn't go too exotic; Dotti, I think, had calamari, John, a lamb stew. But it all was a big hit.

I've written about my Rome marketing elsewhere. It was easy, with markets and stores everywhere; somehow I found things we needed with little problem. I pointed to meats, I could pick up familiar, labeled things in the supermarket, some good prepared dishes, cooking was fairly easy. We even had Maria and Arnoldo to dinner one night for a pasta *carbonera.* (I wedged us all in the kitchen, figuring that tight spaces make a better party than a more formal attempt in the living room.)

Vienna was different. First, the kitchen was out of a magazine: totally new with expensive appliances, service for eight, silverware in both luncheon and dinner sizes, those good pots and pans so heavy I couldn't lift them. There were 24 different wine glasses, eight each for champagne, white and red wines. The obvious irony was we knew no one in Vienna with whom to share this largesse.

With all the dishes and glasses and carving sets, a few basics were omitted; no potholders, potato peeler, paring knives, little things. My theory, which could be totally wrong, was that Barbara, the apartment owner, didn't cook much, or maybe she had a maid. She had equipped the kitchen from the viewpoint of the lady-of-the-house, not from the help. I just went out and bought the stuff; it wasn't Barbara's thing.

But, all the wonderful appliances etc. aside, the constant was me. I was the chef, the grocery buyer, and the meal planner in a slightly downscale neighborhood with a local market to match. I generally shopped at the Billa, a chain store a block away…you saw it all over Vienna in various sizes. Nothing was bad, it just wasn't too appetizing. (It had the same grocery carts as home, same check-out procedure. As I remember, it was all in cash; no debit or credit cards in the markets.)

The meats were labeled, in plastic, just like home…I could recognize most of them. We had veal scallopini and pork chops (no roasts, it was too hot), I never bought hamburger, through some kind of prejudice. There probably was lamb in some shape, always very expensive. You can see my limitations here. The store did have good dried soups, Knorr, and I think Maggi, that I found later in Paris.

We discovered, in a nicer part of town, off the Kaerntnerstrasse, a wonderful store like Gristede's in New York. Also expensive. Again, it's what we could carry, even both of us…and we only went there sporadically…never thought of a cab home. And an open-air fresh market appeared shortly before we left…but it was farther away than was practicable.

The scene changes; we move to London for six weeks, leaving most of the cooking behind. The kitchen, although pretty well equipped, was literally a one-man operation. Add another foot in width to my outstretched arms, and you've got the picture…and that includes the tiny counters. We were in the City, which we loved, but there's not much there in the way of fresh markets. And, it was chilly November, so we weren't interested in hunting them down. I didn't do too much cooking here, except to heat up frozen dinners from Sainsbury's, a huge chain, just up the street. They sold good frozen stuff, Indian dishes that were new to us. I must have gotten some fresh meats, but very rarely. Another city I didn't do cooking justice to.

Now it's Paris, for six months. And while I wasn't into *haute cuisine*, we definitely moved up a notch or two…probably because we had that good market three days a week literally in front of the apartment. And I could walk between all the choices…fish in one block, a good meat butcher just across the street…which made planning and buying a lot easier. (That's the list preceding this story.) Being able to see it all helped a lot. Our market was big; it went on for blocks, both sides of the street, selling everything you ever wanted, with all kinds of meats, fresh fish, chicken, vegetables, fruit, pastries, crêpes…we ate pretty well in Paris.

Again, a small, functional kitchen: gas stove, refrigerator, microwave, plenty of hot water…but no disposal, and no dishwasher. I'm sure more expensive apartments had these niceties as did the kitchens of people we met there. We had our own garbage chute, a wonderful help. You had to bag it properly (the French are very fussy about that)…but then, to toss that bundle down, to hear that satisfactory thud as it hit the bottom…that warms an American heart in Paris. And the green truck, with the matching green-suited men, came by every night…M. le Gardien saw to it that the big baskets were set out daily. When I told him that our garbage was collected at home, usually, just once a week, he was horrified.

We even entertained. And a lot. We had friends from the States for dinner, we had Parisian friends of friends, we had friends' parents; in Paris I was magnificent in the kitchen. Broiled fish, served on a bed of *mirepoix*, was one of my favorites. I got good at soups, seafood entrees, salads, a new world was dawning. I never did desserts, the *pâtisseries* were everywhere. It was the markets right under our window that made it so easy to design a meal, to buy it, to prepare it. And city living made it even easier…once, as the guests were ready to sit down to dinner, I raced across the street to find the *crème fraiche* I'd forgotten.

The main irony in my tale is that just as I've found this new world of food, a lot of my friends…(all of that "certain" age)…are through with that life. They've stopped cooking, don't want to cook, only have people in under duress. I'm alone in the kitchen, still valiantly trying to make the perfect meal at 72, still struggling to learn. I should hurry!

– #77 –
Haute Cuisine
in the 'Hood

*L*e Cordon Bleu, the famous cooking school in Paris, was three blocks from our apartment, and we didn't find it until ten days before we left Paris. We'd seen this tiny store on nightly walks, closed, of course, with two small display windows showing some pot holders and some dishes. I just assumed it was a store for kitchen equipment and forgot about it.

One day I saw the little store was open. I went in and discovered that "*oui, Madame, nous sommes le Cordon Bleu en Paris, l'école pour cuisine, bien sur, aussi pour les débutantes.*" It not only was the famous *Cordon Bleu*, but they had classes, and for beginners! Which was me. Think what I could have been learning and eating all these months!

For this, my second cooking demonstration ever, I signed up for two sessions, each at 3-1/2 hours and 39 euros. I figured I'd do a basic one on soups and stocks. Then, for the second (and really more interesting one) I chose their menu of a complete dinner: first a tomato tart with shrimp and *pistou*, then a herbcrusted salmon *supreme* with a mushroom flan and a red wine sauce, finishing up with Peach Melba. If I could just do one of those dishes, it might make up for my years of Chef Boyardee Spaghetti-O's.

Eager to learn about my *Tarte Croustillante a la Tomate,* I appeared on the appointed day, to yet another discovery. I had signed up for the one demonstration that month given in French. Plus it was advanced, to be taken after all the basic courses, which I definitely needed. (These glitches were due to the fact that we were leaving in ten days…I had to take what I could get.) I decided to see what I could absorb…who knows, maybe the professor would speak slowly, maybe the techniques were possibly within my grasp.

I joined the group, with my pen and paper, but no dictionary. There wouldn't have been time anyway for that, the presentation was so fast. The room had regulation student desks, the ones with the built-in writing arm, maybe six rows of six each. There were two television screens, one on either side of the cooking area, plus two large slanted mirrors overhead, giving close-ups of everything happening.

The room filled with young people (I was two or three times older than everyone, but who's counting). Half were women, most everyone was in the white apprentice smocks, speaking all languages. I heard some English, a lot of French, but there was also German, Spanish, and some I couldn't recognize. There was much activity happening up in the front, before the presentation even started: pots of water were steaming on the big eight-burner gas stove, utensils and bowls and ingredients were coming in, several wine bottles, uncorked and at the ready.

The chef, wearing a white toque, walked briskly into the kitchen, rustled a few pans, assembled his notes. "*Bon jour, ca va*?" he said, looking up. "*Ca va!*" the class replied, and off we went. It was in French, of course, but I understood a lot, since it was coupled with the accompanying motion, ingredient, seasoning, or wine. It wasn't as hard as I expected. Now, I know I missed a lot of important asides, little hints and tips that would have made it special. But I got the bones of the lecture, really more; maybe my French was getting better.

He started with the dessert, the Peach Melba, which now I wish I had paid more attention to. I guess I'm not a dessert person. I dutifully wrote down the essence of what he was doing: making a '*glace vanille,*' stewing the 13-15 peaches, a sauce with sugar, jelly, Kirsch, cook, put in the fruit, cook, puree, strain. OK.

Now he went through some fancies with the salmon dish, some trimmings that I also wrote down, again knowing it was out of my league. One was the careful removal of the black skin from the large salmon, out of which he carved small triangles, diamonds, different shapes, then baked them as decoration. Triangles! Diamonds! I knew I'd never try these. I didn't want frills, I just wanted simple, but French, food to wow a dinner party at home.

Pans, utensils, parchment paper, lids, processors, dishtowels, strainers…all would appear, disappear…a helper was constantly bringing it all in, pans, ingredients, tools, just in time for use, and then quietly removing all detritus. It was beautifully choreographed, she was never in the way, had perfect timing, neither too early nor too late. Speed was the essence; the chef even did a fast splash of water on the mushrooms to clean them, explaining that wiping took too much time. His motions were fast but precise; he just looked casual, made it look easy. He was constantly explaining, talking, joking. It was theatre, it was show business!

He used a lot of parchment paper…in many ways. For one, lining baking tins, that I knew. Then, for another, as a tight lid cut exactly to fit, placed touching the 20-30 minute simmer of the tomato *coulis*. Making a tiny center hole in the paper circle for escaping steam, he said he preferred that to a regular pan lid.

Now he started on my love, the red wine sauce.

2 TBS butter	any peelings from another prep
2 shallots	salt, pepper
3 cups red wine	1/2 tsp sugar
3 cups veal stock	1 TBS butter

The chef threw (literally) the butter to melt in a large pan, added the shallots to sauté, then splashed in the red wine (I think he said it was of a medium quality), to reduce as he went on to something else. Periodically he'd toss into the simmer any peelings he might have from another preparation: garlic skins, onions, mushroom stems. It took maybe an hour, give or take, to reduce to half volume. Then he added the veal stock, again to simmer for an hour, more reduction. He strained it all through a *chinois,* added salt, pepper, sugar. The 1 TBS butter was heated and added at the end.

And *voilà*: a syrupy, exquisite, meaty red wine sauce. He used tiny portions around the mushroom flan, perfect! Now I realize we're not talking rocket science here; most good cooks have produced a red wine sauce. I, however, had not, which is why I wish, really wish that we'd found the school earlier. Nor have I made it since. But...some day...

I'm not describing here the other recipes of that day. I could fill a book with my 3-1/2 hours of note-taking, but I wasn't as precise as I should have been, so I'd hate to lead anyone astray. I'm shaky on the measurements, God knows on techniques, and I'm sure many other shortcomings. But I did pay close attention to the red wine sauce. Trust me.

At the end of the demonstration, the ubiquitous student helper handed us each small paper plates, with bites of everything prepared that afternoon. In my notes I wrote *"Bravo! Magnifique!"* It was a four-star dinner, and the best meal I'd had in Paris.

– #78 –
Fibrillation

On Wednesday, July 30 (four days before we were scheduled to leave Paris) I took the Metro to the Club Med gym where I worked out three times a week. I came home to our apartment, had soup and lay on the sofa with the International Herald Tribune, checking the situation in Iraq. Feeling angina in my chest, I countered with a nitroglycerine tablet and an aspirin. But this was unusual and pills didn't help. Now I was sweaty with a rapid heart beat. I said "Dana, I think we should go to the American Hospital." It was 2 o'clock in the afternoon. (I had checked the hospital behind our apartment months before, just in case, and they advised me to go to the American Hospital. I could never disassociate it from Scott and Zelda Fitzgerald, often ill in the 1920s.) Fifteen euros and 20 minutes and a taxi had us at the hospital. Easy entrance, little bureaucracy, the magic words "chest pains" opened doors. I was taken straight to intensive care where Doctor Jais (a *cardiologue* with good English) talked to us.

Dana said quickly, "He has been taking Timolol by eye drop. Does that matter?"

Yes, it mattered. The doctor quickly ordered an IV for Cordorone to regulate the beat. He checked blood pressure and took a cardiogram. Nurse Valerie stacked my clothes, glasses, and valuables in the corner of the room. I felt better in an hour. Jais returned late in the afternoon to verify improvement and said I would stay the night. I could choose the time for dinner. At 7:00 p.m., I had salmon, rice, tomatoes and *courgettes,* a nectarine and plain yogurt. Ponytailed nurse Rodney from New Bern, North Carolina, helped smooth things with his joking and Southern accent. He had worked here for 12 years. He took my breakfast order in the evening: *chocolat chaud, deux croissants, jus d'orange et café crème.* The French have their priorities in order. A little Xanax, and I slept from 11:00 p.m. until 5:00 a.m. Soon nurse Eric arrived.

"You will be going home today," he said. All signs were normal; the IVs were removed. We could make the plane to Pittsburgh on Saturday! Feeling very lucky and now streetwise, I walked out of the hospital, caught bus 82 to École Militaire and switched to line 12, getting off at rue de la Convention. I was carrying a large envelope with my x-rays.

What happened? For years I have taken Timolol pills to regulate my beating heart. When I used my prescription in France, I received eye drops, "the way it's delivered in Europe," said the pharmacist.

"But the eye drop gives you only one-tenth of the amount you need," said Dr. Jais. This, however, was my only heart incident during 18 months in Europe. The care I received at the American Hospital was superb. Dr. Jais said fibrillation was not uncommon for a 74 year-old with a heart and stroke background. IVs appeared in minutes, the right drug was administered, the cardiogram was taken quickly, the nursing and the hot chocolate were perfect. On Friday we rested and packed; on Saturday we flew to Pittsburgh.

The time in the hospital, the tests and Dr. Jais' service totalled less than $2,000 and we were reimbursed by our health insurance.

– #79 –
Winding Down
in Paris

With only 10 days left in Paris, after being here almost six months, we became a little anxious about not seeing "everything." For example, we had been to the new Opera House but never saw the Opera Garnier, the elegant old one near the Café de la Paix. Carved into its broad staircase were the initials EN for Emperor Napoleon. You must look up to see the ceiling painted by Matisse above the small theater with its maroon velvet chairs on four levels. Under construction from 1860 to 1875, the theater's acoustics are excellent. But its stage was too small for modern ballets and today's staging of opera, so that the new one was built on Place Bastille. And, of course, Parisians cannot agree on any word in that statement except "the" and "and."

We had walked to the post office from our apartment many times. But we had to wait until a few days before we left to discover a fresh route and the cooking school, Cordon Bleu. I liked its address: rue des Gentilhommes, gentlemen's street. Dana made time for a cooking lesson and, she said, her best meal in Paris, described nearby.

One hobby is hanging out in music stores, but I hadn't seen one in Paris until the end. On the right bank, at 175 rue St. Honorè behind the rue Rivoli, I found the music store of my dreams, with the requisite books of Bach but also American jazz from most of the 20th century. After a lot of "just looking," I bought arrangements of songs by Jobim, the Brazilian master of bossa nova.

An unfulfilled love in Paris was chewing on dark country breads. I had never visited the original store where Max Poilane started. He now supplies *tout Paris* with artisanal breads, thick and crusty, some full of nuts and raisins, choices far beyond the ubiquitous baguette. Having bought a small bread stick, I was chewing away when oops! what's this in my mouth? A tack. If I had swallowed it…well, I didn't but decided to return it to Max. After presenting it to the young clerk, he apologized profusely (law suits passing between our eyes) and handed me a free loaf of raisin bread. (I wasn't sure about this tradeoff: your life or a loaf of bread.) I bought a quart of milk for Dana's breakfast porridge. Then I visited the photo shop to order blow-ups of pictures to be turned into jigsaw puzzles.

At the photo shop I balanced the raisin bread and the quart of milk while passing the photos across the glass case of instant cameras. Yes, the unthinkable happened: while choosing prints, I spilled the milk all over the cameras, leaving me feeling very 74, very embarrassed. I helped clean it up; the young woman was very gracious. To apologize for my ineptness, I crossed the street to the florist and bought her a dozen pink roses.

Our biggest surprise in six months was learning the tide comes into Mont-St-Michel only twice a month. The second biggest: the winner of the Tour de France is determined the day before the last. Although the race finished on the Champs Elysees, only 20 minutes away on the Metro, we chose to watch it on TV. And there was Lance Armstrong just calmly winding in and out of bikers, dropping behind, chatting; everyone knew he was the winner. (We felt a little ownership in Lance after meeting Kristin, later his wife, while studying French at the Institut de France in 1998.) The surprise was learning the end of the race was about celebration and show business. The peak excitement happened days before in the mountains.

– #80 –
Favorite and Affordable
French Hotels

*W*e stayed in these hotels and auberges for varying lengths of time, from a one-nighter to a week at the Hotel Welcome. Most of them came from the 2003 Michelin Guide, one from Rick Steves France; others were recommended by friends, one we just happened upon and it looked good. We can be chintzy on accommodations, usually between 2-3 stars. Prices, between $100—$150 per night; some exceptions here.

–   Villefranche-sur-Mer: Hotel Welcome. Small hotel, in perfect location on waterfront in Côte d'Azur suburb of Nice. Old world charm with modern bathrooms, in heart of old-town down several levels to water-side. Steps from cafés, restaurants, Jean Cocteau chapel; the Sunday market has 20th century antiques, prints, linens; car access. My all-time favorite for hotel and town in southern France.
February single, 65 euros
April double, 130 euros

–   Loire Valley: Chez Marcheroux. An *auberge* adjacent to woods for hunters, just off the road to Chenonceaux; plus rooms in main house. Found this just from sign on road, and loved it. A resourceful owner had made 4 small rooms with bath from a former stable; his wife was a passing-fair chef, and the 3-year-old was a charmer. Summer amenities, total peace and quiet.
March double, under 50 euros

–   Mont-St-Michel: Hotel du Guesclin. Totally tourist, but charming hotel in historical steep town. Parking only outside city gates; not for the 'walking challenged.' Hotel on the mount, a short hike up main street. Small hotel, small rooms, vertiginous, with many stairs, good dining room open to public. Two-hour drive from Caen and Normandy beaches; also close to Bayeux tapestries.

April double, approx. 100 euros

—   Sarlat: Le Renoir. On the main street in interesting town. Old charm hotel, pretty rooms, now a Best Western, which is a plus, not a minus. Heart of Dordogne, famous for small charming towns, scenery, mountain roads, caves. 40 minutes from caves at Font-de-Gaume.

May double, $130.00

—   Vernon: le Normandy. Train stop for Giverny (Monet's garden). Interesting old northern town. Adequate hotel near Seine, basically clean bed/bath. Not much else, but we needed an overnight.

June double, $90.00

(Our advice on seeing Monet's gardens: arrive Vernon in the afternoon, by train or car; perhaps an hour from Paris. Explore town, have a good dinner, go to bed. Need car/cab to Giverny, go earliest, lines should be minimal. We did it in reverse, so had 90-minute stand-up wait, in sun, at Giverny at 2:00 p.m. Not good. It's a 10 for Monet lovers and back garden/woods; 5 for the rest of us. Front formal gardens somewhat ordinary.)

—   Biot: Domaine du Jas. Small, movie-set inn, a south-of-France hotel in countryside. Yellow/white striped awnings, pool, nice outside lounging spaces. Small room. In hills behind Antibes, mile from Biot.

June double, approx. $150.00

–   Dijon: Libertel Phillippe le Bon. Old historical inn, located well, walk to bustling old town. Has good restaurant, Les Oenophiles, with dining outside on lawn; great food. On our way to the Burgundy wine country, friends had said not to overlook Dijon, interesting town.

July double, $150.00

–   Beaune: Grillon. Old family house, well-converted, a mile out of town. Old-time charm, pretty gardens, pool, nice owners.

July double, $90.00

I would happily go back to all of these hotels.

RETURNING

*New apartment
in old house
in Pittsburgh.*

– #81 –
Coming Home

On Saturday August 2, the taxi arrived to take us to Charles de Gaulle airport. We had plenty of time. Our only Security moment was Dana's taking off her shoes. Tickets and passports in order, in Dana's fanny pack. Soon our luggage is being boarded, people are boarding, now it's time for us.

Dana can't find our passports! The USAir man said "I'm sure you have them, Madam. I go through this every day." Then the loudspeaker calls for Mr. "Monzhe"—my last name, to the French, looks like part of their verb "to eat"—the airline has bumped us into Business Class! But the passports: I checked the men's room to see if they had fallen from my pocket. The USAir man: "We'll have to take your bags off in a minute if you don't find the passports."

They were in Dana's fanny pack on the inner side! We do this all the time, put important things in special places. Who says we can't handle stress well? We marched into the plane—another self-created crisis averted—to a glorious big space in the front row of Business Class. We devoured our lunch, monkfish, with plenty of champagne. Even a crying baby behind us couldn't disturb our naps.

In Pittsburgh, a taxi took us to our stored car. We had the clicker and the right keys—the Chevy Prizm started right up after sitting for six months. The city was green and wooded, like a park. We repeated our beer and pizza that started this whole odyssey, amazed at the prices, only $10 for two of us. It would have been two or three times that in Paris.

A friend, Ann Hazlett, had thoughtfully asked us to stay in her house while we looked for an apartment. We crept into her large house in Fox Chapel, loading our bags into a spare bedroom.

The next morning we wrote down first impressions of the U.S. after six months away:

–   Pittsburgh was green! June and July had been very wet and rainy, so everything growing came in many shades of green, and Fox Chapel, zoned to be as natural as possible, was even greener.

–   The people were fat and sloppily dressed. In the airport, big men in tee shirts to their knees walked with their thighs apart like two-year olds. One heavy, short woman wore loose sandals and a heavily-flowered blouse.

–   Waiters were more casual. They were chatting us up, which was nice and very different. One called us "hon." We had French friends who would not have enjoyed this misplaced camaraderie.

–   We were in a small city, it was quieter and the people looked older. (Pittsburgh's Allegheny County is second to Florida's Dade Country in the percentage of older people.)

–   Pittsburgh is much less dense than any city we were in and, of course, smaller. If Fox Chapel, our suburban setting, were in Europe, hundreds of thousands of people would live here. As it was, we saw only big, old oak trees, birds and squirrels, occasionally deer and wild turkeys.

–   The air conditioning was cold in the airport and in restaurants. We needed sweaters.

In our idyllic setting, what did we read in the papers? Paris and much of France were having record temperatures, *une crise veritable.* Over 100 degrees Fahrenheit in some places. Few apartments had air conditioning, stores had sold all their electric fans, older people were dying, their children were feeling guilty for leaving them alone. We had gotten out just in time.

We had dinner with our Pittsburgh "kids:" David and Margaret, Alexandra and Scott. Smiling Scott looked older. We had just pulled Alex off the Ferris Wheel in the Tuileries. Margaret was having a mural painted in the entrance hallway. David was building muscle by installing a stone wall beside the stream in his yard. Times were good.

To find an apartment, we grabbed the Sunday newspaper real estate section but also went looking specifically for the duplex apartment mentioned by a friend. It was part of three totally-rehabilitated Victorian houses. The apartment we liked was on the second and third levels. With 12 foot ceilings and three bedrooms, everything else was new: flooring, windows, appliances, and a bath and a half. And only two blocks from chic shopping and cappuccinos. All this for less than we had been paying in Europe for a one-bedroom apartment...signed up and sealed in two weeks.

We realized that living in Europe for two years made us appreciate the space we were getting much more than simply moving directly from suburb to city. We were now living one block from where David was born in 1958, with grocery stores and restaurants we could walk to. Although our garden was now a small deck, we had universities, concert halls and the original Carnegie library only 30 minutes away. The dream that started in August 2001 was fulfilled two years later. We had left home at 72 and returned at 74. What else could we do but stay and write this book?

The One Thing You Don't Want to Bring Home From Paris

July 4, 2003 was cool and dark in Paris. I celebrated by going to see Anne de Vericourt, a *dermatologue*. For a month I had been getting tiny red spots near my ankles which were starting to climb up my legs. Voraciously itchy. I have to see someone, I said to Dana, and the pharmacist told me where to go. Fortunately, I could walk just eight blocks down rue de la Convention to find Dr. Vericourt. She was thin, quiet and had no receptionist. She worked with one other partner in a narrow, five-story building, the kind you see all over Paris.

"Le problem: pour un mois, les eruptions dans mes jambes demangeaisons…ennuie…je besoin un diagnostic et quelqun aide." "For a month, spots on my legs, itchy, I need a diagnosis and some help." She nodded and asked to look at my legs. Her English was slow but elegant. She wanted to know my general health and the drugs I was taking. I emphasized no changes for months.

"I think it is an insect," said Dr. Vericourt. She prescribed an antiseptic cream, an antihistamine pill and a bath cream. Her fee was 50 euros. She had no secretary; she typed out the prescriptions and the bill.

I had tried to imagine where I might have picked up a skin rash. Perhaps a rogue towel at the Club Med gym. Or I had sat on the grass at Parc George Brassens. Perhaps as I sat in shorts on our living room rug.

The baths helped but the itching spread. By the time we got to Pittsburgh in early August, I made a quick date with our family dermatologist, John McSorley. Dana had worked as a secretary for him in the 1980s. He suspected scabies.

"Do nice people get scabies?" I said half jokingly. "Oh yes," he said. "Even doctors' wives."

He prescribed Permithrin, which you put all over your body, then climb into clean pajamas and sheets, throwing everything you have touched into the washer. That should do it, said John McSorley.

One week later, it was still there. Then I found a dermatologist from Ireland, Mary Sheehan, who took a culture with a knife and said, "Yes, definitely, scabies. Take Permithrin cream in two successive nights, washing all bedding, towels, underwear, everything you've touched. It should be gone. Easy for you to say, I thought.

Well, it wasn't gone until October. Dr. Sheehan said I probably contacted it on the subway where I wore tee shirts and shorts and rubbed up against *tout Paris!*

Scabies. The one thing I didn't plan on bringing back from Paris.

– #83 –
Optimism and Denial

The words just popped out of my mouth. We were having our five minutes of fame, being interviewed on WQED, Pittsburgh's educational TV station, as a result of an article we'd written for the Pittsburgh Post-Gazette. The host, Eleanor Shano of Pittsburgh's Channel 13, had been talking about our ability to chuck it all and live in Europe for 18 months, and was just ready to run the credits, when I found myself interrupting her, trumpeting, "Optimism and denial, that's what got us through!" And on that note, the host said "Well, that certainly sums up your views," and quickly wrapped up the show.

It does sum up my views, probably on most of life. I do feel optimistic about most things. Right or wrong, I've always thought that things will turn out generally favorably, given the right input. Which instantly puts you in the land of platitudes: 'the glass is half full,' 'hope for the best,' 'look for the silver lining.' We all know, however, that a platitude is just an affirmation of majority thinking; a proverb is a proverb because it generally is true.

When Don got cancer, some fifteen years ago, it never occurred to either of us that death would be a possibility. In the far reaches of my brain, I realized it could happen, but I knew Don was taking the right steps, seeing the best doctors, and we just assumed it would work. It did work, through a lot of luck and good medical care. And our optimism saved us both months of needless worry and sleepless nights.

And as for its sister, 'denial,' they work well together. If there is a problem, I don't deny its existence, I just figure that it's not as bad as it may or may not be. I'll work to cure whatever the problem, I try to figure it out, I have to muddle through it. And while all this is happening, I tend to forget about it, I don't worry it to death. Maybe the third attribute should be a 'bad memory,' which can often keep you from living on the dark side. If my tooth doesn't hurt at the moment, I forget that future surgery is in the picture; if Don keeps exercising religiously, and remembers to take the pills, we both forget about all the negative possibilities, and just assume he'll make it, at least for the foreseeable future.

When we started thinking about the various steps it would take to pull off this dream of living in Europe, it never occurred to us that we couldn't do it. We knew some negatives would appear, that it would take a lot of planning and list-making, but then our other mantra took center stage, asking, "If not now, when?" I realize that such thinking can be deemed shallow, cavalier, and/or fairly mindless. Also, it's the product of luck, maybe good genes. Nor will it be forever; I can see that circumstances can intrude. But, when you consider the alternatives, it's not a bad way to live.

– #84 –
Itinerary
✦
August 2001–August 2003

	August 2001	Decision to sell the house and rent in Europe
I.	**February-May 2002**	**Rome**
	April	Naples, Pompeii, Sorrento, Amalfi Drive
	May	Week in Orvieto
	May	4 days in Venice
II.	**May-August 2002**	**Vienna**
	June	3 days in Budapest
	June	3 days in Prague
	August-October	Surgery/Convalesence Pittsburgh, Rockport, MA
III.	**November-December**	**London**
	Dec-Jan **2003**	Pittsburgh
IV.	**February-Aug 2003**	**Paris**
	February	Dana, week in Nice
	March	4 days Loire Valley
	April	5 days at Normandy Beaches, Mont St. Michel
	May	4 days Dordogne
	June	5 days Biot, Antibes, Route Napoleon
	June	Overnight Giverney
	July	3 days Burgundy
	July	Overnight Amiens
	July	Day-trip Vaux-le-Vicomte
V.	**August 2003**	Return to Pittsburgh apartment

– #85 –
Volunteering in Lithuania, Turkey and Armenia

In the middle of writing this book, I spent six weeks volunteering in Armenia, consulting with non profit groups on fund raising. Cynics ask why I don't volunteer more in Pittsburgh. Well, it's the foreign travel. Here's how it started.

"I want to do that when I retire." I was talking to a man who worked with the International Executive Service Corps in Stamford, Connecticut back in the 1980s. My sister Lois was having a party in Westport. When I retired in 1997, I contacted IESC, filled out a form, sent in my resume.

"We don't need advertising people in the third world," explained an IESC representative, "but we're interested in your fund raising expertise." (I started a division for non-profits in our advertising agency. While I focused on marketing communications, partners Dotty Beckwith and Marian Weil consulted in development, the broader term for fund raising. I learned it from them.) It wasn't long before a phone call came.

"How would you like an assignment in Lithuania?" asked IESC. I had the time; both Dana and I would go. We were excited. Although IESC pays no fee, they provide housing and a per diem. For four weeks I would write a development plan for the Lithuanian Free Market Institute, a Libertarian think tank. I knew nothing about Libertarianism. Quick Googling turned up articles about the Austrian school of economics promulgating low taxes, a free market and as little government as possible. How did this square with a country that had just become free of the Soviet regime? I would soon learn.

I asked friends about Vilnius. The capital of Lithuania, the bottom of the three small Baltic nations, it was known as "North Jerusalem" because of the many Jews who passed through from

Russia, Poland or Germany, leaving concert halls, libraries and a respected university.

IESC, founded by David Rockefeller in the early 60s to educate Eastern Europeans about democracy, sent plane tickets and a check to cover our expenses for four weeks. Arriving in May, 1998, we were greeted by Vygintas Gontas from IESC. With flowers in his hand for Dana, he took us in a taxi to an apartment building in the middle of the city. The grounds were littered; the playground equipment was broken down. A few blocks away was the statue of Lenin pulled down in 1989, one of the first symbols of the end of the Soviet regime.

On Monday morning, the driver arrived in a Jeep to take me to work. I met a dozen bright and driven women and men in their 30s, specialists in taxes, pensions, social security, trade and more abstruse issues. It took a few days to meet the founder, Elena Lyonteva, with whom I forged a good relationship both in Vilnius and in Pittsburgh. Elena, a beautifully-dressed and put-together Russian woman who had grown up in Lithuania, was a media star who consulted with President Valdas Adamkus every morning. She and the legislative specialists advised the government and were watchdogs for the public.

After I met the staff at the Lithuanian Free Market Institute, I was introduced to my computer. What's this? An old IBM with Windows, that I had heard of, just heard of, because I had been weaned only on a Macintosh. Apple was the only fruit I knew.

I had never seen a two-sided mouse before. And, being in Vilnius, Lithuania, the keyboard was different. Well, I coped, thanks to a tall, blond, friendly, young secretary named Vaida. I would send her everything I typed by internally-networked e-mail and she would put it into reader-friendly English.

I also got help daily from my roommate, Audronia, another tall, blond woman, very smart, who has moved into a higher plane of work. Now, she's head of the Pension Plan for the entire country of Lithuania.

With the help of both of them, I could type my plans and ideas for increasing income and, after four weeks there, we all parted with smiles on our faces.

I broadened the goal from "fund raising" to increasing gross income. Through interviews, I learned that LFMI was highly regarded by business leaders. So I recommended several links between the business community and LFMI; one was the Business Roundtable, a common idea in America but new to Vilnius. All told, after the plan had been implemented, total income increased by more than three and a half times.

Elena visited us twice in Pittsburgh where I introduced her to the foundations of Richard Mellon Scaife, the controversial Libertarian philanthropist pitted against the Clintons, who made donations and offered to underwrite her writing a book of a young girl growing up in a Soviet state, becoming an enthusiastic promoter of the free market and modeling herself on the super-conservative, Libertarian novelist, Ayn Rand.

Day-to-Day in Lithuania

Vilnius was our first peek behind the Iron Curtain, so different from the Europe we'd seen before. The language was the most challenging. It was our first time out of the U.S. into a language with no Latin roots…we literally had no words. Not only were we speechless, we couldn't even read it. Menus were usually translated into English, but it was still anybody's guess. Early on, I had a "vegetable with a peel…and balls." That turned out to be a baked potato and fish cakes…and pretty good, too. For "thank you," we had *aicu*, pronounced achoo, like a sneeze; *praisom* (pryshom) is "please," and *laba diena* is "good day." And I was lazy and didn't learn any more.

The main streets of Vilnius were handsome…Gedemino, leading to the Old Town, looked good, was up-to-date, modern, with our favorite café, computer shops and even a McDonald's. Farther on was the Old Town, a charming nest of curving streets, shops, cafés and interesting old buildings, lots of people, activity, café-sitting. Twice we saw music groups: one, in a park, an 8-girl group singing Irving Berlin's "Puttin' on the Ritz;" another, on a side street, was a 12-piece Dixieland band playing Fats Waller. The Old Town was being renovated at a frantic pace. Workmen were everywhere laying stone in decorative patterns on the streets, old wood facades being painted in bright colors, new buildings going up. The restoration schedule was aimed for an early July festival; we heard the city hoped to become known as the "next Prague."

A mile out of town was different; we saw a lot of half-finished buildings, scaffolded and generally dilapidated with crumbling cement, stemming from a Soviet occupation that had only ended 8-9 years before. Our apartment was functional, in no way decorative. We were told not to complain, as ours was apparently nicer than the average. A standard furnished one-bedroom, it had an equipped kitchen, hall, bath and living room with heavy uncomfortable furniture and a heavy hand in decorating. The hallways were dark, and the public areas surrounding our building, unkempt and sad. Everything needed washing, or painting, or just new light bulbs. The grounds, if not cement, were covered in weeds; "landscaping" is not a verb here. I think it stems from several generations accustomed to big government: the somebody-else-will-do-it syndrome.

A green, wooded capital city lying 200 miles inland from the Baltic Sea, Vilnius is large, with over a half-million people. The country of Lithuania itself is small, squeezed between the Baltic Sea and Russia, Latvia to the north, Poland to the south. The country dates from early B.C. and has had a rugged history, at times in control of Russian lands down to the Black Sea, other times periodically overrun by Poles, Russians and Germans. The country made a bad turn in 1939, trying to resist the German onslaught. They went to the Soviets for protection, which led to more annihilation, and a total annexation by the USSR in 1944.

Now a heavily Catholic country, it came to Christianity late. Not until a Lithuanian leader married into the Polish royal family did Christianity finally penetrate the pagan tribes. A friend told us "they were tree-huggers until the early 1400s," and one of the last European countries to convert.

Winters can be long and dark here; the city is fairly far north, on a latitude with Amsterdam. One clue was the number of nice restaurants and cafés housed in basements…they must be cozy and warm in the cold months. We were there in June, fortunately, but even then the weather could be anything. One week I wore a turtle neck sweater and a wool jacket for my shopping walks across the park into town, another week was 90 degrees. Into that high heat one morning, appeared the landlord's sister to clean the apartment. A big woman, she entered puffing in the warm air. And, with no English but an apologetic look on her face, she stepped out of her dress and slip, right there in the front hall, leaving her cleaning costume as a large pair of pink bloomers and an industrial-strength brassiere.

My food shopping was mainly catch-as-catch-can…if you see it, buy it, as it often won't be there the next day. Supplies were low, or rather sporadic. On Gedemino, the main street, was a modern supermarket with shopping carts and freezer cases…but also with days-old vegetables. Even the roots, as carrots or potatoes, were limp and had rotten spots on them; the open-air market was a little better, but it should have been a <u>lot</u> better.

With no language, I got along by pointing, holding up fingers to indicate quantities, and it usually worked. However, one day I did the pointing into a deli case, buying what I thought was a potato gratin and a roast chicken. At the apartment, up bubbled an unmistakable fish smell from the heating gratin (it was a herring salad) and the roast chicken was some kind of ham molded into a poultry-shape. Again, not all bad, just not as expected.

As a "spouse," I had basically nothing to do. Don was picked up every morning by a silent, speechless driver and disappeared into the traffic. I read, food-shopped almost daily, sat in the park, walked the Old Town. And here was the old University, over 400 years old, all restored for a big anniversary celebration a few years before.

Wandering the old courtyards of the University was one of my favorite expeditions. The University had grown out of an original 1500s Jesuit school; as it expanded through the centuries, the newly acquired buildings were joined to the existing structures by using open spaces as transitions. The resulting 12 courtyards represent every architectural style from Gothic, into Renaissance, Baroque and Classic. Arcades sometimes line the buildings and often form an entry into the courtyards, some of which are small, stone-paved and intimate; others are huge quadrangles of grass and trees and flowers.

One night we heard a Verdi Requiem in Skarga, one of the oldest of these charming open yards. Skarga was small, the 200 chairs filling the space. It was arcaded and ivied on three sides, a wonderful setting for an open-air concert. At the fourth wall of the courtyard sat the orchestra, covered, providentially, by a partial roof. When the apparently expected rain started halfway through the performance, most of the audience was prepared with umbrellas; the rest of us ran to the arcades, and the music continued. (Neither of us knew the music; Don was expecting a Bach-like requiem, and was disappointed, but I loved Verdi's operatic touches.)

Vilnius, termed the "Jerusalem of the East," originally had a big Jewish population, which the Germans were terribly efficient in eradicating; the 32 synagogues of pre-war years have disappeared, leaving only one remaining. But their influence is still there, seen in the thriving cultural life and in the emphasis on education...the University of Vilnius is one of the best in Europe.

It's a young people's town; you see very few gray heads on the street or in the cafés. We were told that the old are trapped by their tiny pensions set in Soviet times and have no clue to the dynamic atmosphere springing up in the country, or any money to enjoy the flourishing cultural life of symphonies, museums, jazz nightclubs, concerts, always well-attended. We noticed that the audiences are 90% young people, again very few of the old, as opposed to most American classical concerts.

Two vivid pictures remain in my mind. The first is on Gedimino, the nice, heavily populated main street. A regular fixture there was an older woman who tended a huge scale set up on the sidewalk, the kind with a large round face. She looked like all the pictures you've seen of Russian peasants, white-haired, roundish, in a shapeless dark dress covered with an apron, a sweater on chilly days. Standing by this old-fashioned six-foot scale, she collected money, a *lita* at a time (25 cents) from the passers-by who would weigh themselves. It seemed to be her occupation, definitely a source of income, as she was always there every time we passed that block. Late at night we would also see her supervising the removal of the heavy scale into a waiting truck.

The other was on our walk to the park and the Old Town, where we would pass a small garden tended by, again, an older woman. She was often there, determinedly willing flowers to grow in an arid, dusty soil; but her other interest was to update the pebbles she had arranged to form the day's date. No month, or year, just the day. We saw a big brown-pebbled "2" change into "3" and so on; we were leaving as she reached "30."

To me, both these women personified the perseverance, the doggedness in the face of adversity, of a country determined to grow and prosper despite wars, systematic annihilations and years of Soviet oppression.

In Istanbul, Sabanci University Rises From The Ground

In 1999, another call from International Executive Service Corps: we'd like you to go to Istanbul. The assignment would be for six weeks to research and write a development plan for a new university just rising, funded by the Sabanci family, wealthiest in

Turkey. Dana and I would live in the Istanbul Hilton, overlooking the Bosporus and indeed Asia.

I worked in a gleaming glass building, the Sabanci tower, with airport security. One of the members of the family had been shot in his office only several months before. I would work with the young development director, a woman named Zeynep Turel, who had been educated in California. The building was filled with U.S. consultants advising and planning every aspect of the new university.

I wore a tie and jacket to work, carried a briefcase and took a taxi. It was not too different from being in New York. I met many of the professors newly hired from good schools in the West: MIT, Berkeley, Penn and others from Britain and Germany who had been persuaded to head departments in this ambitious Turkish startup.

Although I met several times with Guler Sabanci, the female head of many divisions of the family company and one of Forbes magazine's 400 richest people in the world, she let me know that some of my ideas might work in the U.S. but not necessarily in Turkey. An example: with the new buildings rising, they virtually cried out "name me." I contacted the development department of my university, Michigan State, to get details on naming rights of buildings. They were forthcoming about what one might pay to name a department, or a laboratory, a concert hall or the computer science building. And in the last case, the price was, of course, millions of dollars. I made these recommendations but they were never implemented.

Helping 21 NGOs in Armenia

Honestly now, where is Armenia? I first had to go to the map. I found it off the northeast corner of Turkey with a history of loss of land and people. One million were killed in a war with Turkey in 1915, the war termed a genocide by Armenia but not by Turkey. Then in 1920 it was swallowed up into the Soviet Union, which lasted until 1989. If that wasn't sufficient to cause disarray in the 20th century, an earthquake hit the second largest city, Gyumri, in 1988.

Armenia is located between the Black and Caspian Seas in the Trans Caucusus, an ancient and proud Christian land surrounded mainly by the Muslim countries of Azerbaijan, Turkey and Iran, with a strong cadre of eight million Armenian "Diasporans" who visit and support. (While Armenia has a population under three million, eight million more have emigrated to the U.S., Australia, Canada, and Europe. Wealthy American-Armenians like Kirk Kerkorian send money to rebuild roads and reinstall pipelines. Forty percent of the country's income is donated from abroad.)

My job was to help strengthen NGOs—non-governmental oranizations—making them self-sufficient and savvy about fund raising, an initiative led by World Learning and funded by USAID, part of the State Department. Dana, unlike the two previous times, did not go. Her transportation wouldn't be covered nor would she receive emergency medical insurance.

I arrived in Yerevan, the capital, after midnight to be greeted by a driver waiting with a card carrying my last name. (Few things in life equal seeing your name on a card in a foreign airport.) The government travel agency had routed me through London, where I had an overnight rest, then flew six more hours to Armenia. The Ani Plaza was a first-world hotel, with a large corner room with a bright, tiled bathroom, my home for the next six weeks. The next day I got my assignments from World Learning and met my interpreter, Anahit, a 40ish woman who, weeks later, surprised our group after a late dinner and a vodka singing "Show Me the Way to To Go Home."

I was assigned to community centers, groups helping refugees, disabled children and older people (like me) located in cities and towns anywhere from two hours away, like Gyumri, to a five-hour drive and an overnight like Goris, south toward the Iran border, and a few in Yerevan. The first few days were a blur of strange Armenian names, meeting people with widely-different levels of sophistication and working through an interpreter. The first week ended with a four-day, Memorial Day weekend and a similar holiday for Armenia, allowing me to separate the competing names and agendas, to read up and at least think about giving to the hungry, the homeless, the orphans, the refugees, etc.

Beginning work, I found the countryside was rough. "Our land is rocks" said Anahit, with roads that rose to 8,000 feet. The sandy mountains easily caved in. A few miles from Yerevan stands Mt. Ararat where Noah debarked after The Flood. A twin-peaked mountain, snow-covered year round, Ararat, the very logo of Armenia, isn't even located within the country. It's behind a closed border, in Turkey.

The diet consists of grilled lamb, pork and beef, grains, good salads of cucumbers and sweet tomatoes, yogurt, good beers. If you're lucky enough to be invited into a home, as I was, I hope you'll receive a shot of homemade mulberry vodka. The people are generous; the less they have, the more they give. They're also long-lived. I bought a watercolor of a woman 103 years old, done by a 12-year-old girl, that captures the force and vitality of some old Armenians.

With a well-regarded symphony orchestra, an opera company and a chamber music hall, the capital has a flourishing cultural life. A seat in the orchestra, seven rows from the conductor, cost only two dollars, a positive leftover from Soviet times. A stunning museum of ancient manuscripts sits on a high hill. In 301, a certain Mashtots designed an original alphabet for Armenia, eschewing both the Greek and Latin alphabets and still in use. A line of type resembles mirror handwriting, something like *mnunnubuump* with an occasional backward 3. I learned *badev* for hello, and *inch bes es*, how are you?

This consulting differed from previous assignments in two ways: here I had 21 clients instead of one and I worked with other volunteers. Tammie was there with her 14-year old daughter Chelsea from Seattle, Gary and Jeff from St. Petersburg, Florida, and others from Holland and Canada. In the evening we discussed our work over shish kabobs and wine and had time to laugh at ourselves. Several volunteers had worked here before, returning to good Armenian friends; some said they would work in Armenia with the right job.

Another difference was seeing historic and cultural sights on our drives around the country: a pagan temple from the first century A.D., a Christian church from the fourth century, a monastery hiding on a mountaintop near Azerbaijan, and more. On a Sunday near Yerevan I observed a long and solemn Armenian Apostolic church service with monks in hoods and singers in embroidered dresses. Outside the cathedral, people were buying caged doves, having them blessed by a priest and then letting the doves fly free. Someone said it was symbolic of sins being forgiven.

I could never spend my $40-a-day per diem. Lunch was often two or three dollars, dinner eight or ten. The Armenians I worked with were living on less than $200 a month in conditions that had been better during Soviet times. When Anahit invited me to her apartment in the center of Yerevan, she told me that water was available only three or four hours a day. She had to carry cooking fuel into the apartment. Four in her family lived in a one-bedroom apartment; her daughter, a surgeon, slept on a cot in the living room.

What did I actually do? I brought with me a computer disc containing names and information of scores of U.S. foundations that have a history of supporting Eastern European or Armenian endeavors, and I helped them quantify strategic plans and foundation requests, sharpen their missions and find more ways to produce income, not just wait for donations.

Two extremes show the range of the groups I worked with. One, a community center in Charentsavan, had the services of a

Peace Corps man for two years, a business man from New York City. Through his help, they have a thriving community center with printers, faxes, scanners and eight computers plus a large conference room. They have also formed a legal entity that enables them to charge small fees for renting this equipment. This is the best it gets in Armenia in the USAID drive to be "self-sufficient."

Contrarily, I met on three different occasions in Vanadzor with a history professor, a local government official, and a computer operator, none paid and all working on their own time, trying to form a sports and cultural center for after-school activities. Not knowing how to arrange the necessary legal entity, they could not charge for games or art exhibits. Their strategic plan was written in unintelligible English and the history professor waved off the protocol for a foundation request as unnecessary "paper-work."

Many differences between U.S. and Armenian attitudes surfaced. One day, I was angry after leaving an NGO. The group had resisted strongly my suggestions to work together more, to find volunteers, not focus solely on the money. In the car, Anahit said, "well, Armenians don't like to work together." Aha! A bulb went on, another attitude encouraged by the Soviets. And then another: a love of abstract language. One group trying to provide job training called their mission "peace." I said, "you'll do better with a foundation when you acknowledge that your mission is job training." A handful of both Armenians and Lithuanians agreed that yes, it was a Soviet practice to raise language to an inordinately high, abstract level.

– #86 –
Looking Back

While writing this book, we discovered this quote of Lytton Strachey from Eminent Victorians. With more poetry, he describes our wading through an "ocean" of notes and e-mails for this book. (Although difficult to believe, we haven't printed everything.)

> *It is not by the direct method of scrupulous narration that the explorer of the past can hope to depict a singular epoch. If he is wise, he will adopt a subtler strategy. He will attack his subject in unexpected places; he will fall upon the flank and the rear; he will shoot a sudden revealing searchlight into obscure recesses, hitherto undevined. He will row out over the great ocean of material and lower down into it, here and there, a little bucket which will bring up to the light of day some characteristic specimen, from those far depths, to be examined with a careful curiosity.*

We have rediscovered a smaller truth. If you want to relive where you've been, write a book.

Don and Dana

978-0-595-37362-8
0-595-37362-3

Lightning Source UK Ltd.
Milton Keynes UK
UKOW041036020413

208526UK00001B/191/A